William Shakespeare's

ROMEO & JULIET

A new approach for a new course

EDUCATE.IE

SHAKESPEARE

SERIES

Annotations, analysis and activities by

Catherine O'Donovan

educate.ie

PUBLISHED BY:

Educate.ie
Walsh Educational Books Ltd
Castleisland, Co. Kerry, Ireland
www.educate.ie

EDITOR:
Donna Garvin

DESIGN & LAYOUT:
Kieran O'Donoghue

COVER DESIGN:
Kieran O'Donoghue

PROOFREADER:
Jennifer Armstrong

PRINTED AND BOUND BY:
Walsh Colour Print, Castleisland

PHOTOGRAPHS:

Front cover photograph: Pictorial Press Ltd./Alamy

AF Archive/Alamy; Bigstock; Classic Image/Alamy;
Imagebroker/Alamy; Moviestore Collection Ltd./Alamy;
Paris Pierce/Alamy; Photo Yoko Aziz 2/Alamy; Photos 12/
Alamy; Pictorial Press Ltd./Alamy; Prisma Archivo/Alamy;
The Protected Art Archive/Alamy; Travelib Europe/Alamy;
United Archives/Topfoto; Welcome Images/Welcome
Trust; World History Archive/Alamy

ILLUSTRATIONS:

Bigstock

ACKNOWLEDGEMENT:

'Romeo and Juliet. The stage as cemetery and tomb' from
*Enter the Whole Army: A Pictorial Study of Shakespearean
Staging, 1576–1616* by C. Walter Hodges (1999) by
permission of Cambridge University Press.

The author and publisher have made every effort to trace
all copyright holders. If any have been overlooked we
would be happy to make the necessary arrangements at
the first opportunity.

ISBN: 978-1-910052-87-7

Contents

Teacher's Introduction

The *Specification for Junior Cycle English* focuses on the development of language and literacy in and throughout the three strands: Oral Language, Reading and Writing.

These strands aim to promote **active engagement** with the texts for students. The aim of this edition of *Romeo and Juliet* is to explore the play in a way that helps to engage learners, while also focusing on the following key objectives:

1. Communicating as a speaker, reader and writer,
2. Exploring and using language, and
3. Understanding the content and structure of language.

This edition of the play is designed to facilitate exploration by including strategies and activities that encourage active engagement and interaction with the play. The overarching aim is to encourage students to see the play as a dramatic script to be explored and performed. While there are many activities and exercises included throughout the play text and the portfolio, it is not expected that all will be completed. It is hoped that there will be suggestions to complement the teacher's own approach to the play, bearing in mind the uniqueness of each class group.

The Portfolio

The portfolio is designed to provide a **personal learning log/journal** for students to visit as they read through the play. It provides a forum for reflection on the characters, plot and key themes of the play, allowing students to take personal ownership of the learning process. The written tasks help them to engage imaginatively with the play and explore the language of William Shakespeare.

Character File

The Character File section of the portfolio provides a template for students to reflect on their feelings about the main characters as they progress through the play. They are encouraged to record their responses to the characters in each key scene. They may focus on something that stands out to them. They may notice a significant change in the character, or may wish to note something that confuses them about a character in a particular scene.

Student's Introduction

Key Points About *Romeo and Juliet*

Romeo and Juliet was inspired by the poet Arthur Brooke's poem *The Tragicall Historye of Romeo and Juliet*, which was written in 1562.

- Shakespeare wrote his play *Romeo and Juliet* in 1595.
- It is a **tragedy**, but it does have some light-hearted moments of **comedy**.

What is a tragedy?

A tragedy is a play that deals with unfortunate events and usually features the death of the main character(s). As we will discover in the prologue before we even begin reading the play, this play ends with the tragic deaths of two 'star-crossed lovers' named Romeo and Juliet.

- The **play** is divided into five **acts**. Unlike prose, a play is essentially a script to be performed.
- Each **act** is divided into **scenes**.
- The **language** is archaic (old-fashioned). Some words will be unfamiliar to you at first, but you will get used to them as the play progresses.

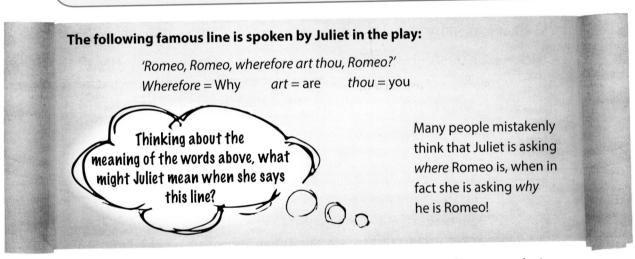

The following famous line is spoken by Juliet in the play:

'*Romeo, Romeo, wherefore art thou, Romeo?*'

Wherefore = Why   *art* = are   *thou* = you

Thinking about the meaning of the words above, what might Juliet mean when she says this line?

Many people mistakenly think that Juliet is asking *where* Romeo is, when in fact she is asking *why* he is Romeo!

The play is rich in **imagery**, which comes from Shakepeare's use of language devices (techniques) such as **metaphor, simile, personification, oxymoron** (opposites) and **hyperbole** (exaggeration). These terms will be explained as you read through the play.

Shakespeare's Theatre

In Elizabethan times (when Shakespeare wrote his plays), the stage in a theatre was usually quite bare. Often the audience had to rely on the characters' lines to figure out whether the scene was set during the day or at night. Shakespeare's Globe Theatre (which has been rebuilt in London close to the site of the original building) was an open-air theatre.

Globe Theatre >

Key Themes in *Romeo and Juliet*

There are many themes in *Romeo and Juliet*, but some of the main ones are:

- Conflict
- Love
- Fate
- Death.

The play is full of **opposites**, such as:

- Love versus hate
- Youth versus old age
- Peace versus conflict
- Life versus death.

Your Portfolio

When looking at the play, try to form your own ideas about the **characters** and **themes**, and the **language** used. The activities in the book and portfolio should help you with this.

P = **portfolio activity**

Character File

As you read through the play, record your responses to the main characters in the **Character File** section of your portfolio. Write down anything that you think is important about each character's personality. Use the **list of useful adjectives** in the **Character File** section to help you.

Think about:

- What the character **does** in each key scene.
- The **adjectives** you would use to describe the character.
- **Something that stands out** to you in a key scene.
- How the character **reacts to situations** that arise.
- Significant **change** in the character.
- Something that **confuses or surprises you** about the character in a particular scene.
- How the character interacts with other characters, i.e. **relationships**.

Important Characters in the Play

- Romeo
- Juliet
- Tybalt
- Mercutio
- The Nurse
- Friar Laurence
- Prince Escalus

Why Is *Romeo and Juliet* Such a Popular Play? |P|

What do you already know about the play *Romeo and Juliet*? Turn to **page 3** of your portfolio and write down as many points as you can.

Overview of the Play

The following grid shows the number of scenes in each act of the play. At the end of each act, you will write one phrase to summarise each scene of that act on **pages 4–5** of your portfolio. When completed, it will form your own **personal overview** of the play.

 = **key scene**

	SCENE 1	SCENE 2	SCENE 3	SCENE 4	SCENE 5	SCENE 6
ACT 1					🔑	
ACT 2		🔑				
ACT 3	🔑					
ACT 4			🔑			
ACT 5			🔑			

Glossary of Important Terms

ANTITHESIS Antithesis (plural **antitheses**) is when two opposite things are used in a sentence to form a contrast. Juliet's line 'My grave is like to be my wedding bed' (Act 1, Scene 5) is an example of antithesis. This device is used to highlight conflicting or opposing ideas in the character's language.

ASIDE An aside is a remark that the audience is supposed to hear but that is not supposed to be heard by the other characters on stage.

DRAMATIC IRONY Dramatic irony is when the audience or characters on stage have information or knowledge that the other character(s) on stage do(es) not.

HYBERBOLE Hyberbole is using **exaggerated, over-the-top language** for a dramatic effect. For example, in Act 2, Scene 2, Romeo says that Juliet's eyes would shine so brightly that the birds would think it was daytime:
> Her eyes in heaven
> Would through the airy region stream so bright
> That birds would sing and think it were not night.

IMAGERY Imagery uses words and phrases to create pictures in your mind. Much of the imagery in the play comes from other language devices such as metaphors, personification, oxymorons, etc.
Imagery can:
- Tell us more about a **character**
- Create a certain **mood or atmosphere**
- Reinforce certain **themes** (of love or conflict, for example).

In *Romeo and Juliet* we have religious imagery, nature imagery, imagery of death, etc.

LISTS Lists are groups of words or phrases used by a character to achieve a certain dramatic effect. For example, Juliet lists all the things she would rather do than marry Paris in Act 4, Scene 1, which is very dramatic.

METAPHOR A metaphor is a figure of speech used to make a comparison, usually saying one thing is another, which is not literally true, e.g. *Her eyes **are** sparkling diamonds.*

OXYMORON An oxymoron is a figure of speech which uses opposites to achieve a certain effect. Examples: 'loving hate', 'cold fire' (Romeo, Act 1, Scene 1).

PERSONIFICATION Personification is when we give non-human things human characteristics. For example, *The wind was **whistling** in the trees. The autumn leaves **danced** in the wind.*

SIMILE A simile is a figure of speech used to compare two things. A simile uses the words 'like', 'as' or 'than'. For example, *Her eyes are **like** sparkling diamonds.* (Compare with **metaphor** above.)

SOLILOQUY A soliloquy is a speech spoken by a character alone on stage. It gives us an **insight into the character's thoughts and feelings** at that particular time.

SONNET A sonnet is a 14-line poem, typically having ten syllables per line. There are two main types of sonnet: the Shakespearean sonnet and the Petrarchan (Italian) sonnet. As this play was written by William Shakespeare, we will be discussing the Shakespearean sonnet in this play.

*The most excellent
and lamentable tragedy of*

ROMEO & JULIET

By William Shakespeare

Setting: Verona, Italy.

'In fair Verona, where we lay our scene' (Act 1, Prologue, line 2)

Characters in the Play

Chorus

Prince Escalus, Ruler of Verona

Mercutio, *Prince Escalus's cousin; Romeo's friend*

Count Paris, *Prince Escalus's cousin; suitor to (admirer of) Juliet*

House of Capulet

Juliet

Lord Capulet

Lady Capulet

Tybalt, *Juliet's cousin*

Nurse to Juliet

Servants

Sampson

Gregory

Peter

House of Montague

Romeo

Lord Montague

Lady Montague

Benvolio, *Romeo's cousin*

Friar Laurence, Franciscan priest

Friar John, Franciscan priest

Servants

Abraham

Balthasar, *Romeo's servant*

Guests and followers of the Montague and Capulet families

Musicians

An apothecary (a person who sells medicines)

Who's Who?

Pair Activity |P|

Study the list of characters for a few minutes. Turn to **page 6** of the portfolio. With your partner, fill in as many characters as you can remember. When you have finished, look at the character list again and fill in the ones you might have missed.

'In fair Verona, where we lay our scene...'

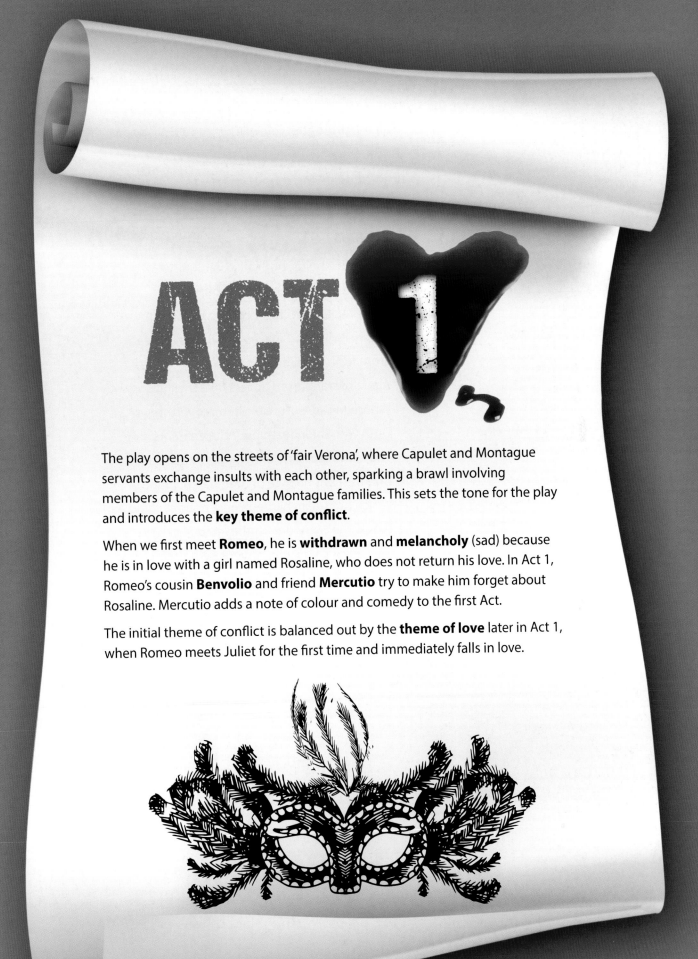

ACT 1

The play opens on the streets of 'fair Verona', where Capulet and Montague servants exchange insults with each other, sparking a brawl involving members of the Capulet and Montague families. This sets the tone for the play and introduces the **key theme of conflict**.

When we first meet **Romeo**, he is **withdrawn** and **melancholy** (sad) because he is in love with a girl named Rosaline, who does not return his love. In Act 1, Romeo's cousin **Benvolio** and friend **Mercutio** try to make him forget about Rosaline. Mercutio adds a note of colour and comedy to the first Act.

The initial theme of conflict is balanced out by the **theme of love** later in Act 1, when Romeo meets Juliet for the first time and immediately falls in love.

PROLOGUE

In the **prologue**, you will:

- Learn about the **plot** of the play.
- Explore the **sonnet** form.

CHORUS

Two households, both alike in dignity[1]
In fair Verona, where we lay[2] our scene,
From ancient grudge[3] break to new mutiny,[4]
Where civil blood makes civil hands unclean.[5]
5   From forth the fatal[6] loins of these two foes
A pair of star-cross'd[7] lovers take their life,
Whose misadventured[8] piteous overthrows
Doth with their death bury their parents' strife.
The fearful passage of their death-mark'd love
10   And the continuance of their parents' rage –
Which but their children's end, nought could remove –
Is now the two-hours' traffic[9] of our stage;
The which if you with patient ears attend,
What here shall miss, our toil shall strive to mend.[10]

Exeunt.

1. rank (equal in status)
2. set
3. feud 4. fighting
5. everyone has blood on their hands
6. ill-fated
7. unlucky
8. unfortunate
9. two hours' performance
10. We will try to fill you in in more detail during the course of the play.

PROLOGUE

The prologue is a **sonnet**.

What is a sonnet?

- A sonnet is a 14-line poem.
- Typically, there are ten syllables in each line.
- The rhyming scheme for a Shakespeare sonnet is: ABAB/CDCD/EFEF/GG.

Structure of the sonnet

We can divide the 14 lines into three groups of four lines, called **quatrains** and one group of two lines, called a **couplet**.

A. EXPLORING

Pair Activity |P|

What does the prologue tell us about the plot of the play?
In pairs, summarise the prologue. Turn to **page 7** of the portfolio to help you.

B. ORAL LANGUAGE

Choral Reading of the Prologue

Pair Activity

In groups, prepare to read the prologue aloud. Which lines/phrases will you emphasise?
What tone will you use? Will you read it all together, or will you take turns?

ACT 1, SCENE 1

Setting: Verona; a public place.

In this **scene**, you will:

- Be introduced to three important characters: **Benvolio**, **Tybalt** and **Romeo**.
- Find out about the key **themes** of **conflict** and **love**.
- Explore a feature of language – the **metaphor**.

Action – What Happens?

In this scene, the Capulet servants Sampson and Gregory see the Montague servants Abraham and Balthasar on the street. They provoke each other and a fight breaks out. We are introduced to the characters of **Benvolio** (a Montague) and **Tybalt** (a Capulet), who become involved in the fighting. The fighting soon spreads and a riot breaks out on the streets of Verona. Prince Escalus arrives and warns that if there is further violence, those responsible will be put to death. Later in the scene, we meet **Romeo**, who is depressed because the girl he loves does not love him in return.

Useful Words

tyrant – a cruel and controlling ruler   **tyrannous** – cruel   **kinsmen** – relatives

counsellor – a person who gives advice   **counsel** – advice

Enter SAMPSON and GREGORY, of the house of Capulet, armed with swords and bucklers.[1]

SAMPSON

Gregory, on my word, we'll not carry coals.[2]

GREGORY

No, for then we should be colliers.[3]

SAMPSON

I mean, an we be in choler, we'll draw.[4]

GREGORY

Ay, while you live, draw your neck out of collar.[5]

SAMPSON

I strike quickly, being moved.[6]   5

GREGORY

But thou art not quickly moved to strike.

SAMPSON

A dog of the house of Montague moves me.

GREGORY

To move is to stir, and to be valiant is to stand,[7]

therefore, if thou art moved, thou runn'st away.

SAMPSON

A dog of that house shall move me to stand. I will   10

take the wall of any man or maid of Montague's.[8]

GREGORY

That shows thee a weak slave, for the weakest goes to the wall.

SAMPSON

'Tis true, and therefore women, being the weaker vessels,

are ever thrust to the wall; therefore I will push

Montague's men from the wall, and thrust his maids   15

to the wall.[9]

---

1. shields

2. we won't be humiliated

3. coal porters/sneaky people

4. If we are angry, we will draw our swords
   (choler = anger; collar = noose).

5. a noose

6. when I am annoyed

7. to be brave is to stand up for yourself

8. I will walk in the inside of the footpath, which is
   the cleaner side. (This would allow him to show
   that he is superior to the Montagues.)

9. push the women to the wall to assault them

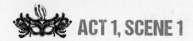
GREGORY

The quarrel is between our masters and us their men.

SAMPSON

'Tis all one, I will show myself a tyrant:[10] when I
have fought with the men, I will be civil with the
20 maids – I will cut off their heads.

GREGORY

The heads of the maids?

SAMPSON

Ay, the heads of the maids, or their maidenheads,[11]
take it in what sense thou wilt.

GREGORY

They must take it in sense that feel it.

SAMPSON

25 Me they shall feel while I am able to stand, and
'tis known I am a pretty piece of flesh.

GREGORY

'Tis well thou art not fish. If thou hadst, thou hadst been
poor-john.[12] Draw thy tool. Here comes of the house
of the Montagues.

SAMPSON

30 My naked weapon is out. Quarrel, I will back thee.

GREGORY

How – turn thy back and run?

SAMPSON

Fear me not.

GREGORY

No, marry[13] – I fear thee!

SAMPSON

Let us take the law of our side. Let them begin.

10. a cruel, oppressive ruler; a bully

11. virginity

12. cheap dried fish

13. by the Virgin Mary (another way of saying 'indeed')

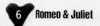

GREGORY

I will frown as I pass by, and let them take it as   35
they list.

SAMPSON

Nay, as they dare. I will bite my thumb at them,
which is disgrace to them if they bear it.[14]
[*He bites his thumb.*]

Enter ABRAHAM and BALTHASAR.

ABRAHAM

Do you bite your thumb at us, sir?

SAMPSON

I do bite my thumb, sir.   40

ABRAHAM

Do you bite your thumb at us, sir?

SAMPSON

[*aside to GREGORY*] Is the law of our side[15] if I say 'Ay'?

GREGORY

No.

SAMPSON

No, sir, I do not bite my thumb at you, sir, but I
bite my thumb, sir.   45

GREGORY

Do you quarrel, sir?

ABRAHAM

Quarrel, sir? No, sir.

SAMPSON

But if you do, sir, I am for you. I serve as good
a man as you.

ABRAHAM

No better.   50

14. (Flicking the thumb from behind the upper teeth was a rude gesture. They are trying to provoke the Montague servants.)

15. on our side

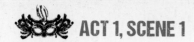
SAMPSON

Well, sir.

Enter BENVOLIO.

16. relatives (He sees Tybalt approaching.)

GREGORY

Say 'better'. Here comes one of my master's kinsmen.[16]

SAMPSON

[*to ABRAHAM*] Yes, better, sir.

ABRAHAM

You lie.

SAMPSON

17. violent/slashing stroke

55 Draw, if you be men. Gregory, remember thy
washing blow.[17]

They fight.

BENVOLIO

[*drawing*] Part, fools.
Put up your swords. You know not what you do.

Enter TYBALT.

TYBALT

18. cowardly servants ('Heartless' is a pun on 'hart', which is a stag. These servants (hinds) are without their master, and so are vulnerable.)

What, art thou drawn among these heartless hinds?[18]
60 Turn thee, Benvolio, look upon thy death.

BENVOLIO

I do but keep the peace. Put up thy sword,

19. use

Or manage[19] it to part these men with me.

TYBALT

What, drawn and talk of peace? I hate the word
As I hate hell, all Montagues, and thee.

20. Let's fight!

65 Have at thee,[20] coward!

*They fight. Enter three or four CITIZENS,
with clubs or partisans.*

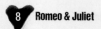

'What, drawn and talk of peace? I hate the word
As I hate hell, all Montagues, and thee.'
(Tybalt, Act 1, Scene 1, lines 63–64)

CITIZENS

Clubs, bills, and partisans![21] Strike! Beat them down!
Down with the Capulets. Down with the Montagues!

21. spears

Enter CAPULET in his gown, and LADY CAPULET.

CAPULET

What noise is this? Give me my long sword, ho!

LADY CAPULET

A crutch, a crutch – why call you for a sword?[22]

22. You are too old to be fighting; you should be looking for a crutch, not a sword.

CAPULET

My sword, I say! Old Montague is come,
And flourishes his blade in spite of me.[23]

70

23. waves his sword to provoke me

Enter MONTAGUE with his sword drawn, and LADY MONTAGUE.

MONTAGUE

Thou villain Capulet! [*his WIFE holds him back*] Hold me not, let
me go.

LADY MONTAGUE

Thou shalt not stir one foot to seek a foe.

Enter PRINCE ESCALUS with his train.[24]

PRINCE

Rebellious subjects, enemies to peace,

75   Profaners of this neighbour-stainèd steel[25] –

Will they not hear? What ho, you men, you beasts,

That quench the fire of your pernicious[26] rage

With purple fountains issuing from your veins:

On pain of torture, from those bloody hands

80   Throw your mistempered[27] weapons to the ground,

And hear the sentence of your movèd[28] Prince.

*MONTAGUE, CAPULET, and their followers throw down their
weapons.*

Three civil brawls,[29] bred of an airy word[30]

By thee, old Capulet, and Montague,

Have thrice[31] disturbed the quiet of our streets

85   And made Verona's ancient[32] citizens

Cast by their grave-beseeming ornaments[33]

To wield old partisans in hands as old,

Cankered[34] with peace, to part your cankered[35] hate:

If ever you disturb our streets again

90   Your lives shall pay the forfeit[36] of the peace.

For this time, all the rest depart away.

You, Capulet, shall go along with me;

And Montague, come you this afternoon

To know our farther pleasure in this case

95   To old Freetown, our common judgement-place.[37]

Once more, on pain of death, all men depart.

Exeunt all but MONTAGUE, LADY MONTAGUE and BENVOLIO.

24. followers

25. You who have stained your swords with the blood of your neighbours

26. destructive

27. misshapen
28. furious

29. fights
30. unsubstantial/started by a few words

31. three times

32. elderly

33. Put away their staffs

34. rusty
35. evil/malignant

36. penalty

37. public court

MONTAGUE

Who set this ancient quarrel new abroach?[38]

Speak, nephew: were you by when it began?

BENVOLIO

Here were the servants of your adversary,[39]

And yours, close fighting ere[40] I did approach: 100

I drew[41] to part them. In the instant came

The fiery[42] Tybalt with his sword prepared,

Which, as he breathed[43] defiance to my ears,

He swung about his head and cut the winds

Who nothing hurt withal[44] hissed him in scorn.[45]   105

While we were interchanging[46] thrusts and blows,

Came more and more,[47] and fought on part and part,[48]

Till the Prince came, who parted either part.

LADY MONTAGUE

O, where is Romeo – saw you him today?

Right glad I am he was not at this fray.[49]   110

BENVOLIO

Madam, an hour before the worshipped sun

Peered forth[50] the golden window of the east,

A troubled mind drive[51] me to walk abroad,

Where, underneath the grove of sycamore

That westward rooteth[52] from this city side,   115

So early walking did I see your son.

Towards him I made, but he was ware[53] of me

And stole into the covert[54] of the wood.

I, measuring his affections[55] by my own –

Which then most sought where most might not be found,[56]   120

Being one too many by my weary self –

Pursued my humour[57] not pursuing his,

And gladly shunned who gladly fled from me.[58]

MONTAGUE

Many a morning hath he there been seen,

With tears augmenting[59] the fresh morning's dew,   125

Adding to clouds more clouds with his deep sighs.

But all so soon as the all-cheering sun

Should in the farthest east begin to draw

---

38. Who restarted this fight?

39. enemy
40. before

41. drew my sword

42. quick-tempered/aggressive

43. uttered/spoke

44. by that
45. mockery/contempt
46. exchanging

47. people
48. both sides

49. fight/riot

50. out from (rose)

51. drove/caused me to

52. grows out

53. aware

54. covering/thicket (The sycamore woods were associated with unhappy lovers.)
55. mood

56. in a place where I was unlikely to be found

57. mood

58. I gladly avoided Romeo, as he wished to avoid me too.

59. adding to

60. (goddess of the dawn in classical mythology)

61. sad/melancholy

62. ominous/worrying

63. advice

The shady curtains from Aurora's[60] bed,

130 Away from the light steals home my heavy[61] son,

And private in his chamber pens himself,

Shuts up his windows, locks fair daylight out

And makes himself an artificial night.

Black and portentous[62] must this humour prove,

135 Unless good counsel[63] may the cause remove.

BENVOLIO

My noble uncle, do you know the cause?

MONTAGUE

I neither know it nor can learn of him.

BENVOLIO

Have you importuned[64] him by any means?

64. questioned

MONTAGUE

Both by myself and many other friends,

But he, his own affections' counsellor,[65]   140

65. advisor (He keeps to himself.)

Is to himself – I will not say how true,

But to himself so secret and so close,

So far from sounding and discovery,[66]

66. He will not reveal what the matter is

As is the bud bit with an envious worm,

Ere he can spread his sweet leaves[67] to the air,   145

67. petals

Or dedicate his beauty to the sun.

Could we[68] but learn from whence[69] his sorrows grow

68. If we could
69. where

We would as willingly give cure as know.

Enter ROMEO.

BENVOLIO

See, where he comes. So please you, step aside,

I'll know his grievance[70] or be much denied.   150

70. the cause of his distress/his problem

MONTAGUE

I would[71] thou wert so happy[72] by thy stay

To hear true shrift.[73] Come, madam, let's away.[74]

71. I wish
72. successful/fortunate
73. confession
74. let's leave

Exeunt MONTAGUE and LADY MONTAGUE.

BENVOLIO

Good morrow, cousin.

ROMEO

              Is the day so young?

BENVOLIO

But new[75] struck nine.

75. only just

ROMEO

              Ay me, sad hours seem long.

Was that my father that went hence so fast?   155

BENVOLIO

It was. What sadness lengthens Romeo's hours?

ROMEO

Not having that, which, having, makes them short.

BENVOLIO

In love?

ROMEO

Out.

BENVOLIO

160   Of love?

ROMEO

Out of her favour where I am in love.

BENVOLIO

Alas, that love, so gentle in his view,[76]
Should be so tyrannous[77] and rough in proof.[78]

ROMEO

Alas that love, whose view is muffled[79] still,
165   Should without eyes see pathways to his will.
Where shall we dine? O me! What fray[80] was here?
Yet tell me not, for I have heard it all.
Here's much to do with hate, but more with love.
Why then, O brawling love, O loving hate,[81]
170   O anything of nothing first create;
O heavy lightness, serious vanity,
Misshapen chaos of well-seeming forms,
Feather of lead, bright smoke, cold fire, sick health,
Still-waking sleep, that is not what it is!
175   This love feel I, that feel no love in this.[82]
Dost[83] thou not laugh?

BENVOLIO

No, coz,[84] I rather weep.

ROMEO

Good heart, at what?

76. appearance
77. cruel
78. in reality

79. who cannot see (This is a reference to Cupid, the god of love, who was depicted as being blindfolded.)

80. fight

81. (Romeo is outlining the contradictions of love. He uses contradictory words to show how he is confused by love.)

82. The love I feel is not returned and this causes me pain.
83. Do

84. cousin

Cupid

BENVOLIO

At thy good heart's oppression.[85]

85. distress/sadness

ROMEO

Why, such is love's transgression.[86]

86. fault (That is the problem with love.)

Griefs of mine own lie heavy in my breast,

Which thou wilt propagate[87] to have it pressed   180

87. increase

With more of thine. This love that thou hast shown

Doth add more grief to too much of mine[88] own.

88. my

Love is a smoke made with the fume[89] of sighs,

89. smoke/breath

Being purged,[90] a fire sparkling in lovers' eyes,

90. cleansed/purified (when love is returned)

Being vexed,[91] a sea nourished with lovers' tears.   185

91. annoyed/agitated (when love is not returned)

What is it else? A madness most discreet,[92]

92. wise

A choking gall[93] and a preserving sweet.[94]

93. poison
94. healing sweetness

Farewell, my coz.

95. Wait!

96. an if = if

97. seriously

98. marksman (archer who hits the target)

99. target

100. (Diana was the goddess of hunting and chastity [virginity]. She avoided Cupid's arrows.)
101. She is immune to love. (She is able to resist love.)
102. endure (listen to)

103. Nor give up her chastity for golden gifts, which are very tempting.

104. Her beauty will not continue on, as she will not have any children.

BENVOLIO

Soft![95] I will go along;
An if[96] you leave me so, you do me wrong.

ROMEO

190 Tut, I have lost myself. I am not here.
This is not Romeo; he's some other where.

BENVOLIO

Tell me in sadness,[97] who is that you love?

ROMEO

What, shall I groan and tell thee?

BENVOLIO

Groan? Why, no; but sadly tell me who.

ROMEO

195 Bid a sick man in sadness make his will,
A word ill urged to one that is so ill.
In sadness, cousin, I do love a woman.

BENVOLIO

I aimed so near when I supposed you loved.

ROMEO

A right good markman;[98] and she's fair I love.

BENVOLIO

200 A right fair mark,[99] fair coz, is soonest hit.

ROMEO

Well, in that hit you miss. She'll not be hit
With Cupid's arrow; she hath Dian's wit,
And, in strong proof of chastity well armed,[100]
From love's weak childish bow she lives unharmed.[101]
205 She will not stay[102] the siege of loving terms,
Nor bide the encounter of assailing eyes,
Nor ope her lap to saint-seducing gold.[103]
O, she is rich in beauty, only poor
That when she dies, with beauty dies her store.[104]

BENVOLIO

Then she hath sworn that she will still live chaste?[105]

ROMEO

She hath, and in that sparing makes huge waste;

For beauty starved with her severity

Cuts beauty off from all posterity.[106]

She is too fair, too wise, wisely too fair,[107]

To merit bliss[108] by making me despair.

She hath forsworn to love,[109] and in that vow

Do I live dead, that live to tell it now.

BENVOLIO

Be ruled by me;[110] forget to think of her.

ROMEO

O, teach me how I should forget to think!

BENVOLIO

By giving liberty[111] unto thine[112] eyes.

Examine other beauties.

ROMEO

          'Tis the way

To call hers, exquisite, in question more.[113]

These happy masks that kiss fair ladies' brows,

Being black, puts us in mind they hide the fair.

He that is strucken blind cannot forget

The precious treasure of his eyesight lost.

Show me a mistress that is passing[114] fair,

What doth her beauty serve but as a note

Where I may read who passed that passing fair?[115]

Farewell, thou canst not teach me to forget.

BENVOLIO

I'll pay that doctrine, or else die in debt.[116]

Exeunt.

215

220

225

230

105. always remain chaste

106. future generations (As she will not have children, she will not pass on her beauty.)
107. just/moral

108. earn heaven's blessing

109. taken an oath to never fall in love

110. Take my advice

111. freedom
112. your

113. That would only cause me to reflect more on her beauty.

114. exceedingly

115. Looking at other beautiful women only emphasises how superior she is in comparison.

116. I'll challenge your belief about that or die trying.

OVERVIEW OF ACT 1, SCENE 1

There are two distinct parts to this scene.

Part 1 – The street brawl breaks out.

- This is a very dramatic opening scene, which launches us straight into the action of the play and establishes one of the main themes: conflict.

- The ancient feud between the Capulets and Montagues has been reignited. Sampson and Gregory, servants of the Capulets, see the Montague servants Abraham and Balthasar on the streets of Verona and provoke them. Sampson 'bites his thumb' at them, which is an extremely rude and offensive gesture. The Montague servants do not tolerate this and a fight ensues.

- Benvolio (a Montague) and Tybalt (a Capulet) enter the scene. Benvolio tries to keep the peace:

  I do but keep the peace. Put up thy sword,

  Or manage it to part these men with me. (lines 61–62)

- However, in contrast, Tybalt wishes to become **embroiled** (involved) in the conflict. Many other people become involved in the riot and even Capulet and Montague try to join the action. This shows just how tense the scene is and how the feuding – the 'ancient grudge' (Prologue, line 3) – affects everyone, from master to servant.

- Next, Prince Escalus arrives with his followers (his train) to break up the fight. He is **incensed** (angry), as this is the third fight that has broken out in recent times. He demands that everyone put down their weapons and warns that if there is any further violence on the streets of Verona, those involved will be put to death.

Part 2 – Romeo reveals the cause of his distress to Benvolio.

- We get an insight into another type of conflict in this scene: Romeo's **inner conflict**.

- Romeo's parents express their concerns about their son to Benvolio. They tell him that Romeo seems sad and **melancholy**, but they cannot find out the cause of his distress.

- Benvolio tells them that he saw Romeo walking in the sycamore woods early in the morning. Realising that Romeo did not want to be disturbed, Benvolio decided to avoid him. Benvolio promises Romeo's parents that he will try to find out what is bothering Romeo.

- Romeo is troubled and melancholy because the girl he loves (who we later find out is named Rosaline) does not love him back. She has decided never to fall in love.

- Romeo is heart-broken and finds love confusing. His language reflects a contradictory attitude to love. In theory, love is supposed to be a wonderful thing, but in reality, it causes him a lot of pain and distress.

- Romeo notices blood on the street, which makes him even more disillusioned with the world.

- As the scene unfolds, we get an insight into Romeo's character. He appears to be isolating himself from his family.

- Romeo's language contrasts with the servants' bawdy (indecent) language.

A. REVIEWING

1. Who do you think is responsible for starting the fight?
2. What is the Prince's reaction to the violence?
3. What warning does the Prince give?
4. What is the cause of Romeo's sadness?
5. What information do we find out about the girl that Romeo is in love with?
6. What advice does Benvolio give Romeo at the end of the scene?
7. What is Romeo's response to this advice?

B. EXPLORING

Romeo's Language – Metaphors /P\

Romeo's **language** is rich in imagery. He uses metaphors extensively in this scene.

What is a metaphor?

A metaphor is a figure of speech that is used to make a comparison by saying that one thing is another. A metaphor is not literally true. For example: Her eyes *are* sparkling diamonds.

Turn to **page 9** of your portfolio to find out more about Romeo's language and to complete the tasks.

C. REFLECTING

1. Character File /P\

Turn to the Character File section of your portfolio and record your first impressions of **(a) Romeo (page 82)**, **(b) Tybalt (page 96)** and **(c) Benvolio (page 97)** based on this scene.

2. My Reflection on Act 1, Scene 1 /P\

Turn to **page 10** of your portfolio and write a short reflection on Act 1, Scene 1.

3. Considering Key Themes /P\

Turn to **page 11** of your portfolio and answer the questions on the themes in the play.

4. Key Quotes /P\

Turn to **page 12** of your portfolio and complete the task on key quotes from this scene.

ACT 1, SCENE 2

Setting: Verona; a street.

In this **scene,** you will:

- Be introduced to the characters of **Capulet** and **Paris.**
- Find out more about the theme of **love.**
- Write a short **script** and read it aloud.

Action – What Happens?

In this scene, Paris, a nobleman, has come to ask for Juliet's hand in marriage. Capulet tells Paris that Juliet is too young to marry, but that he should woo her at his 'old accustomed feast' that evening. A Capulet servant, who cannot read, meets Romeo and Benvolio by chance. Romeo discovers that the girl he loves – Capulet's niece Rosaline – will be at the feast. Benvolio and Romeo decide to go to the Capulet feast.

Useful Words

whither – where   **thither** – there

Enter CAPULET, PARIS and a SERVANT.

CAPULET

But Montague is bound[1] as well as I,

In penalty alike, and 'tis not hard, I think,

For men so old as we to keep the peace.

PARIS

Of honourable reckoning[2] are you both,

And pity 'tis you lived at odds so long.   5

But now, my lord, what say you to my suit?[3]

CAPULET

But saying o'er what I have said before:

My child is yet a stranger in the world;

She hath not seen the change[4] of fourteen years.

Let two more summers wither in their pride   10

Ere we may think her ripe[5] to be a bride.

PARIS

Younger than she are happy mothers made.

CAPULET

And too soon marred[6] are those so early made.

Earth hath swallowed all my hopes but she,[7]

She's the hopeful lady of my earth.   15

But woo her, gentle Paris, get her heart,

My will to her consent is but a part,[8]

And, she agreed,[9] within her scope of choice

Lies my consent and fair-according[10] voice.

This night I hold an old accustomed[11] feast,   20

Whereto[12] I have invited many a guest

Such as I love, and you among the store,[13]

One more, most welcome, makes my number more.

At my poor house look to behold[14] this night

Earth-treading stars[15] that make dark heaven light.   25

Such comfort as do lusty young men feel

When well-apparelled[16] April on the heel

Of limping winter treads – even such delight

Among fresh female buds shall you this night

Inherit[17] at my house; hear all, all see,   30

1. under oath/ordered

2. reputation

3. request to marry

4. passing

5. ready

6. harmed

7. She is the only child I have left

8. My wishes are just a small part of it

9. if she agrees

10. approving

11. customary/traditional

12. To which

13. guests

14. see

15. Stunning ladies

16. well-dressed (Here, he imagines spring dressed in flowers.)

17. Enjoy

18. (lines 31–33) Give your love to the girl whom you think is most deserving. When you compare Juliet with the other girls, you may not think so highly of her.

19. yardstick
20. shoe form
21. paintbrush (lines 38–41: The servant is mixing up workers and their tools. A shoemaker, not a tailor, uses a last. A fisherman uses a net, not a pencil [paintbrush], etc.)
22. figure out

23. I must go and find someone who can read.

24. Great timing!

25. Turn until you are dizzy
26. helped (Meaning: You will cure your dizziness by turning in the reverse direction.)
27. A terrible pain is lessened by the start/onset of a greater pain.
28. An old eye infection will seem insignificant in comparison to a new one.

29. (a plant whose leaves were used to heal cuts and grazes)

30. grazed

And like her most whose merit most shall be,
Which on more view of many, mine, being one,
May stand in number, though in reckoning none.[18]
Come, go with me. [*giving SERVANT a paper*] Go, sirrah, trudge about

35 Through fair Verona; find those persons out
Whose names are written there, and to them say
My house and welcome on their pleasure stay.

Exeunt CAPULET and PARIS.

SERVANT
Find them out whose names are written here? It is
written that the shoemaker should meddle with his

40 yard,[19] and the tailor with his last,[20] the fisher with
his pencil,[21] and the painter with his nets; but I am sent
to find those persons, whose names are here writ,
and can never find[22] what names the writing person
hath here writ. I must to the learned.[23]

Enter BENVOLIO and ROMEO.

45 In good time.[24]

BENVOLIO
Tut, man, one fire burns out another's burning,
One pain is lessened by another's anguish.
Turn giddy,[25] and be holp[26] by backward turning.
One desperate grief cures with another's languish.[27]

50 Take thou some new infection to thy eye,[28]
And the rank poison of the old will die.

ROMEO
Your plantain[29] leaf is excellent for that.

BENVOLIO
For what, I pray thee?

ROMEO
For your broken[30] shin.

BENVOLIO

Why, Romeo, art thou mad?

ROMEO

Not mad, but bound more than a madman is; 55

Shut up in prison, kept without my food,

Whipped and tormented, and –

Good-e'en,[31] good fellow.

31. Good evening (afternoon)

SERVANT

God gi'good-e'en.[32] I pray, sir, can you read?

32. God give you a good evening. (This was a greeting.)

ROMEO

Ay, mine own fortune[33] in my misery. 60

33. I can predict my own future

SERVANT

Perhaps you have learned it without book.[34] But,

I pray, can you read any thing you see?

34. by heart (by memorising it)

ROMEO

Ay, if I know the letters and the language.

SERVANT

Ye say honestly.[35] Rest you merry.

35. (The servant thinks that Romeo means he cannot read, and so thanks him for being honest.)

ROMEO

Stay, fellow, I can read. 65

[*He reads the letter:*]

'Signior Martino and his wife and daughters. County

Anselme and his beauteous sisters. The lady Widow

of Vitruvio. Signior Placentio and his lovely nieces.

Mercutio and his brother Valentine. Mine uncle

Capulet, his wife and daughters. My fair niece 70

Rosaline and Livia. Signior Valentio and his cousin

Tybalt. Lucio and the lively Helena.'

A fair assembly: whither[36] should they come?

36. where

SERVANT

Up.

ROMEO

75 Whither? To supper?

SERVANT

To our house.

ROMEO

Whose house?

SERVANT

My master's.

ROMEO

Indeed, I should have asked you that before.

SERVANT

80 Now I'll tell you without asking. My master is the great rich
Capulet, and if you be not of the house of Montagues, I
pray, come and crush[37] a cup of wine. Rest you merry.

Exit SERVANT.

BENVOLIO

At this same ancient[38] feast of Capulet's,
Sups the fair Rosaline, whom thou so loves,
85 With all the admirèd beauties of Verona.
Go thither,[39] and with unattainted[40] eye
Compare her face with some that I shall show,
And I will make thee think thy swan a crow.

ROMEO

When the devout[41] religion of mine eye
90 Maintains such falsehood,[42] then turns tears to fires;
And these[43] who, often drowned, could never die,
Transparent heretics, be burnt for liars.
One fairer than my love! – The all-seeing sun
Ne'er saw her match since first the world begun.

BENVOLIO

95 Tut, you saw her fair, none else being by,
Herself poised with herself in either eye;[44]

37. drink

38. traditional

39. there
40. innocent/impartial

41. sincere

42. Accepts such a lie

43. eyes (Romeo is saying that he does not believe
he could ever think Rosaline is not beautiful. If
that day ever came, he says, his tears should turn
to fire and his eyes should be burned for being
traitors/liars. Rosaline is unrivalled in her beauty,
he claims.)

44. poised = balanced against (Benvolio claims that
as there was no other lady present with whom to
compare Rosaline, there was no real competition.)

But in that crystal scales[45] let there be weighed
Your lady's love against some other maid
That I will show you shining at this feast,
And she shall scant[46] show well that now seems best.   100

45. your eyes

46. hardly/scarcely

ROMEO

I'll go along, no such sight to be shown,
But to rejoice in splendour of mine own.

Exeunt.

'Compare her face with some that I shall show,
And I will make thee think thy swan a crow.'

(Benvolio, Act 1, Scene 2, lines 87–88)

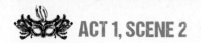

OVERVIEW OF ACT 1, SCENE 2

- At the start of the scene, Paris has come to ask Capulet for his daughter, Juliet's, hand in marriage.
- Capulet informs Paris that Juliet is still too young to marry. She is only 13 years old. He says that Juliet is the only child he has left:

    Earth hath swallowed all my hopes but she (line 14)

- Capulet suggests that it will be two more years before Juliet is old enough to marry:

    Let two more summers wither in their pride

    Ere we may think her ripe to be a bride. (lines 10–11)

- He invites Paris to an 'old accustomed feast' (line 20), which he will host that evening. He gives Paris permission to woo Juliet (win her heart), but warns him that when he sees Juliet among so many beautiful ladies, he may not think she is the most desirable girl there.
- Capulet gives a servant a list of guests to be invited to the feast. However, the servant cannot read.
- Luckily, the servant meets Benvolio and Romeo, who read the names on the list to him. They notice that Rosaline has been invited to the feast and decide to go too.
- Benvolio believes that Romeo will forget about Rosaline once he sees the other beautiful women there:

    Compare her face with some that I shall show,

    And I will make thee think thy swan a crow. (lines 87–88)

A. REVIEWING

1. Why has Paris come to see Capulet?
2. What is Capulet's response to Paris's request?
3. We have not met Juliet yet, but what do we find out about her in this scene? Write down two points.
4. Why does Romeo decide to go to the Capulet feast?

B. ORAL LANGUAGE

Pair Activity

When we join this scene, Capulet and Paris are having a conversation. We find out that Capulet has already discussed what the Prince said to him, and that Paris has mentioned marrying Juliet. Write the few lines of conversation that are missing from the scene. Read your script aloud, or simply improvise!

C. REFLECTING

My Reflection on Act 1, Scene 2 |P|

Turn to **page 13** of your portfolio and write a short reflection on Act 1, Scene 2.

ACT 1, SCENE 3

Setting: Verona; a room in Capulet's house.

In this **scene,** you will:

- Meet the characters of **Lady Capulet** (Juliet's mother), the **Nurse** and **Juliet**.
- Find out more about the theme of **love and marriage**.

Action – What Happens?

In this scene, Lady Capulet broaches (discusses) the topic of marriage with her daughter Juliet. She informs her that Paris wishes to marry her and that he will be at the feast that evening. We are also introduced to the Nurse, who reminisces about Juliet's childhood.

Useful Words

bade – asked　　　**quoth he** – he said　　　**I warrant** – I guarantee

Enter LADY CAPULET and NURSE.

LADY CAPULET

Nurse, where's my daughter? Call her forth[1] to me.

1. here

NURSE

Now, by my maidenhead,[2] at twelve year old,

2. virginity

I bade[3] her come. What, lamb! What, ladybird! –

3. told

God forbid! – Where's this girl? What, Juliet!

Enter JULIET.

JULIET

How now! Who calls?   5

NURSE

Your mother.

JULIET

Madam, I am here. What is your will?[4]

4. What do you want?

LADY CAPULET

This is the matter. – Nurse, give leave[5] awhile.

5. leave us/excuse us

We must talk in secret. – Nurse, come back again.

I have remembered me, thou's hear our counsel.[6]   10

6. you shall hear our conversation/secrets

Thou knowest my daughter's of a pretty age.

NURSE

Faith[7], I can tell her age unto an hour.[8]

7. Indeed
8. to the hour

LADY CAPULET

She's not fourteen.

NURSE

        I'll lay fourteen of my teeth –

And yet to my teen[9] be it spoken I have but four –

9. sorrow

She is not fourteen. How long is it now   15

To Lammas-tide?[10]

10. August 1st (a day that used to be celebrated by the church as a harvest festival)

LADY CAPULET

        A fortnight and odd days.

NURSE

Even or odd, of all days in the year,

Come Lammas-eve at night shall she be fourteen.[11]

Susan and she – God rest all Christian souls! –

20 Were of an age. Well, Susan is with God;[12]

She was too good for me. But, as I said,

On Lammas-Eve at night shall she be fourteen;

That shall she, marry, I remember it well.

'Tis since the earthquake now eleven years,

25 And she was weaned – I never shall forget it –

Of all the days of the year, upon that day,

For I had then laid wormwood to my dug,[13]

Sitting in the sun under the dove-house wall.

My lord and you were then at Mantua.

30 Nay, I do bear a brain![14] But, as I said,

When it did taste the wormwood on the nipple

Of my dug and felt it bitter, pretty fool!

To see it tetchy[15] and fall out wi'th'dug!

'Shake,' quoth the dove-house![16] 'Twas no need, I trow,

35 To bid me trudge.[17]

And since that time it is eleven years.

For then she could stand high-lone.[18] Nay, by th'rood,[19]

She could have run and waddled all about,

For even the day before, she broke her brow,[20]

40 And then my husband – God be with his soul!

A[21] was a merry man – took up the child.

'Yea,' quoth[22] he, 'dost thou fall upon thy face?

Thou wilt fall backward when thou hast more wit,[23]

Wilt thou not, Jule?' And, by my halidom,[24]

45 The pretty wretch left[25] crying and said 'Ay'.[26]

To see now how a jest[27] shall come about![28]

I warrant,[29] an[30] I should live a thousand years,

I never should forget it. 'Wilt thou not, Jule?' quoth he,

And, pretty fool, it stinted[31] and said 'Ay'.

LADY CAPULET

50 Enough of this. I pray thee hold thy peace.

NURSE

Yes, madam. Yet I cannot choose but laugh

To think it should leave crying, and say 'Ay'.

11. (Therefore, Juliet's birthday is July 31st.)

12. (The Nurse nursed [breastfed] Juliet after her own daughter, Susan, died.)

13. (She put a bitter-tasting plant on her breast to wean Juliet.)

14. I still have a great memory!

15. irritable/annoyed

16. The dove-house shook because of the earthquake. (Here, the dove-house is personified, and it tells the Nurse to move quickly away from danger.)

17. remove myself

18. she could stand upright by herself

19. By the cross

20. cut her forehead

21. He

22. said

23. knowledge/sense

24. holiness/holy relic

25. stopped

26. 'Yes'

27. joke

28. come true

29. I guarantee you/I tell you

30. if

31. she stopped (crying)

And yet, I warrant, it had upon it brow

A bump as big as a young cockerel's stone.[32]

A perilous knock,[33] and it cried bitterly.   55

'Yea,' quoth my husband, 'fall'st upon thy face?

Thou wilt fall backward when thou com'st to age,

Wilt thou not, Jule?' It stinted and said 'Ay'.

JULIET

And stint thou too, I pray thee, Nurse, say I.[34]

NURSE

Peace, I have done. God mark thee to his grace!   60

Thou wast the prettiest babe that e'er I nursed.

An I might live to see thee married once,

I have my wish.

LADY CAPULET

Marry, that 'marry' is the very theme

I came to talk of. Tell me, daughter Juliet,   65

How stands your disposition to be married?[35]

JULIET

It is an honour that I dream not of.

NURSE

An honour! Were not I thine only nurse,

I would say thou hast sucked wisdom from thy teat.[36]

LADY CAPULET

Well, think of marriage now. Younger than you,   70

Here in Verona, ladies of esteem,

Are made already mothers. By my count,

I was your mother much upon these years

That you are now a maid.[37] Thus then, in brief:

The valiant Paris seeks you for his love.   75

NURSE

A man, young lady! Lady, such a man

As all the world – why, he's a man of wax.[38]

32. a rooster's testicle

33. a terrible lump

34. Please stop talking.

35. How do you feel about marriage?

36. from the breast that nourished you

37. (lines 72–74) I was around your age when you were born.

38. he is perfect (It is as if he was sculpted, not born.)

LADY CAPULET

Verona's summer hath not such a flower.

NURSE

Nay, he's a flower; in faith, a very flower.

LADY CAPULET

80   What say you? Can you love the gentleman?

This night you shall behold him at our feast.

Read o'er the volume[39] of young Paris' face,

And find delight writ[40] there with beauty's pen.

Examine every married lineament,[41]

85   And see how one another lends content.

And what obscured in this fair volume lies

Find written in the margin of his eyes.

This precious book of love, this unbound[42] lover,

To beautify him, only lacks a cover.

39. book

40. written

41. harmonious feature

42. unmarried

The fish lives in the sea, and 'tis much pride 90

For fair without the fair within to hide.[43]

That book in many eyes doth share the glory,

That in gold clasps locks in the golden story.

So shall you share all that he doth possess

By having him, making yourself no less. 95

NURSE

No less? Nay, bigger. Women grow by men.[44]

LADY CAPULET

Speak briefly: can you like of Paris' love?

JULIET

I'll look to like, if looking liking move;

But no more deep will I endart mine eye

Than your consent gives strength to make it fly.[45] 100

Enter a SERVINGMAN.

SERVINGMAN

Madam, the guests are come, supper served up, you
called, my young lady asked for, the nurse cursed in
the pantry, and everything in extremity.[46] I must
hence[47] to wait. I beseech[48] you, follow straight.

LADY CAPULET

We follow thee.

Exit SERVINGMAN.

> Juliet, the County stays.[49] 105

NURSE

Go, girl, seek happy nights to[50] happy days.

Exeunt.

---

43. Something beautiful on the outside is also beautiful on the inside.

44. increase in size when they become pregnant

45. I will look out for him, but only pay him as much attention as you wish me to.

46. is chaotic

47. leave here
48. beg

49. Count Paris is waiting

50. at the end of

OVERVIEW OF ACT 1, SCENE 3

- In this scene, we meet Lady Capulet, the Nurse and Juliet for the first time.
- Lady Capulet has come to ask Juliet about her thoughts on marriage. Juliet says it 'is an honour that I dream not of' (line 67), meaning that she has not given it much thought.
- The Nurse **reminisces** about (looks back on) Juliet's childhood and recounts a funny story about a time when Juliet fell on her face and cut her forehead. It is clear that the Nurse has genuine affection for Juliet, because she can recall exact details from her childhood.
- In contrast to her relationship with the Nurse, Juliet has a very formal relationship with her mother: 'Madam, I am here. What is your will?' (line 7).
- Juliet appears to be a very obedient, dutiful daughter in this scene.
- Lady Capulet tells Juliet that Paris will be at the feast and that he is interested in her. Lady Capulet and the Nurse proceed to lavish praise on Paris, claiming that he is 'a man of wax' (line 77) and 'Verona's summer hath not such a flower' (line 78).
- The scene ends with a servant urging Lady Capulet to join the feast as the guests have arrived.

A. REVIEWING

1. Why has Juliet's mother come to see her?
2. How does Juliet react to the news that Paris is interested in her?

B. EXPLORING

Imagery of Paris |P|

Turn to **page 14** of your portfolio and complete the activity.

C. REFLECTING

Character File |P|

Turn to the Character File section of your portfolio and record your first impressions of **(a) Juliet (page 89)** and **(b) the Nurse (page 99)** based on this scene. Write a paragraph for each.

ACT 1, SCENE 4

Setting: Verona; a street.

In this **scene,** you will:

- Meet the character of **Mercutio.**
- Explore **imagery** and **language.**

Action – What Happens?

In this scene, we are introduced to the character of Romeo's friend Mercutio. Romeo, Mercutio and Benvolio are on their way to the Capulet feast. Mercutio and Benvolio are in a jovial (cheerful) mood, but Romeo is disturbed by a dream he had. Mercutio mocks Romeo by telling him about Queen Mab, a mischievous fairy. At the end of the scene, Romeo is resigned to his fate. He agrees to go to the ball, despite his fears.

Useful Words

masquer – a person taking part in a masquerade or masked ball (dress-up ball)

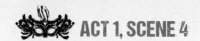
Enter ROMEO, MERCUTIO, BENVOLIO, with five or six MASQUERS, TORCH-BEARERS and OTHERS.

ROMEO

What, shall this speech be spoke for our excuse?

Or shall we on without apology?[1]

BENVOLIO

The date is out of such prolixity:[2]

We'll have no Cupid hoodwinked[3] with a scarf,

5   Bearing a Tartar's painted bow of lath,[4]

Scaring the ladies like a crow-keeper;[5]

Nor no without-book[6] prologue, faintly spoke

After the prompter, for our entrance:

But, let them measure[7] us by what they will,

10   We'll measure[8] them a measure,[9] and be gone.

ROMEO

Give me a torch. I am not for this ambling.[10]

Being but heavy,[11] I will bear the light.[12]

MERCUTIO

Nay, gentle Romeo, we must have you dance.

ROMEO

Not I, believe me. You have dancing shoes

15   With nimble soles. I have a soul of lead

So stakes[13] me to the ground I cannot move.

MERCUTIO

You are a lover. Borrow Cupid's wings,

And soar with them above a common bound.[14]

ROMEO

I am too sore enpiercèd with his shaft[15]

20   To soar with his light feathers, and so bound

I cannot bound a pitch[16] above dull woe;[17]

Under love's heavy burden do I sink.

MERCUTIO

And, to sink in it, should you burden love –

Too great oppression for a tender thing.

---

1. (lines 1–2) Should we excuse ourselves for intruding, or should we just go in without saying anything?

2. Such boring speeches (excuses) are outdated

3. blindfolded

4. a short bow (shaped like an upper lip)

5. scarecrow

6. memorised/learnt off by heart

7. judge

8. perform
9. dance

10. dancing

11. sad/melancholy
12. I will carry the torch

13. ties

14. leap (jump higher than the average dancer's leap)

15. I am too deeply wounded by Cupid's arrow

16. height
17. my sadness

ROMEO

Is love a tender thing? It is too rough,   25

Too rude, too boisterous, and it pricks like thorn.

MERCUTIO

If love be rough with you, be rough with love;

Prick love for pricking and you beat love down.

Give me a case,[18] to put my visage[19] in.

A visor for a visor![20] What care I   30

What curious eye doth quote deformities?[21]

Here are the beetle brows[22] shall blush for me.

They put on visors.

BENVOLIO

Come, knock and enter, and no sooner in,[23]

But every man betake him to his legs.[24]

ROMEO

A torch for me. Let wantons light of heart,   35

Tickle the senseless rushes[25] with their heels,

For I am proverbed with a grandsire phrase[26] –

I'll be a candle-holder, and look on.[27]

The game was ne'er so fair, and I am done.[28]

MERCUTIO

Tut, dun's the mouse,[29] the constable's own word.   40

If thou art Dun, we'll draw thee from the mire,[30]

Or – save your reverence – love, wherein thou stickest

Up to the ears. Come, we burn daylight,[31] ho!

ROMEO

Nay, that's not so.

MERCUTIO

       I mean, sir, in delay

We waste our lights in vain, like lamps by day.   45

Take our good meaning for our judgement sits

Five times in that ere once in our five wits.

18. mask
19. face
20. A mask to hide an ugly face!

21. What do I care about curious eyes that stare at me?
22. protruding/bushy eyebrows

23. as soon as we are inside

24. Let everyone dance

25. floor mats

26. an old saying

27. (lines 37–38) I follow the old saying that those who look on, lose nothing.
28. (Romeo is quoting another proverb, which says: 'When play is best it is time to leave'.)

29. Keep as quiet as a mouse (pun on the word 'dun')

30. mud (Mercutio is calling Romeo a stick-in-the-mud [a dull, unadventurous person].)

31. we are wasting time

32. Even though we are going to his masked ball with good intentions, I think it is unwise to go.

33. last night

34. (This is a pun on the word 'lie', i.e. to lie sleeping, or to tell a lie.)

35. a ring with precious stones, which featured a carving of a human figure
36. member of council

37. tiny creatures

38. spiders'

39. canopy

40. harness

41. gossamer (cobwebs)

42. driver
43. (a type of fly resembling a mosquito)

ROMEO

And we mean well in going to this masque,
But 'tis no wit to go.[32]

MERCUTIO

      Why, may one ask?

ROMEO

I dreamt a dream tonight.[33]

MERCUTIO

50   And so did I.

ROMEO

Well, what was yours?

MERCUTIO

      That dreamers often lie.[34]

ROMEO

In bed asleep, while they do dream things true.

MERCUTIO

O, then I see Queen Mab hath been with you.

BENVOLIO

Queen Mab, what's she?

MERCUTIO

55 She is the fairies' midwife, and she comes
In shape no bigger than an agate-stone[35]
On the fore-finger of an alderman,[36]
Drawn with a team of little atomies[37]
Over men's noses as they lie asleep.
60 Her waggon-spokes made of long spinners'[38] legs;
The cover,[39] of the wings of grasshoppers;
Her traces,[40] of the smallest spider web;
Her collars, of the moonshine's watery beams;
Her whip, of cricket's bone; the lash, of film;[41]
65 Her waggoner,[42] a small grey-coated gnat,[43]
Not half so big as a round little worm

Pricked from the lazy finger of a maid.

Her chariot is an empty hazelnut,

Made by the joiner[44] squirrel or old grub,[45]

Time out o' mind[46] the fairies' coach-makers.   70

And in this state[47] she gallops night by night

Through lovers' brains, and then they dream of love;

O'er courtiers' knees, that dream on curtsies straight;[48]

O'er lawyers' fingers, who straight dream on fees;

O'er ladies' lips, who straight on kisses dream;   75

Which oft the angry Mab with blisters plagues,[49]

Because their breaths with sweetmeats tainted are.[50]

Sometime she gallops o'er a courtier's[51] nose,

And then dreams he of smelling out a suit.[52]

And sometime comes she with a tithe-pig's[53] tail,   80

Tickling a parson's[54] nose as 'a[55] lies asleep;

Then dreams he of another benefice.[56]

Sometime she driveth o'er a soldier's neck,

And then dreams he of cutting foreign throats,

Of breaches,[57] ambuscadoes,[58] Spanish blades,[59]   85

Of healths five fathom deep;[60] and then anon[61]

Drums in his ear, at which he starts and wakes;

And, being thus frighted, swears a prayer or two,

And sleeps again. This is that very Mab

That plaits the manes of horses in the night   90

And bakes the elf-locks in foul sluttish hairs,[62]

Which once untangled much misfortune bodes.[63]

This is the hag, when maids lie on their backs,

That presses them and learns[64] them first to bear,

Making them women of good carriage.[65]   95

This is she –

ROMEO

        Peace, peace, Mercutio, peace!

Thou talkest of nothing.

MERCUTIO

        True, I talk of dreams,

Which are the children of an idle brain,

Begot[66] of nothing but vain fantasy;[67]

Which is as thin of substance as the air,   100

And more inconstant than the wind, who woos

---

44. carpenter
45. maggot/caterpillar
46. A time so long ago that people have no memory of it
47. fashion/manner

48. straight away (immediately)

49. gives them blisters (cold sores)

50. Because they have eaten too many sweet things.

51. advisor to the king/queen

52. petition

53. a pig paid as an offering to the parish to support the priest
54. a vicar's
55. he
56. permanent church position

57. breaking down fortifications/defences
58. ambushes/surprise attacks
59. swords from Spain (which were said to be the best quality)
60. large cups of alcohol
61. soon

62. entangles the manes of horses

63. (Disentangling the manes was said to anger the mischievous elves.)

64. teaches

65. deportment/childbearing

66. Caused by/brought about by
67. empty imagination

68. there

Even now the frozen bosom of the north,
And, being angered, puffs away from thence,[68]
Turning his face to the dew-dropping south.

BENVOLIO

105 This wind you talk of blows us from ourselves.
Supper is done, and we shall come too late.

ROMEO

I fear too early, for my mind misgives[69]
Some consequence yet hanging in the stars
Shall bitterly begin his fearful date[70]

69. fears

70. period/phase

71. celebrations/party
72. finish/end

73. premature/early (lines 107–112: Romeo fears that his fate has already been decided and that a period of bad luck, which will start tonight at the feast, will end with his premature death.)
74. God in heaven, who is in charge of my life, guide me.
75. merry

110 With this night's revels,[71] and expire[72] the term
Of a despisèd life, closed in my breast,
By some vile forfeit of untimely[73] death.
But he that hath the steerage of my course
Direct my sail![74] On, lusty[75] gentlemen!

BENVOLIO

115 Strike, drum.

They march about the stage and exeunt.

'I'll be a candle-holder, and look on.'
(Romeo, Act 1, Scene 4, line 38)

OVERVIEW OF ACT 1, SCENE 4

- At the start of this scene, Romeo, Mercutio and Benvolio are on their way to the Capulet feast. Romeo wonders if they should say something before entering, but Benvolio says that such excuses and speeches are not fashionable.

- Romeo informs the others that he is too sad and melancholy to dance, so he will carry the torch (light) instead.

- We are introduced to Romeo's friend Mercutio, who tries to cheer Romeo up. He tells him that he must dance and should borrow Cupid's wings to soar high above the ground. Romeo feels that love is a burden: 'Under love's heavy burden do I sink' (line 22).

- Romeo and Mercutio's language is full of witty puns (words with many possible meanings).

- Mercutio tries to cheer Romeo up by telling him about Queen Mab, a mischievous fairy, 'the fairies' midwife', who visits people when they are asleep and affects their dreams.

- Romeo also reveals that he had a bad dream last night, which seemed to predict his death. He is apprehensive (anxious/worried) about going to the feast, as he feels it will have terrible consequences for him and eventually lead to his death:

    > I fear too early, for my mind misgives
    >
    > Some consequence yet hanging in the stars
    >
    > Shall bitterly begin his fearful date
    >
    > With this night's revels, and expire the term
    >
    > Of a despisèd life, closed in my breast,
    >
    > By some vile forfeit of untimely death. (lines 107–112)

- However, Romeo still wants to go to the feast and seems resigned to (accepting of) his fate:

    > But he that hath the steerage of my course
    >
    > Direct my sail! (lines 113–114)

A. REVIEWING

1. How would you describe Romeo's mood at the start of this scene? Use a quote to support your answer.

2. **(a)** What was Romeo's dream about on the previous night?
   (b) How has this affected his mood?

3. At the end of the scene, Romeo decides to go to the feast despite his fears. Which lines tell us this? Quote the lines and explain them in your own words.

B. ORAL LANGUAGE

1. Performing Mercutio's Queen Mab Speech

Pair Activity

Mercutio's speech about Queen Mab (lines 55–96) is full of vivid imagery. Perform the speech in pairs. Change speaker at each punctuation mark. Are there certain lines you would read faster than others? Discuss this with your partner.

2. Imagery: Drawing Queen Mab │P│

Pair Activity

Turn to **page 15** of your portfolio and **draw a picture** to illustrate your impressions of Queen Mab. Look back over lines 55–96 and **use quotes to label your picture**.

C. EXPLORING

Research: Cupid, God of Love │P│

Find out more about Cupid, the god of love in Roman mythology. Turn to **page 16** of your portfolio to help you with this task.

D. REFLECTING

Character File │P│

Turn to the Character File section of your portfolio and record your first impressions of **Mercutio (page 103)** based on this scene.

ACT 1, SCENE 5

Setting: Verona; a hall in Capulet's house.

In this **scene,** you will:

- Learn more about the **characters of Romeo and Juliet**.
- Find out more about two key **themes**: **love** and **conflict**.
- Explore the **language** and **imagery** in the scene.
- Create a **magazine article** based on the events in this scene.

Action – What Happens?

This is a key scene. Romeo and Juliet meet for the first time and fall in love. At the Capulet feast, everyone is dancing. Tybalt recognises Romeo by his voice and threatens to kill him. However, Capulet calms him down, reminding him that he is the master and does not want a scene. Tybalt is very unhappy and vows to get revenge on Romeo for intruding on the feast. Meanwhile, Romeo sees Juliet and it is love at first sight. They kiss without realising their true identities.

Useful Words

pilgrim – a person who travels to a sacred place for religious reasons (also known as a palmer)

masque – a masquerade/masked ball

anon – soon

1. clear the tables
2. wooden plate

3. bad

4. sideboard
5. silverware

6. (girls whom he wishes to invite to the servants' quarters)

7. (a proverb that means 'life is short')

8. dance

9. who is reluctant to dance

10. Am I close to the truth?

11. mask

SERVINGMEN come forward with napkins.

FIRST SERVINGMAN

Where's Potpan, that he helps not to take away?[1]
He shift a trencher,[2] he scrape a trencher!

SECOND SERVINGMAN

When good manners shall lie all in one or two men's
hands, and they unwashed too, 'tis a foul[3] thing.

FIRST SERVINGMAN

5   Away with the joint-stools, remove the court-cupboard,[4]
look to the plate.[5] Good thou, save me a piece of
marzipan, and, as thou lovest me, let the porter let in
Susan Grindstone and Nell.[6] Antony and Potpan!

SECOND SERVINGMAN

Ay, boy, ready.

FIRST SERVINGMAN

10   You are looked for and called for, asked for and
sought for, in the great chamber.

THIRD SERVINGMAN

We cannot be here and there too.

SECOND SERVINGMAN

Cheerly, boys, be brisk awhile, and the longer liver
take all.[7]

*Enter CAPULET and FAMILY, and all of the GUESTS and
GENTLEWOMEN to the MASQUERS.*

CAPULET

15   Welcome, gentlemen! Ladies that have their toes
Unplagued with corns will walk a bout[8] with you.
Aha, my mistresses, which of you all
Will now deny to dance? She that makes dainty,[9]
She, I'll swear, hath corns. Am I come near ye now?[10]
20   Welcome gentlemen! I have seen the day
That I have worn a visor,[11] and could tell

A whispering tale in a fair lady's ear

Such as would please. 'Tis gone, 'tis gone, 'tis gone.

You are welcome, gentlemen! Come, musicians, play.

Music plays, and they dance. ROMEO stands apart [to the side].

A hall, a hall! Give room, and foot it,[12] girls.   25

More light, ye knaves,[13] and turn the tables up,[14]

And quench the fire, the room is grown too hot.

Ah sirrah, this unlooked-for sport[15] comes well.

Nay, sit, nay, sit, good cousin Capulet,

For you and I are past our dancing days.   30

How long is't now since last yourself and I

Were in a masque?

COUSIN CAPULET

      By'r Lady,[16] thirty years.

CAPULET

What, man, 'tis not so much, 'tis not so much.

'Tis since the nuptial[17] of Lucentio,

Come Pentecost[18] as quickly as it will,   35

Some five-and-twenty years; and then we masqued.

COUSIN CAPULET

'Tis more, 'tis more. His son is elder, sir.

His son is thirty.

CAPULET

      Will you tell me that?

His son was but a ward[19] two years ago.

ROMEO

[to a SERVINGMAN] What lady's that which doth enrich the hand   40

Of yonder knight?[20]

SERVINGMAN

      I know not, sir.

ROMEO

O, she doth teach the torches to burn bright![21]

---

12. dance

13. fools
14. remove the tables

15. unexpected enjoyment

16. By the Virgin Mary

17. wedding
18. Whit Sunday (50 days after Easter)

19. minor (a person under the age of 21)

20. lord/nobleman

21. She is so dazzling that she outshines the torches!

22. Ethiopian's (a term used for any black African in Shakespeare's time)
23. normal life
24. beauty too good for this world, and too precious to die and be buried in earth
25. flocking

26. dance

27. unworthy

28. before
29. Deny
30. eyes

It seems she hangs upon the cheek of night
As a rich jewel in an Ethiop's[22] ear –
45 Beauty too rich for use,[23] for earth too dear![24]
So shows a snowy dove trooping[25] with crows
As yonder lady o'er her fellows shows.
The measure[26] done, I'll watch her place of stand,
And, touching hers, make blessèd my rude[27] hand.
50 Did my heart love till[28] now? Forswear[29] it, sight,[30]
For I ne'er saw true beauty till this night.

TYBALT

This, by his voice, should be a Montague.
Fetch me my rapier,[31] boy. What, dares the slave

31. sword

32. here
33. mask
34. mock
35. celebration/festivity
36. family

Come hither,[32] covered with an antic face,[33]
55 To fleer[34] and scorn at our solemnity?[35]
Now, by the stock and honour of my kin,[36]
To strike him dead I hold it not a sin.

CAPULET

Why, how now, kinsman?[37] Wherefore[38] storm you so?

37. cousin
38. Why

TYBALT

Uncle, this is a Montague, our foe,[39]

39. enemy/adversary

60 A villain that is hither come in spite,
To scorn[40] at our solemnity this night.

40. sneer

CAPULET

Young Romeo, is it?

TYBALT

'Tis he, that villain Romeo.

CAPULET

Content thee, gentle coz, let him alone.
A[41] bears him like a portly gentleman,[42]

41. He
42. behaves like a well-mannered/dignified person

65 And, to say truth, Verona brags of him
To be a virtuous and well-governed[43] youth.

43. well-behaved

I would not for the wealth of all this town
Here in my house do him disparagement.[44]

44. do him disparagement = insult him/humiliate him
45. notice

Therefore be patient, take no note[45] of him.
70 It is my will, the which if thou respect,

Show a fair presence and put off these frowns,

An ill-beseeming semblance[46] for a feast.

TYBALT

It fits[47] when such a villain is a guest.

I'll not endure him.

CAPULET

　　　He shall be endured.

What, goodman[48] boy, I say, he shall. Go to,[49]

Am I the master here, or you? Go to –

You'll not endure him! God shall mend my soul.

You'll make a mutiny[50] among my guests!

You will set cock-a-hoop![51] You'll be the man!

75

TYBALT

Why, uncle, 'tis a shame.

46. an unsuitable expression

47. It is appropriate (a suitable expression)

48. yeoman (i.e. not a gentleman) ('Goodman boy' is a double insult to Tybalt.)

49. (an expression of impatience or anger)

50. trouble

51. You will create chaos

52. cheeky/impertinent

53. harm (Capulet is warning Tybalt that his fiery temper may get him into trouble.)
54. go against
55. it's time to teach you a lesson

56. cheeky, arrogant boy

57. friends

58. forced
59. anger (lines 89–90: The fact that I am forced to control myself even though I am furious makes me shake with anger.)
60. leave
61. poison (Tybalt is seething with rage and says that although he will leave now, this conflict between himself and Romeo is not over.)

CAPULET

80   Go to, go to,
You are a saucy[52] boy. Is't so, indeed?
This trick may chance to scathe[53] you. I know what,
You must contrary[54] me. Marry, 'tis time[55] –
[*to GUESTS*] Well said, my hearts!
85 [*to TYBALT*] You are a princox,[56] go. Be quiet, or –
[*to SERVINGMEN*] More light, more light! –
[*to TYBALT*] For shame! I'll make you quiet.
[*to GUESTS*] What, cheerly, my hearts![57]

TYBALT

Patience perforce[58] with wilful choler[59] meeting
90 Makes my flesh tremble in their different greeting.
I will withdraw,[60] but this intrusion shall
Now seeming sweet convert to bitterest gall.[61]

Exit TYBALT.

ROMEO

[*to JULIET*] If I profane[62] with my unworthiest hand

This holy shrine, the gentle sin is this:

My lips, two blushing pilgrims,[63] ready stand

To smooth that rough touch with a tender kiss.

JULIET

Good pilgrim, you do wrong your hand too much,

Which mannerly devotion shows in this.

For saints[64] have hands that pilgrims' hands do touch,

And palm to palm[65] is holy palmers' kiss.

ROMEO

Have not saints lips, and holy palmers, too?

JULIET

Ay, pilgrim, lips that they must use in prayer.

ROMEO

O then, dear saint, let lips do what hands do:

They pray, grant thou, lest faith turn to despair.[66]

JULIET

Saints do not move, though grant for prayers' sake.[67]

ROMEO

Then move not, while my prayers' effect I take.[68]

[*He kisses her.*]

95

100

105

62. disrespect

63. someone who travels to a sacred place for religious reasons

64. statues or pictures of saints

65. a handshake

66. (lines 103–104) My lips are praying; please answer my prayers (by returning my love) or my faith will turn to despair.

67. Statues of saints cannot move, but saints in heaven will try to answer your prayers.

68. If that is the case, stay still while I kiss you and have my prayers answered.

ACT 1, SCENE 5

69. Kissing you has cleansed me of my sin.

70. Now, I have your sin on my lips.

71. You tell me that I have sinned so sweetly!
72. Give back

73. according to the rules/with poetic language and flattery

74. wants

75. Who

76. with
77. marry her
78. plenty of money

79. What a price to pay!
80. My life is now in the power of my family's enemy.

Thus from my lips, by thine my sin is purged.[69]

JULIET
Then have my lips the sin that they have took.[70]

ROMEO
Sin from my lips? O trespass sweetly urged![71]
Give me[72] my sin again.
[*He kisses her.*]

JULIET
⠀⠀⠀⠀⠀⠀⠀⠀You kiss by th' book.[73]
NURSE
Madam, your mother craves[74] a word with you.

ROMEO
What[75] is her mother?

NURSE
⠀⠀⠀⠀⠀⠀Marry, bachelor,
Her mother is the lady of the house,
And a good lady, and a wise, and virtuous.
I nursed her daughter that you talked withal.[76]
I tell you, he that can lay hold of her[77]
Shall have the chinks.[78]

ROMEO
⠀⠀⠀⠀⠀⠀[*aside*] Is she a Capulet?
O dear account![79] My life is my foe's debt.[80]

110

115

50 **Romeo & Juliet**

BENVOLIO

Away, be gone, the sport is at the best.

ROMEO

Ay, so I fear, the more is my unrest.[81]   120

81. my uneasiness is increasing

CAPULET

Nay, gentlemen, prepare not to be gone.
We have a trifling foolish banquet towards.[82]

82. We have more food on the way.

They whisper in his ear.

Is it e'en so?[83] Why then, I thank you all.
I thank you, honest gentlemen. Good night.
More torches here! Come on then, let's to bed.   125
Ah, sirrah, by my fay,[84] it waxes late.[85]
I'll to my rest.[86]

83. Really?

84. faith
85. it's getting late
86. I'll go to bed.

Exeunt all except JULIET and NURSE.

JULIET

Come hither, Nurse. What is yon[87] gentleman?

87. yonder (that)

NURSE

The son and heir of old Tiberio.

JULIET

130   What's he that now is going out of door?

NURSE

Marry, that, I think, be young Petruchio.

JULIET

What's he,[88] that follows there, that would not dance?

88. Who's he

NURSE

I know not.

JULIET

Go, ask his name. If he be marrièd,

89. likely

135   My grave is like[89] to be my wedding bed.

NURSE

His name is Romeo, and a Montague,

The only son of your great enemy.

JULIET

[*aside*] My only love sprung from my only hate!

Too early seen unknown, and known too late!

90. Monstrous/unlucky

140   Prodigious[90] birth of love it is to me

91. hated

That I must love a loathèd[91] enemy.

NURSE

What's this, what's this?

JULIET

           A rhyme I learned even now

Of one I danced withal.

One calls within: 'Juliet!'

92. Coming!

NURSE

           Anon, anon![92]

Come, let's away; the strangers are all gone.

Exeunt

OVERVIEW OF ACT 1, SCENE 5
🔑 KEY SCENE OF LOVE

- At the beginning of this scene, Capulet is welcoming his guests to the feast. The mood is buoyant (cheerful), jovial and light-hearted.

- He discusses how long it has been since he was at a masque with his cousin and is surprised to learn that it has been 30 years.

- Next, Romeo sees Juliet and is immediately mesmerised by her beauty. He is so taken with her that he wonders:

  > *Did my heart love till now? Forswear it, sight,*
  >
  > *For I ne'er saw true beauty till this night.* (lines 50–51)

- It seems that Romeo has completely forgotten about Rosaline.

- The light-hearted, happy mood changes when Tybalt hears Romeo speak and recognises his voice. He is furious that Romeo has come to the feast uninvited and is willing to confront him. He asks for his sword:

  > *Now, by the stock and honour of my kin,*
  >
  > *To strike him dead I hold it not a sin.* (lines 56–57)

- Capulet notices that Tybalt is agitated and asks him why he is so angry:

  > *Wherefore storm you so?* (line 58)

- Tybalt reveals that Romeo, a Montague, has come to the feast. Tybalt threatens the happy atmosphere of the party. Capulet tries to calm him and becomes increasingly angry at the idea that Tybalt might cause trouble at the feast:

  You'll make a mutiny among my guests! (line 78)

- It is interesting to note that Capulet has a very good opinion of Romeo and does not wish to insult him by asking him to leave the party.

- Tybalt reluctantly withdraws, but promises that he will get revenge on Romeo for his intrusion:

  I will withdraw, but this intrusion shall

  Now seeming sweet convert to bitterest gall. (lines 91–92)

- There is a sense of danger lurking even in the midst of the party. This reminds us that there is danger everywhere for the two lovers.

- Romeo approaches Juliet and addresses her using over-the-top, exaggerated language full of religious imagery.

- Romeo imagines himself as a pilgrim at a holy shrine and feels that he is unworthy of Juliet. However, they soon kiss and Juliet tells Romeo, 'You kiss by th' book' (line 110).

- They are interrupted by the Nurse, who informs Juliet that her mother wishes to speak to her. When Romeo asks who her mother is, the Nurse informs him that Juliet is a Capulet, saying that whoever should marry Juliet 'Shall have the chinks' (line 117). Romeo is shocked at the revelation that he has fallen in love with a Capulet: 'My life is my foe's debt' (line 118).

- Capulet is informed that it is very late. He bids goodnight to his guests, and so the crowd disperses.

- At the end of the scene, Juliet asks the Nurse to find out the name of he who 'would not dance' (line 132). She is shocked to find out that Romeo is a Montague. She, like Romeo, seems to have fallen in love at first sight. At the end of the scene, she confirms this when she says:

  My only love sprung from my only hate!

  Too early seen unknown, and known too late!

  Prodigious birth of love it is to me

  That I must love a loathèd enemy. (lines 138–141)

A. REVIEWING

1. How does Tybalt react when he sees Romeo?
2. What does Capulet do when Tybalt informs him that Romeo has come to the feast?
3. How does Romeo react when he sees Juliet for the first time?
4. Describe Romeo's reaction to the news that Juliet is a Capulet, and Juliet's reaction to the news that Romeo is a Montague.

B. ORAL LANGUAGE

Pair Activity ‖P‖

With your partner, read Romeo and Juliet's shared sonnet (lines 93–106). One person should read Romeo's lines and the other should read Juliet's. Turn to **page 17** of your portfolio and complete the activity.

C. REFLECTING

1. My Reflection on Act 1, Scene 5 – a Key Scene |P|

Turn to **page 19** of your portfolio and complete the reflection on this scene.

2. Key Quotes |P|

Turn to **page 21** of your portfolio and complete the grid on key quotes from this scene.

3. Character File |P|

Turn to the Character File section of your portfolio and continue recording your impressions of **(a) Romeo (page 83)** and **(b) Juliet (page 90)** based on this scene.

D. CREATING

Writing a Magazine Article |P|

You are a reporter for the popular, glitzy Veronese magazine, *Good Morrow!* You have been asked to report on the Capulet feast. Refer to **page 22** of your portfolio for guidelines.

E. LOOKING BACK AT ACT 1

1. Overview |P|

Pair Activity

With your partner, turn to **page 4** of your portfolio and write one sentence or phrase in the box for each scene in Act 1. This sentence or phrase should sum up the main action in the scene. For example, in the box for Act 1, Scene 5, you might say: 'The Capulet feast – Romeo and Juliet meet for the first time'.

2. What If…?

Pair Activity

What if **Act 1, Scene 5** were set in modern times? Rewrite the scene for modern times, using modern English. Think about the **appropriate language to use** and where you would **set** the scene. Act out your new script with your partner.

Juliet's Balcony,
Verona, Italy

ACT 2

At this point in the play, Romeo has escaped his friends and climbed one of the walls of the Capulet orchard to try to catch another glimpse of Juliet. The revelation that Juliet is a Capulet and the only daughter of his family's enemy seems to be no **deterrent** (stop) for Romeo, who is already enchanted by her.

Act 2 features the famous **Balcony Scene**, in which Romeo and Juliet declare their love for each other. **Love** is the dominant theme of this act, as Romeo and Juliet decide to be together in spite of the obstacles in their way.

In this act we also meet Romeo's friend and advisor **Friar Laurence**, who is willing to assist the lovers in the hope of bringing about peace and harmony in Verona. Friar Laurence will play a significant part in the fortunes of the two young lovers as the play progresses.

PROLOGUE

CHORUS

1. (Romeo's former desire, i.e. Rosaline)

2. (Romeo's new love, i.e. Juliet)
3. longs to replace this old desire (Rosaline)
4. Rosaline

5. compared

6. loved in return

7. Both are enchanted by each other's good looks,

8. supposed enemy (Juliet)
9. address with loving speeches
10. frightening

11. are used to/accustomed to

12. opportunities

13. The delight and pleasure they experience will balance out the dangers they will meet.

Now old desire[1] doth in his death-bed lie,

And young affection[2] gapes to be his heir;[3]

That fair[4] for which love groaned for and would die,

With tender Juliet matched,[5] is now not fair.

5 Now Romeo is beloved[6] and loves again,

Alike bewitchèd by the charm of looks,[7]

But to his foe supposed[8] he must complain,[9]

And she steal love's sweet bait from fearful[10] hooks:

Being held a foe, he may not have access

10 To breathe such vows as lovers use[11] to swear;

And she as much in love, her means[12] much less

To meet her new-belovèd any where:

But passion lends them power, time means, to meet,

Tempering extremity with extreme sweet.[13]

Exeunt.

About the Prologue

The **prologue** informs the audience about events so far in the play. Romeo no longer loves Rosaline, as he has fallen in love with Juliet. It is important to realise that Juliet returns Romeo's love, whereas Rosaline did not. Romeo's character is changing because of love.

A. ORAL LANGUAGE

Reading and Summarising the Prologue ⎸P⎹

Pair Activity

Read the prologue in pairs. Turn to **page 24** of your portfolio and complete the activity.

ACT 2, SCENE 1

Setting: Verona; a lane by the wall of Capulet's orchard.

In this **scene**, you will:

- Discuss the **differences** between **Mercutio and Benvolio**.

Action – What Happens?

In this short scene, we find out that Romeo has separated from his companions. He is lurking near the walls of the Capulet orchard, hoping for another glimpse of Juliet. Mercutio, meanwhile, is puzzled by Romeo's disappearance, and humorously tries to make him appear by magic.

Useful Words

conjure – to make something appear (by magic); to summon up

befits – suits; matches

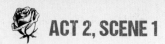
Enter ROMEO alone.

ROMEO

Can I go forward when my heart is here?

Turn back, dull earth,[1] and find thy centre[2] out.

He turns back and withdraws.

Enter BENVOLIO and MERCUTIO.

BENVOLIO

Romeo! My cousin Romeo, Romeo!

MERCUTIO

      He is wise,

And, on my life, hath stolen[3] him home to bed.

BENVOLIO

5   He ran this way, and leapt this orchard wall.

Call, good Mercutio.

MERCUTIO

      Nay, I'll conjure[4] too.

Romeo! Humours![5] Madman! Passion! Lover!

Appear thou in the likeness of a sigh.

Speak but one rhyme and I am satisfied.

10   Cry but 'Ay me!' Pronounce but 'love' and 'dove'.

Speak to my gossip[6] Venus one fair word.

One nickname for her purblind[7] son and heir,

Young Abraham Cupid,[8] he that shot so trim

When King Cophetua[9] loved the beggar-maid.

15   He heareth not, he stirreth not, he moveth not.

The ape[10] is dead, and I must conjure him.

I conjure thee by Rosaline's bright eyes,

By her high forehead, and her scarlet lip,

By her fine foot, straight leg, and quivering thigh,

20   And the demesnes[11] that there adjacent[12] lie,

That in thy likeness thou appear to us.

BENVOLIO

An if[13] he hear thee, thou wilt anger him.

---

1. (Romeo's body)
2. (Romeo's heart, i.e. Juliet)
3. crept
4. make appear by magic
5. Moody lover!
6. old friend
7. partially blind or dim-witted
8. (the god of love in mythology)
9. (The story of a king who fell in love with a beggar-maid was a popular theme of ballads.)
10. foolish creature
11. places (Mercutio is being lewd [rude] here.)
12. next to
13. An if = If

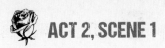

MERCUTIO

This cannot anger him. 'Twould anger him

To raise a spirit in his mistress' circle[14]

Of some strange nature, letting it there stand   25

Till she had laid it and conjured it down.

That were some spite.[15] My invocation[16]

Is fair and honest. In his mistress' name,

I conjure only but to raise up him.[17]

BENVOLIO

Come, he hath hid[18] himself among these trees,   30

To be consorted with[19] the humorous[20] night.

Blind is his love and best befits[21] the dark.

MERCUTIO

If love be blind, love cannot hit the mark.[22]

Now will he sit under a medlar[23] tree

And wish his mistress were that kind of fruit   35

As maids call medlars when they laugh alone.

O Romeo, that she were, O that she were

An open-arse[24] and thou a poppering-pear![25]

Romeo, good night. I'll to my truckle-bed.[26]

This field-bed[27] is too cold for me to sleep: 40

Come, shall we go?

BENVOLIO

        Go, then, for 'tis in vain

To seek him here that means not to be found.

Exeunt BENVOLIO and MERCUTIO.

14. magic circle

15. annoyance
16. summoning of him

17. make him appear

18. hidden

19. in the company of
20. melancholy/moody
21. suits

22. target

23. (a type of fruit)

24. A medlar fruit
25. (a pear from Poperinghe in Belgium)
26. (small child's bed, which was stored under a larger one/camp bed)
27. (a bed out in the open/soldier's bed)

Overview of Act 2, Scene 1

- This is a short transition scene that links the dramatic and energetic Feast Scene with the more intimate and serene Balcony Scene.

- Romeo has broken away from his friends so that he may catch another glimpse of Juliet. Now that he has seen her, he finds it impossible to leave:

    Can I go forward when my heart is here?

    Turn back, dull earth, and find thy centre out. (lines 1–2)

- Mercutio and Benvolio are wondering where Romeo has gone. Benvolio says that he saw Romeo climb the Capulet orchard wall and asks Mercutio to call him. Mercutio calls him and also jokingly says that he will try to make him appear by magic (conjure him). Mercutio's words are full of double meaning and sexual innuendo (references).

- Romeo's romantic language contrasts with Mercutio's lewd, bawdy (rude) language.

A. REVIEWING

1. What do you think Romeo might mean by the following lines?

    Can I go forward when my heart is here?

    Turn back, dull earth, and find thy centre out. (lines 1–2)

2. What do you think Benvolio might mean by the following lines?

    Go, then, for 'tis in vain

    To seek him here that means not to be found. (lines 41–42)

B. ORAL LANGUAGE

Pair Activity

Mercutio and Benvolio are very different characters. Briefly discuss the differences you see between them in this scene.

ACT 2, SCENE 2

Setting: Verona; Capulet's orchard.

In this **scene**, you will:

- Learn more about the key theme of **love**.
- Examine Romeo and Juliet's **soliloquies**.
- Explore many features of **language**.
- Plan how to **stage a key scene**.

Action — What Happens?

This is the famous Balcony Scene, which is a key scene of love. Romeo, who is still in the Capulet orchard, sees Juliet standing on her balcony. He is dazzled by her beauty. Juliet is speaking to herself. Romeo listens for a little while before revealing his presence.

At first, Juliet is shocked, and she worries that Romeo's life will be in danger if her family finds him there. However, they exchange vows of love, and Juliet tells Romeo that if he is serious about their love, they should get married the following day. She says that she will arrange for a messenger to go to him. The scene ends with Romeo saying that he will go to Friar Laurence's cell to inform him of his intentions.

Useful Words

discourses – speaks

doff – take off

tassel-gentle – hawk

nyas – young hawk

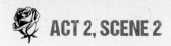
ROMEO comes forward.

ROMEO

He jests at scars that never felt a wound.

Enter JULIET above.

> But, soft!¹ what light through yonder window breaks?
>
> It is the east, and Juliet is the sun!
>
> Arise, fair sun, and kill the envious moon,²
>
> 5 Who is already sick and pale with grief,
>
> That thou her maid art far more fair than she.
>
> Be not her maid, since she is envious.
>
> Her vestal livery³ is but sick and green,
>
> And none but fools do wear it; cast it off.
>
> 10 It is my lady, O, it is my love!
>
> O that she knew she were!
>
> She speaks, yet she says nothing. What of that?
>
> Her eye discourses;⁴ I will answer it.
>
> I am too bold.⁵ 'Tis not to me she speaks.
>
> 15 Two of the fairest stars in all the heaven,
>
> Having some business,⁶ do entreat⁷ her eyes
>
> To twinkle in their spheres⁸ till they return.
>
> What if her eyes were there,⁹ they¹⁰ in her head?
>
> The brightness of her cheek would shame¹¹ those stars
>
> 20 As daylight doth a lamp. Her eyes in heaven
>
> Would through the airy region¹² stream so bright
>
> That birds would sing and think it were not night.
>
> See how she leans her cheek upon her hand!
>
> O, that I were a glove upon that hand,
>
> That I might touch that cheek!

JULIET

       Ay me!

ROMEO

25   She speaks.

O, speak again, bright angel; for thou art

As glorious to this night, being o'er my head,

As is a wingèd messenger¹³ of heaven

Unto the white-upturnèd wondering eyes

30 Of mortals that fall back to gaze on him

1. wait

2. (Diana, goddess of the moon in Roman mythology, was associated with virginity.)

3. virginal clothing

4. speaks

5. presumptuous

6. task to do
7. ask
8. orbits

9. (in the place where the stars are, i.e. the sky)
10. (the two stars)
11. outshine

12. the sky

13. an angel

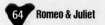

When he bestrides[14] the lazy-passing clouds,

And sails upon the bosom of the air.

JULIET

O Romeo, Romeo, wherefore art thou[15] Romeo?

Deny thy father and refuse[16] thy name,

Or, if thou wilt not, be but sworn my love,   35

And I'll no longer be a Capulet.

ROMEO

[*aside*] Shall I hear more, or shall I speak at this?[17]

JULIET

'Tis but thy name that is my enemy;

Thou art thyself, though not[18] a Montague.

What's Montague? It is nor hand, nor foot,   40

Nor arm, nor face, nor any other part

Belonging to a man. O, be some other name!

What's in a name? That which we call a rose

By any other word would smell as sweet.[19]

So Romeo would, were he not Romeo called,   45

Retain that dear perfection which he owes[20]

Without that title. Romeo, doff[21] thy name,

And for thy name – which is no part of thee –

Take all myself.

ROMEO

       I take thee at thy word.

Call me but love and I'll be new baptised.[22]   50

Henceforth[23] I never will be Romeo.

JULIET

What man art thou that, thus bescreened[24] in night,

So stumblest on my counsel?[25]

ROMEO

       By a name

I know not how to tell thee who I am.

My name, dear saint,[26] is hateful to myself,   55

Because it is an enemy to thee.

Had I it written, I would tear the word.

14. sits on

15. why are you/why do you have to be named

16. reject

17. (This is an aside, meaning that it is not meant to be heard by Juliet. Romeo is wondering if he should make his presence known at this point.)

18. even if you were not

19. A rose would still smell nice, regardless of its name/title.

20. owns

21. take off/reject

22. given a new name

23. From now on

24. hidden

25. private thoughts

26. (This reminds us of how Romeo addressed Juliet in Act 1, Scene 5.)

JULIET

My ears have yet not drunk a hundred words

Of thy tongue's uttering, yet I know the sound.

60   Art thou not Romeo, and a Montague?

ROMEO

Neither, fair maid, if either thee dislike.

JULIET

27. here

How camest thou hither,[27] tell me, and wherefore?

The orchard walls are high and hard to climb,

And the place death, considering who thou art,

28. family   65   If any of my kinsmen[28] find thee here.

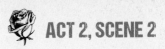

ROMEO

With love's light wings did I o'er-perch²⁹ these walls;

For stony limits cannot hold love out,

And what love can do that dares love attempt.³⁰

Therefore thy kinsmen are no stop³¹ to me.

JULIET

If they do see thee they will murder thee.   70

ROMEO

Alack, there lies more peril³² in thine eye

Than twenty of their swords. Look thou but sweet,

And I am proof³³ against their enmity.³⁴

JULIET

I would not for the world they saw thee here.

ROMEO

I have night's cloak to hide me from their eyes,   75

And but thou love me, let them find me here.

My life were better ended by their hate,

Than death proroguèd,³⁵ wanting of³⁶ thy love.

JULIET

By whose direction foundest thou out this place?

ROMEO

By love, that first did prompt me to enquire.   80

He lent me counsel,³⁷ and I lent him eyes.

I am no pilot,³⁸ yet wert thou as far

As that vast shore washed with the farthest sea,

I should adventure³⁹ for such merchandise.⁴⁰ ⁴¹

JULIET

Thou knowest the mask of night is on my face,   85

Else⁴² would a maiden blush bepaint⁴³ my cheek

For that which thou hast heard me speak tonight.

Fain⁴⁴ would I dwell on form,⁴⁵ fain, fain deny

What I have spoke; but farewell, compliment!⁴⁶

Dost thou love me? I know thou wilt say 'Ay',   90

And I will take thy word. Yet, if thou swearest,

29. fly over

30. Love will do whatever is possible.

31. obstacle

32. danger

33. protected
34. hostility

35. deferred/postponed
36. lacking/without (lines 77–78: I would rather die now than live a long life without your love.)

37. gave me advice

38. sailor

39. voyage/sail
40. treasure
41. (lines 82–84) I am no sailor, but I would travel to the ends of the Earth in search of you.

42. Or else/otherwise
43. colour

44. Gladly
45. I would gladly behave in a manner that is right and proper.
46. etiquette/politeness (Juliet is saying that she cannot behave according to the proper etiquette/ custom, which would require her to hide her feelings for Romeo.)

47. lies	Thou mayst prove false. At lovers' perjuries,[47]
48. Jupiter, Roman god of oaths	They say, Jove[48] laughs. O gentle Romeo,
49. say	If thou dost love, pronounce[49] it faithfully.
	95 Or if thou think'st I am too quickly won,
50. awkward/difficult	I'll frown and be perverse[50] and say thee nay,
	So thou wilt woo; but else, not for the world.
51. infatuated	In truth, fair Montague, I am too fond,[51]
52. behaviour	And therefore thou mayst think my 'haviour[52] light.
	100 But trust me, gentleman, I'll prove more true
53. distant/aloof ('Those that have more cunning to be strange' means 'Those who play hard to get'.)	Than those that have more cunning to be strange.[53]
	I should have been more strange, I must confess,
54. aware	But that thou over-heard'st, ere I was ware,[54]

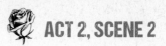

My true-love passion. Therefore pardon me,

And not impute[55] this yielding[56] to light love,   105

Which the dark night hath so discoverèd.

ROMEO

Lady, by yonder blessèd moon I vow

That tips with silver all these fruit-tree tops –

JULIET

O swear not by the moon, th'inconstant[57] moon,

That monthly changes in her circled orb,[58]   110

Lest[59] that thy love prove likewise variable.

ROMEO

What shall I swear by?

JULIET

       Do not swear at all.

Or, if thou wilt, swear by thy gracious self,

Which is the god of my idolatry,[60]

And I'll believe thee.

ROMEO

       If my heart's dear love –   115

JULIET

Well, do not swear. Although I joy in thee,

I have no joy of this contract[61] tonight.

It is too rash, too unadvised, too sudden;

Too like the lightning, which doth cease to be

Ere one can say it lightens.[62] Sweet, good night!   120

This bud of love, by summer's ripening breath,

May prove a beauteous flower when next we meet.[63]

Good night, good night! As sweet repose and rest

Come to thy heart as that within my breast![64]

ROMEO

O, wilt thou leave me so unsatisfied?   125

JULIET

What satisfaction canst thou have tonight?

---

55. attribute
56. forward behaviour

57. ever-changing

58. orbit (of the Earth)

59. In case

60. (Juliet is saying that she worships Romeo like a god.)

61. agreement

62. (lines 118–120) It is too sudden./It is happening as quick as lightning. (The image here is of a bolt of lightning that vanishes before you can say, 'It lightens'.)
63. (lines 121–122) Our love will have developed and blossomed when we next meet, just like flowers in summer.

64. heart

ROMEO

Th'exchange of thy love's faithful vow for mine.

JULIET

I gave thee mine before thou didst request it.

And yet I would it were to give[65] again.

ROMEO

130 Wouldst thou withdraw it? For what purpose, love?

JULIET

But to be frank[66] and give it thee again.

And yet I wish but for the thing I have.

My bounty[67] is as boundless[68] as the sea,

My love as deep. The more I give to thee,

135 The more I have, for both are infinite.[69]

NURSE calls within.

I hear some noise within; dear love, adieu![70]

Anon, good nurse! – Sweet Montague, be true.

Stay but a little,[71] I will come again.

Exit JULIET.

ROMEO

O blessèd, blessèd night! I am afeard,[72]

140 Being in night, all this is but a dream,

Too flattering-sweet to be substantial.[73]

Re-enter JULIET, above.

JULIET

Three words, dear Romeo, and good night indeed,

If that thy bent of love[74] be honourable,

Thy purpose marriage, send me word tomorrow,

145 By one that I'll procure[75] to come to thee,

Where and what time thou wilt perform the rite,[76]

And all my fortunes at thy foot I'll lay,

And follow thee, my lord, throughout the world.

65. I wish I could give it

66. generous

67. generosity/gifts/desire to give
68. bottomless/endless

69. without end

70. goodbye

71. Wait a while

72. afraid

73. Too wonderfully sweet to be real. (Too good to be true.)

74. your intentions

75. arrange

76. marriage ceremony

NURSE [*within*]
Madam!

JULIET
I come, anon[77] – But if thou mean'st not well,   150
I do beseech[78] thee –

NURSE [*within*]
          Madam!

JULIET
              By and by, I come –
To cease thy strife[79] and leave me to my grief.
Tomorrow will I send.

ROMEO
          So thrive[80] my soul –

JULIET
A thousand times good night!

Exit JULIET.

ROMEO
A thousand times the worse, to want[81] thy light.   155
Love goes toward love, as schoolboys from their books,
But love from love, toward school with heavy looks.

77. I'm coming soon
78. beg

79. Trouble yourself no further with trying to win me

80. save

81. lack

82. male falcon (a bird of prey)
83. I cannot raise my voice, because others might hear me
84. (Echo, a nymph in Greek mythology, was in love with Narcissus. He rejected her, and she pined away in a cave until only her voice was left.)

85. listening

86. young hawk

87. time

Re-enter JULIET, above.

JULIET

Hist! Romeo, hist! O for a falconer's voice,

To lure this tassel-gentle[82] back again.

160   Bondage is hoarse,[83] and may not speak aloud,

Else would I tear the cave where Echo[84] lies,

And make her airy tongue more hoarse than mine,

With repetition of my Romeo's name. Romeo!

ROMEO

It is my soul that calls upon my name.

165   How silver-sweet sound lovers' tongues by night,

Like softest music to attending[85] ears!

JULIET

Romeo!

ROMEO

            My nyas![86]

JULIET

                   At what o'clock[87] tomorrow

Shall I send to thee?

ROMEO

            By the hour of nine.

JULIET

I will not fail. 'Tis twenty years till then.

170   I have forgot why I did call thee back.

ROMEO

Let me stand here till thou remember it.

JULIET

I shall forget, to have thee still stand there,

Remembering how I love thy company.

ROMEO

And I'll still stay, to have thee still forget,

Forgetting any other home but this. 175

JULIET

'Tis almost morning. I would have thee gone –

And yet no farther than a wanton's[88] bird,   88. a spoilt child's

That lets it hop a little from her hand,

Like a poor prisoner in his twisted gyves,[89]   89. chains

And with a silken thread plucks it back again, 180

So loving-jealous of his liberty.

ROMEO

I would[90] I were thy bird.   90. wish

JULIET

        Sweet, so would I.

Yet I should kill thee with much cherishing.

Good night, good night! Parting is such sweet sorrow

That I shall say good night till it be morrow.[91]   185   91. day

Exit JULIET.

ROMEO

Sleep dwell upon thine eyes, peace in thy breast!

Would I were sleep and peace, so sweet to rest!

Hence will I[92] to my ghostly sire's[93] close cell,[94]

His help to crave,[95] and my dear hap[96] to tell.

92. I will go
93. my spiritual/holy father's (i.e. Friar Laurence's)
94. private room
95. To ask his help
96. good fortune

Exeunt.

'What's in a name? That which we call a rose
     By any other word would smell as sweet.'

            (Juliet, Act 2, Scene 2, lines 43–44)

Overview of Act 2, Scene 2
🔑 KEY SCENE OF LOVE

The Balcony Scene (Act 2, Scene 2) is considered to be one of the most romantic scenes in English literature. Romeo and Juliet declare their love for each other. Juliet is willing to sacrifice everything for the sake of love.

Part 1 – Romeo sees Juliet on her balcony from a distance and is overwhelmed by her beauty.

- Romeo overhears Juliet talking to herself. In his **soliloquy**, he praises her beauty by comparing her to the sun and claiming that her eyes are brighter than the brightest stars in the sky. His language is **hyperbolic** (deliberately exaggerated), poetic and extravagant as he praises her:

    See how she leans her cheek upon her hand!

    O, that I were a glove upon that hand,

    That I might touch that cheek! (lines 23–25)

- Romeo uses **religious imagery** in this scene to show his love for Juliet. He says, 'O, speak again, bright angel', and refers to Juliet as a 'wingèd messenger' (angel) (lines 26, 28). He also uses many **images of brightness** throughout to communicate Juliet's dazzling beauty.

- Juliet, meanwhile, is trying to come to terms with the news that Romeo is a Montague. This causes her to reflect on the **importance and meaning of names and titles**. She is unaware that Romeo is nearby, listening to every word. Juliet first asks why Romeo has to be a Montague, and suggests that if a rose were called something else, it would still smell as sweet. It would retain its **essential characteristics**. This is exactly the same situation for Romeo, she argues. If he were not named Romeo, he would still be the same person. She concludes that if he is not willing to reject his family name, she will gladly give up hers to be with him:

    O Romeo, Romeo, wherefore art thou Romeo?

    Deny thy father and refuse thy name,

    Or, if thou wilt not, be but sworn my love,

    And I'll no longer be a Capulet. (lines 33–36)

Part 2 – Romeo reveals his presence.

Juliet is shocked that someone (Romeo) has overheard her private musings (thoughts). However, as soon as she realises that it is Romeo, her shock turns to concern, as she worries that her family will find him and kill him. Romeo seems **unfazed** by this, saying that as long as Juliet loves him, he is protected against all harm:

    Look thou but sweet,

    And I am proof against their enmity. (lines 72–73)

Part 3 — Romeo and Juliet declare their love for one another and Juliet becomes worried that they are moving too fast.

- Juliet reminds Romeo that it is night and says that otherwise he would see her blushing over the things he overheard her saying:

  Else would a maiden blush bepaint my cheek

  For that which thou hast heard me speak tonight. (lines 86–87)

- However, she says she cannot undo what has been done and would rather be forthright and honest about her feelings for him. She declares her love for Romeo:

  But trust me, gentleman, I'll prove more true

  Than those that have more cunning to be strange. (lines 100–101)

- However, Juliet is also more **realistic** and **practical** than Romeo:

  O swear not by the moon, th'inconstant moon,

  That monthly changes in her circled orb,

  Lest that thy love prove likewise variable. (lines 109–111)

Part 4 — Juliet proposes marriage and says she will send a messenger to Romeo the next day.

- As Juliet is about to leave, Romeo asks her, 'wilt thou leave me so unsatisfied?' (line 125). He needs more reassurance of Juliet's love. She playfully insists that she has already given her love to him, but would like to take it back in order to have the pleasure of giving it to him again. She tells him that her love for him is deep and sincere:

  My bounty is as boundless as the sea,

  My love as deep. The more I give to thee,

  The more I have, for both are infinite. (lines 133–135)

- At this point, the Nurse calls Juliet. Juliet asks Romeo to wait a little while until she returns.

Part 5 — Juliet returns — 'Parting is such sweet sorrow…'

- When Juliet returns, she tries to whisper to Romeo so that she will not be overheard. She compares him to a bird, saying that she would like to keep him attached to a silken thread so that he could never go far away from her. She decides to send someone to Romeo at nine o'clock the next morning. They say good night. Juliet says, 'Parting is such sweet sorrow that I shall say good night till it be morrow' (lines 184–185), which means that she would prefer to keep saying good night until the next day.

- The scene ends with Romeo saying that he will go to Friar Laurence's cell to inform him about his good news.

A. REVIEWING

1. What do you think Juliet might mean by the following lines?

   O Romeo, Romeo, wherefore art thou Romeo?

   Deny thy father and refuse thy name,

   Or, if thou wilt not, be but sworn my love,

   And I'll no longer be a Capulet. (lines 33–36)

2. How does Juliet react when she realises that Romeo has overheard her? (Use a quote in your answer.)

3. Why does Juliet object to Romeo's swearing on the moon (lines 109–111)?

4. What do Romeo and Juliet decide to do the next day?

B. ORAL LANGUAGE

What is a soliloquy?

A soliloquy is a speech spoken by a character to him/herself. It gives us an **insight into the character's thoughts and feelings** at that particular time.

1. Romeo's Soliloquy ⎰P⎱

Pair Activity

Turn to **page 26** of your portfolio and complete the activities on Romeo's soliloquy.

2. Juliet's Soliloquy

Pair Activity

What point is Juliet making about Romeo's name in her soliloquy (lines 33–36, 38–49)? How does she develop this idea? Pick out the lines that show her reasoning.

3. Discussion

Pair Activity

Do you agree with Juliet? Do you think a name is simply a label that has nothing to do with the thing itself or the person?

C. EXPLORING

Imagery and Language Devices in the Balcony Scene

Imagery gives us an **insight into characters** and helps **create the mood or atmosphere** of a scene. Much of the imagery in the Balcony Scene comes from the **language devices** that are used by the characters, such as hyperbole, metaphor, simile and personification.

What is hyperbole?

Hyperbole is **exaggerated, over-the-top language** that is used for dramatic effect. For example, in Act 2, Scene 2, Romeo says that Juliet's eyes would shine so brightly that the birds would think it was daytime:

> *Her eyes in heaven*
> *Would through the airy region stream so bright*
> *That birds would sing and think it were not night.* (lines 20–22)

Turn to the **glossary section** on **page viii** of this book for definitions of **simile**, **metaphor** and **personification**.

1. Language Devices in the Balcony Scene |P|

Turn to **page 28** of your portfolio to complete an activity on the language devices used in this scene.

2. The Language of Love in the Balcony Scene |P|

Pair Activity

Compare and contrast Romeo's and Juliet's **attitudes to love** in this scene. For example, is Juliet as romantic as Romeo? What does the type of language that each of them uses say about his/her character? Turn to **page 29** of your portfolio to help you with this task.

D. REFLECTING

1. My Reflection on Act 2, Scene 2 – a Key Scene |P|

Complete the brief scene reflection on **pages 31–32** of your portfolio.

2. Character File |P|

Turn to the Character File section of your portfolio and add to your impressions of **(a) Romeo** **(page 84)** and **(b) Juliet (page 91)** based on this scene.

E. PROJECT

Producing and Presenting a Scene |P|

Group Activity

Imagine that you are one of the directors/producers of *Romeo and Juliet*. You are going to stage either the **Capulet Feast Scene (Act 1, Scene 5)**, or the **Balcony Scene (Act 2, Scene 2)**. In **groups**, design, plan and prepare for how you would produce your chosen scene. Try to bring the scene to life as much as possible using visual and sound effects. You will make an **oral presentation** to the class when you have completed the project. Each person will be required to speak.

Turn to **pages 33–37** of your portfolio to help you with this task. When you have given your presentation to the class, complete your reflection on the project on **pages 38–39** of your portfolio.

ACT 2, SCENE 3

Setting: Verona; Friar Laurence's cell.

In this **scene**, you will:

- Meet the character of **Friar Laurence**.
- Explore two language features: **antithesis** and **personification**.

Action – What Happens?

In this scene, we meet Friar Laurence. It is morning, and he is gathering herbs when Romeo approaches him. He is very surprised to hear that Romeo's love for Rosaline has been replaced by his love for Juliet. Friar Laurence is sceptical about the nature of young men's love. He is reluctant to marry Romeo and Juliet, but agrees to do so in the hope that this will unite their feuding families.

Useful Words

nought – nothing

aught – anything

rancour – bitterness/resentment

virtue – a good quality

vice – a bad quality

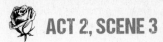

Enter FRIAR LAURENCE, with a basket.

FRIAR LAURENCE

The grey-eyed morn smiles on the frowning night,

Chequering the eastern clouds with streaks of light,

And fleckled[1] darkness like a drunkard reels

From forth[2] day's path and Titan's[3] fiery wheels.

Now, ere the sun advance his burning eye   5

The day to cheer and night's dank[4] dew to dry,

I must up-fill this osier cage[5] of ours

With baleful[6] weeds and precious-juicèd flowers.

The earth that's nature's mother is her tomb.

What is her burying grave that is her womb,   10

And from her womb children of divers[7] kind

We sucking on her natural bosom[8] find,

Many for many virtues excellent,

None but for some, and yet all different.

O mickle[9] is the powerful grace that lies   15

In plants, herbs, stones, and their true qualities,

For nought[10] so vile that on the earth doth live

But to the earth some special good doth give;

Nor aught[11] so good but strained[12] from that fair use,

Revolts from true birth,[13] stumbling on abuse   20

Virtue itself turns vice being misapplied,

And vice sometime's by action dignified.[14]

Within the infant rind of this weak flower

Poison hath residence and medicine power,

For this, being smelt, with that part cheers each part;   25

Being tasted, slays[15] all senses with the heart.

Two such opposèd kings encamp them still

In man as well as herbs[16] – grace and rude will;[17]

And where the worser is predominant,

Full soon the canker death eats up that plant.[18]   30

Enter ROMEO.

ROMEO

Good morrow,[19] father!

1. dappled (spotted with light or colour)
2. out of
3. (Helios, the sun god in Greek mythology, who travelled across the sky in a blazing chariot from east to west)
4. damp/wet
5. willow basket
6. harmful
7. different
8. breasts
9. great
10. nothing
11. anything
12. altered/diverted
13. turns away from its true nature if it is misused
14. (lines 21–22) Good qualities can be bad if misused, and bad qualities can be positive in certain situations.
15. kills
16. (lines 27–28) Two opposing 'kings' are to be found in human beings as well as plants (i.e. the capacity for doing both good and harm)
17. good and evil
18. (lines 29–30) Where the bad part is dominant, it destroys the whole plant.
19. Good day

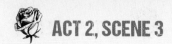
20. God bless you!
21. greets

22. To be up so early suggests a troubled mind.

23. (lines 35–38) Older people, who have a lot on their mind, may find it difficult to sleep, but younger people, who have no cares in the world, have no trouble sleeping.
24. disturbance/problem

25. holy
26. sorrow/distress

27. holy remedy (i.e. the marriage ceremony)

28. request
29. benefits

30. direct in your meaning
31. absolution/forgiveness (after confession)

FRIAR LAURENCE

      Benedicite![20]

What early tongue so sweet saluteth[21] me?

Young son, it argues a distempered head

So soon to bid good morrow to thy bed.[22]

35   Care keeps his watch in every old man's eye,

And where care lodges, sleep will never lie.

But where unbruisèd youth with unstuffed brain

Doth couch his limbs, there golden sleep doth reign.[23]

Therefore thy earliness doth me assure

40   Thou art uproused with some distemperature;[24]

Or if not so, then here I hit it right –

Our Romeo hath not been in bed tonight.

ROMEO

That last is true. The sweeter rest was mine.

FRIAR LAURENCE

God pardon sin! Wast thou with Rosaline?

ROMEO

45   With Rosaline, my ghostly[25] father? No,

I have forgot that name, and that name's woe.[26]

FRIAR LAURENCE

That's my good son; but where hast thou been then?

ROMEO

I'll tell thee, ere thou ask it me again.

I have been feasting with mine enemy,

50   Where on a sudden one hath wounded me,

That's by me wounded. Both our remedies

Within thy help and holy physic[27] lies:

I bear no hatred, blessèd man, for lo,

My intercession[28] likewise steads[29] my foe.

FRIAR LAURENCE

55   Be plain, good son, and homely in thy drift.[30]

Riddling confession finds but riddling shrift.[31]

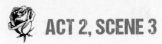

ROMEO

Then plainly know my heart's dear love is set

On the fair daughter of rich Capulet.

As mine on hers, so hers is set on mine,

And all combined, save what thou must combine   60

By holy marriage. When and where and how

We met, we wooed and made exchange of vow,

I'll tell thee as we pass. But this I pray,

That thou consent to marry us today.

FRIAR LAURENCE

Holy Saint Francis![32] What a change is here!   65

Is Rosaline, that thou didst love so dear,

So soon forsaken?[33] Young men's love then lies

Not truly in their hearts, but in their eyes.

Jesu Maria! What a deal of brine[34]

Hath washed thy sallow cheeks for Rosaline!   70

How much salt water thrown away in waste,

To season love, that of it doth not taste!

The sun not yet thy sighs from heaven clears.

Thy old groans yet ring in my ancient ears.

Lo, here upon thy cheek the stain doth sit   75

Of an old tear that is not washed off yet.

If e'er thou wast thyself, and these woes thine,

Thou and these woes were all for Rosaline.

And art thou changed? Pronounce this sentence[35] then:

Women may[36] fall, when there's no strength in men.   80

ROMEO

Thou chidd'st me oft[37] for loving Rosaline.

FRIAR LAURENCE

For doting,[38] not for loving, pupil mine.

ROMEO

And bad'st[39] me bury love.

FRIAR LAURENCE

       Not in a grave,

To lay one in, another out to have.

32. (Friar Laurence is a Franciscan friar and is swearing by Saint Francis.)

33. abandoned/rejected

34. salt water (tears)

35. proverb

36. might well

37. gave out to me frequently

38. being infatuated

39. told me to

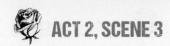

40. Please do not give out to me.

41. (lines 85–87) The person I now love returns my love, unlike Rosaline.

42. (lines 87–88) Rosaline knew that your love was not deep or sincere.

43. union/marriage

44. bitterness/hatred

ROMEO

85   I pray thee, chide me not.[40] Her I love now

Doth grace for grace and love for love allow.

The other did not so.[41]

FRIAR LAURENCE

O she knew well

Thy love did read by rote that could not spell.[42]

But come, young waverer, come, go with me.

90   In one respect I'll thy assistant be;

For this alliance[43] may so happy prove,

To turn your households' rancour[44] to pure love.

ROMEO

O let us hence! I stand on sudden haste.

FRIAR LAURENCE

Wisely and slow. They stumble that run fast.

Exeunt.

Overview of Act 2, Scene 3

- In this scene we are introduced to Friar Laurence for the first time. He is Romeo's confidant (close friend) and spiritual advisor. He will have a very important role in the play from now on, as as moral guide to both Romeo and Juliet.

- The magical night of love and romance of the previous scene now gives way to daylight and we are plunged back to reality. At the beginning of the scene, Friar Laurence tells us that it is early morning. He says:

    The grey-eyed morn smiles on the frowning night (line 1)

- Friar Laurence is gathering herbs and weeds, which he will use in healing.

- He is surprised to see Romeo up so early and wonders where he has been. Romeo says that he has been 'feasting with mine enemy' (line 49). He goes on to say that he has fallen in love with Juliet and asks Friar Laurence to marry them that day:

    Then plainly know my heart's dear love is set
    On the fair daughter of rich Capulet. (lines 57–58)

- Friar Laurence is shocked that Romeo has forgotten about Rosaline. He is concerned about how quickly events have changed.

- Romeo assures Friar Laurence that his love for Juliet is true. Juliet loves him in return, whereas Rosaline did not.

- Despite his fears, Friar Laurence agrees to marry Romeo and Juliet, hoping that the marriage will unite their feuding families and bring peace and harmony:

    For this alliance may so happy prove,
    To turn your households' rancour to pure love. (lines 91–92)

A. REVIEWING

1. (a) What point does Friar Laurence make about the capacity of plants for doing both good and harm?

    (b) How does he link this idea to human beings?

2. How does Friar Laurence react to the news that Romeo is now in love with Juliet?

3. Why does Friar Laurence agree to marry Romeo and Juliet?

4. Do you think he is right to agree to marry the couple?

B. EXPLORING

Antithesis and Personification in Friar Laurence's Language

At the beginning of the scene, Friar Laurence is gathering weeds and herbs, which have both poisonous and medicinal (healing) qualities – 'baleful weeds and precious-juicèd flowers' (line 8). While doing so, he becomes philosophical, reflecting on nature and human nature. He suggests that, like plants, human beings have the capacity for doing both good and harm:

> *Two such opposèd kings encamp them still*
> *In man as well as herbs – grace and rude will* (lines 27–28)

Through the use of **antithesis**, Father Laurence's language reminds us that **conflict** is a key theme of the play.

> ### What is antithesis?
>
> Antithesis is a literary device in which two opposing/conflicting ideas are used in a sentence to form a contrast.

Turn to the **glossary section** on **page viii** of this book for a definition of **personification**.

Pair Activity ⎮P⎮

Turn to **page 40** of your portfolio and complete the task on antithesis and personification in Friar Laurence's language.

C. REFLECTING

1. Character File ⎮P⎮

Turn to the Character File section of your portfolio and record your first impressions of **Friar Laurence (page 101)** based on this scene.

2. Key Quotes ⎮P⎮

Turn to **page 41** of your portfolio and complete the grid on key quotes from this scene.

ACT 2, SCENE 4

Setting: Verona; a street.

In this **scene**, you will:

- See a change in **Romeo's character**.
- Write a **letter** from Tybalt to Romeo.
- Research **classical references** in this scene.

Action – What Happens?

Mercutio and Benvolio are wondering where Romeo is. They assume that he is still in love with Rosaline. Benvolio informs us that Tybalt has sent a letter to Romeo, containing a challenge to fight. Benvolio and Mercutio joke about Tybalt and his manner of fighting. Later on, a much-changed Romeo arrives and engages in witty banter with his friends. The Nurse arrives with her servant, Peter, to speak privately to Romeo about his marriage to Juliet.

Useful Words

pricksong – printed music

hams – legs

shrift – confession

jest – a joke; a witty remark

vexed – agitated/annoyed

Enter BENVOLIO and MERCUTIO.

MERCUTIO

Where the devil should this Romeo be?

Came he not home tonight?[1]

1. last night

BENVOLIO

Not to his father's. I spoke with his man.[2]

2. servant

MERCUTIO

Why, that same pale hard-hearted wench,[3] that Rosaline,

Torments him so, that he will sure run mad.   5

3. (an insulting term for a woman)

BENVOLIO

Tybalt, the kinsman of old Capulet,

Hath sent a letter to his father's house.

MERCUTIO

A challenge, on my life.

BENVOLIO

Romeo will answer[4] it.

4. accept

MERCUTIO

Any man that can write may answer a letter.   10

BENVOLIO

Nay, he will answer the letter's master, how he dares,

being dared.

MERCUTIO

Alas, poor Romeo, he is already dead – stabbed with a

white wench's black eye, run through the ear with a love-

song, the very pin[5] of his heart cleft[6] with the blind   15

bow-boy's butt-shaft;[7] and is he a man to encounter Tybalt?

5. centre
6. split
7. Cupid's arrow

BENVOLIO

Why, what is Tybalt?

MERCUTIO

More than Prince of Cats,[8] I can tell you. O, he's the

courageous captain of compliments.[9] He fights as you

8. (The name 'Tybalt' was a popular name for a cat.)

9. (the formal aspects of duelling/fighting)

 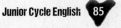

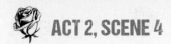
10. (from sheet music, which is more precise than improvised music)

11. the best fencing school

12. reason for the duel/fight

13. (In Italian fencing terms, the word *'passado'* means a forward thrust, the phrase *'punto reverso'* means a back-handed thrust and the word *'hai'* refers to the sword striking an opponent.)

14. a plague on/a disease on (meant as a curse)

15. (lines 27–28: Mercutio is criticising pretentious men with elaborate/ostentatious language.)

16. regrettable/very bad

17. have to put up with

18. insist
19. fashion

20. (lines 33–34) that their bones are aching on the furniture of those who went before them

21. (Roe [fish eggs] are removed from fish during the curing process. This is a pun on Romeo's name. If the first part of the name 'Romeo' is taken away, this leaves 'Me, O', which is a way of poking fun at Romeo's sadness.)
22. poetry
23. wrote
24. compared to
25. write poems about her

26. (lines 38–41: The names here are references to beautiful women in poetry and mythology, about whom verses were written. These beautiful women are insignificant compared to Romeo's great love, i.e. Rosaline.)
27. pants
28. You gave us the slip (You escaped from us)

29. a counterfeit/fake coin (also known as a 'slip')
30. Do you follow me?

---

20 sing pricksong:[10] keeps time, distance, and proportion. He rests his minim rests: one, two, and the third in your bosom; the very butcher of a silk button. A duellist, a duellist; a gentleman of the very first house,[11] of the first and second cause.[12] Ah, the immortal *passado*, the *punto*
25 *reverso*, the *hai*![13]

BENVOLIO

The what?

MERCUTIO

The pox of[14] such antic, lisping, affecting phantasims, these new tuners of accents![15] 'By Jesu, a very good blade, a very tall man, a very good whore'. Why, is not this a
30 lamentable[16] thing, grandsire, that we should be thus afflicted[17] with these strange flies, these fashionmongers, these 'pardon-me's, who stand[18] so much on the new form[19] that they cannot sit at ease on the old bench? O, their bones, their bones![20]

Enter ROMEO.

BENVOLIO

35 Here comes Romeo, here comes Romeo!

MERCUTIO

Without his roe, like a dried herring.[21] O, flesh, flesh, how art thou fishified! Now is he for the numbers[22] that Petrarch flowed in.[23] Laura to[24] his lady was a kitchen-wench – marry, she had a better love to berhyme her[25] – Dido a
40 dowdy, Cleopatra a gipsy, Helen and Hero hildings and harlots, Thisbe a grey eye or so, but not to the purpose.[26] Signor Romeo, *bonjour!* There's a French salutation to your French slop.[27] You gave us the counterfeit[28] fairly last night.

ROMEO

45 Good morrow to you both. What counterfeit did I give you?

MERCUTIO

The slip, sir, the slip.[29] Can you not conceive?[30]

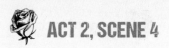

ROMEO

Pardon, good Mercutio, my business was great,

and in such a case as mine a man may strain courtesy.[31]

31. bend the rules of courtesy

MERCUTIO

That's as much as to say such a case as yours constrains a

man to bow in the hams.[32]   50

32. forces a man to bend his legs

ROMEO

Meaning – to curtsy.

MERCUTIO

Thou hast most kindly hit it.

ROMEO

A most courteous exposition.[33]

33. explanation

MERCUTIO

Nay, I am the very pink of courtesy.[34]

34. a most courteous person

ROMEO

Pink for flower.   55

MERCUTIO

Right.

ROMEO

Why, then is my pump[35] well flowered.[36]

35. shoe
36. decorated

MERCUTIO

Sure wit, follow[37] me this jest[38] now till thou hast worn out

thy pump, that when the single[39] sole of it is worn, the jest

may remain, after the wearing, solely singular.[40]   60

37. reply to
38. witty joking
39. thin
40. completely unique

ROMEO

O, single-soled jest,[41] solely singular for the singleness![42]

41. bad joke
42. which stands out because it is so bad

MERCUTIO

Come between us, good Benvolio; my wits faint.[43]

43. Step in for me, Benvolio; I am becoming tired of this game.

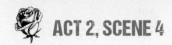

ROMEO

Switch and spurs, switch and spurs, or I'll cry a match.[44]

MERCUTIO

Nay, if our wits run the wild-goose chase, I am done, for
65 thou hast more of the wild goose[45] in one of thy wits than,
I am sure, I have in my whole five. Was I with you there for
the goose?[46]

ROMEO

Thou wast never with me for anything when thou
wast not there for the goose.

MERCUTIO

70 I will bite thee by the ear[47] for that jest.

ROMEO

Nay, good goose, bite not.

MERCUTIO

Thy wit is a very bitter sweeting,[48] it is a most sharp sauce.

ROMEO

And is it not then well served in to a sweet goose?

MERCUTIO

O, here's a wit of cheverel, that stretches from
75 An inch narrow to an ell broad.[49]

ROMEO

I stretch it out for that word 'broad', which, added to the
goose, proves thee far and wide a broad goose.[50]

MERCUTIO

Why, is not this better now than groaning for love?
Now art thou sociable, now art thou Romeo. Now art
80 thou what thou art,[51] by art[52] as well as by nature, for this
drivelling love is like a great natural[53] that runs lolling up
and down to hide his bauble[54] in a hole.

---

44. Continue on, or I win!

45. foolishness

46. Was I even with you with the goose joke?

47. (This was considered to be an affectionate/playful gesture.)

48. apple

49. (Cheverel was a type of soft leather. A one-inch length of cheverel could be stretched to an ell, which was a length measuring 45 inches.)

50. an idiot

51. you are
52. skill
53. idiot

54. (a stick carried by a jester)

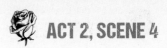

BENVOLIO

Stop there, stop there.

MERCUTIO

Thou desirest me to stop in my tale against the hair.[55]

55. You want me to stop my story before it is finished.

BENVOLIO

Thou wouldst else have made thy tale large.   85

MERCUTIO

O, thou art deceived, I would have made it short, for I was
come to the whole depth of my tale, and meant indeed
to occupy the argument[56] no longer.

56. topic of discussion (Mercutio is saying that Romeo is wrong, as he was nearly finished his story.)

ROMEO

Here's goodly gear![57]

57. (This is a reference to the Nurse's large appearance.)

Enter NURSE and PETER.

A sail, a sail![58]   90

58. (This was something a sailor said when he saw another ship on the water.)

MERCUTIO

Two, two – a shirt and a smock.[59]

59. (He is referring to Peter as a 'shirt' [a man's garment], and to the Nurse as a 'smock' [a woman's garment].)

NURSE

Peter!

PETER

Anon![60]

60. Coming!

NURSE

My fan, Peter.

MERCUTIO

Good Peter, to hide her face, for her fan's the fairer face.   95

NURSE

God ye good morrow,[61] gentlemen.

61. Good morning

MERCUTIO

God ye good e'en,[62] fair gentlewoman.

62. Good afternoon

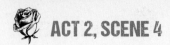
NURSE

Is it good e'en?

MERCUTIO

'Tis no less, I tell ye: for the bawdy[63] hand of the dial is
100 now upon the prick[64] of noon.

NURSE

Out upon you! What a man are you!

ROMEO

One, gentlewoman, that God hath made for himself
to mar.[65]

NURSE

By my troth,[66] it is well said. 'For himself to mar,' quoth a?[67]
105 Gentleman, can any of you tell me where I may find the
young Romeo?

ROMEO

I can tell you, but young Romeo will be older when you
have found him than he was when you sought him. I am
the youngest of that name, for fault[68] of a worse.

NURSE

110 You say well.

MERCUTIO

Yea, is the worst well? Very well took, i' faith,[69] wisely,
wisely.

NURSE

If you be he, sir, I desire some confidence[70] with you.

BENVOLIO

She will indite[71] him to some supper.

MERCUTIO

115 A bawd, a bawd, a bawd! So ho![72]

ROMEO

What hast thou found?[73]

63. vulgar
64. mark (lines 99–100: It is noon.)

65. ruin

66. Upon my word
67. he said

68. lack

69. indeed

70. (The Nurse means to say 'conference', meaning a conversation.)

71. (Benvolio is mocking the Nurse by using the word 'indite', instead of the correct word: 'invite'.)

72. (a call made by hunters when they spied the animal they were hunting)

73. spotted

MERCUTIO

No hare, sir; unless a hare, sir, in a lenten pie,[74] that is

something stale and hoar[75] ere it be spent.[76]

[*He walks by them and sings:*]

An old hare hoar[77]

And an old hare hoar   120

Is very good meat in Lent

But a hare that is hoar

Is too much for a score[78]

When it hoars ere it be spent.[79]

Romeo, will you come to your father's? We'll to dinner   125

thither.[80]

ROMEO

I will follow you.

MERCUTIO

Farewell, ancient lady. Farewell,

[*singing*] 'Lady, lady, lady.'

Exeunt MERCUTIO and BENVOLIO.

NURSE

I pray you, sir, what saucy merchant[81] was this,   130

that was so full of his ropery?[82]

ROMEO

A gentleman, Nurse, that loves to hear himself talk, and

will speak more in a minute than he will stand to[83] in

a month.

NURSE

An a speak[84] anything against me, I'll take him down, an   135

a were lustier than he is, and twenty such Jacks; an if

I cannot, I'll find those that shall. Scurvy knave![85] I am

none of his flirt-gills,[86] I am none of his skeans-mates.[87]

[*to PETER*] And thou must stand by, too, and suffer every

knave to use me at his pleasure?[88]   140

PETER

I saw no man use you at his pleasure. If I had, my weapon

should quickly have been out. I warrant[89] you, I dare draw

74. a meatless pie

75. mouldy
76. eaten

77. grey

78. too much to pay for

79. When it becomes mouldy before it can be eaten

80. there

81. cheeky, impertinent person

82. rudeness

83. do

84. If he speaks

85. Rude fellow!

86. loose women
87. cut-throat pals

88. And you just stand there and allow them to abuse me like this?

89. guarantee

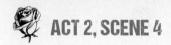
as soon as another man if I see occasion in a good quarrel, and the law on my side.

NURSE

145 Now, afore God, I am so vexed[90] that every part about me quivers. Scurvy knave! Pray you, sir, a word; and as I told you, my young lady bid me enquire you out.[91] What she bid me say I will keep to myself, but first let me tell ye if ye should lead her in a fool's paradise[92] as they say, it were a very

150 gross[93] kind of behaviour, as they say, for the gentlewoman is young; and therefore if youshould deal doubly with her,[94] truly it were an ill thing to be offered to any gentlewoman, and very weak dealing.

ROMEO

Nurse, commend me[95] to thy lady and mistress.

155 I protest[96] unto thee, —

NURSE

Good heart, and i' faith I will tell her as much.
Lord, Lord, she will be a joyful woman.

ROMEO

What wilt thou tell her, Nurse? Thou dost not mark[97] me.

NURSE

I will tell her, sir, that you do protest;[98] which, as I take it, is a gentlemanlike offer.

ROMEO

160   Bid her devise
Some means to come to shrift[99] this afternoon,
And there she shall at Friar Laurence' cell,
Be shrived[100] and married. [*offering money*] Here is for thy pains.[101]

NURSE

No, truly, sir, not a penny.

ROMEO

165 Go to,[102] I say, you shall.

90. annoyed

91. find you

92. lead her on

93. outrageous

94. deceive her

95. give my best wishes

96. I swear

97. listen to

98. (The Nurse is probably confusing the word 'protest' with 'propose', and is excited to tell Juliet this news.)

99. confession

100. confessed
101. Here is some money for your efforts.

102. Go on!

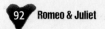

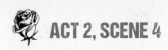

NURSE [*taking the money*]

This afternoon, sir? Well, she shall be there.

ROMEO

And stay,[103] good Nurse, behind the abbey wall.

Within this hour my man[104] shall be with thee

And bring thee cords made like a tackled stair,[105]

Which to the high topgallant[106] of my joy   170

Must be my convoy[107] in the secret night.

Farewell. Be trusty,[108] and I'll quit thy pains.[109]

Farewell. Commend me to thy mistress.

NURSE

Now God in heaven bless thee! Hark you, sir.

ROMEO

What sayst thou, my dear Nurse?   175

NURSE

Is your man secret?[110] Did you ne'er hear say

'Two may keep counsel, putting one away'?

ROMEO

I warrant thee my man's as true as steel.

NURSE

Well, sir, my mistress is the sweetest lady. Lord, Lord,

when 'twas a little prating thing – O, there is a   180

nobleman in town, one Paris, that would fain lay knife

aboard;[111] but she, good soul, had as lief[112] see a toad,

a very toad, as see him. I anger her sometimes and tell her

that Paris is the properer[113] man; but, I'll warrant you,

when I say so, she looks as pale as any clout in the versal   185

world.[114] Doth not rosemary and Romeo begin both

with a[115] letter?

ROMEO

Ay, Nurse, what of that? Both with an 'R'.

NURSE

Ah, mocker – that's the dog's name. 'R' is for the – No, I

103. wait

104. servant

105. rope ladder

106. peak

107. pathway

108. trustworthy
109. I will reward you

110. discreet/trustworthy

111. would love to claim her for himself (In Shakespeare's time, guests brought their own knives to claim a place at the table, i.e. the 'board'.)
112. would rather
113. more handsome

114. cloth in the whole world

115. the same

116. (The Nurse is confused again and means to say 'sentences'.)

190 know it begins with some other letter, and she had the prettiest sententious[116] of it, of you and rosemary, that it would do you good to hear it.

ROMEO

Commend me to thy lady.

NURSE

Ay, a thousand times. Peter!

Exit ROMEO.

PETER

195 Anon!

NURSE

Before, and apace.[117]

117. Lead on, quickly.

Exeunt.

Overview of Act 2, Scene 4

- At the beginning of this scene, we learn that Tybalt has sent a letter to Romeo, challenging him to a duel. This is a very serious development in the play. It introduces a sense of foreboding (uneasiness), as we know that tension is rising in the background. This **conflict** will have a serious impact on the developing relationship between Romeo and Juliet.

- Mercutio and Benvolio engage in witty banter, making puns and jokes. This was a very common activity in Shakespeare's time. Many of the puns and jokes are of a sexual nature. When the Nurse and Peter arrive, the Nurse is outraged and offended by Mercutio's bawdy, disrespectful language.

- This scene shows how Romeo's **character has changed**. He is transformed by love. He is no longer melancholy and sad, but happy and cheerful, as he jokes with his friends. His change of character is so noticeable that it causes Mercutio to say:

  Now art thou sociable, now art thou Romeo. (line 79)

- As was arranged in Act 2, Scene 2, Juliet has sent her messenger – the Nurse – to Romeo to discuss plans for their secret marriage. The Nurse speaks privately to Romeo, who tells her that she should ask Juliet to ask permission of her parents to go to confession. He then tells the Nurse to wait near the abbey (church) wall, where, within the hour, he will send someone with a rope ladder. This will be used to ascend (go up to) Juliet's chamber later that night.

- This is a scene of **comedy** overall, with plenty of joking and jesting. However, the ominous threat of Tybalt lurking in the background reminds us that conflict is never far away.

A. REVIEWING

1. Why does Mercutio feel that Romeo is in no fit state to fight Tybalt?

2. How does the Nurse react to Mercutio's rude language?

3. The Nurse is quite protective of Juliet. Where do we find evidence of this in this scene? Use quotes in your answer.

4. What impression do you form of Tybalt from Mercutio's description of him? Use quotes in your answer.

B. EXPLORING

1. Tybalt's Letter to Romeo |P|

Pretend that you are Tybalt. Write the letter to Romeo outlining your grievance (problem) with him, and say what you want to do about it. Turn to **page 42** of your portfolio to complete this task.

2. Research: Classical Lovers |P|

Research the tragic women whom Mercutio mentions in his speech (lines 39–41). Turn to **page 43** of your portfolio to help you with this task.

C. REFLECTING

Character File |P|

Turn to the Character File section of your portfolio and continue recording your impressions of **(a) Romeo (page 85)** and **(b)** the **Nurse (page 99)** based on this scene.

ACT 2, SCENE 5

Setting: Verona; Capulet's garden.

In this **scene**, you will:

- Learn more about the **relationship** between Juliet and the Nurse.
- Explore the **character of Juliet** by writing a diary entry.

Action – What Happens?

Juliet has been waiting over three hours for the return of the Nurse and is growing impatient. When the Nurse arrives, she annoys Juliet by complaining about how sore her back is after her long journey to find Romeo. The Nurse eventually reveals the plan to Juliet and directs her to go to Friar Laurence's cell, where Romeo will be waiting to marry her.

Useful Words

poultice – remedy

wanton – playful

beshrew – curse

jaunce – walk/journey

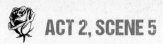

Enter JULIET.

JULIET

The clock struck nine when I did send the Nurse.

In half an hour she promised to return.

Perchance[1] she cannot meet him. That's not so.

O, she is lame! Love's heralds[2] should be thoughts,

Which ten times faster glides than the sun's beams   5

Driving back shadows over louring[3] hills.

Therefore do nimble-pinioned[4] doves draw Love,

And therefore hath the wind-swift Cupid wings.

Now is the sun upon the highmost[5] hill

Of this day's journey, and from nine till twelve   10

Is three long hours, yet she is not come.

Had she affections, and warm youthful blood,

She'd be as swift in motion as a ball.

My words would bandy[6] her to my sweet love,

And his to me.   15

But old folks, many feign[7] as they were dead –

Unwieldy, slow, heavy and pale as lead.

Enter NURSE and PETER.

O, God, she comes! O, honey Nurse, what news?

Hast thou met with him? Send thy man away.

NURSE

Peter, stay[8] at the gate.   20

Exit PETER.

JULIET

Now, good sweet Nurse – O, Lord, why look'st thou sad?

Though news be sad, yet tell them merrily.

If good, thou sham'st the music of sweet news

By playing it to me with so sour a face.[9]

NURSE

I am aweary. Give me leave a while.[10]   25

Fie, how my bones ache. What a jaunce[11] have I!

1. Perhaps

2. messengers

3. dark and threatening

4. nimble-winged

5. highest

6. speed

7. act

8. wait

9. (lines 23–24) You are ruining the good news by telling it with a sad face.

10. Let me alone.

11. trek

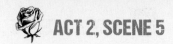

12. I wish

13. wait

14. the tale (news) that you aren't telling me

15. I'll wait for the details

16. foolish

17. though they are not worth mentioning
18. I assure you that he is
19. girl

20. Curse/damn
21. trekking/walking

JULIET

I would[12] thou hadst my bones, and I thy news.

Nay, come, I pray thee, speak, good, good Nurse, speak.

NURSE

Jesu, what haste! Can you not stay[13] a while?

30 Do you not see that I am out of breath?

JULIET

How art thou out of breath when thou hast breath

To say to me that thou art out of breath?

The excuse that thou dost make in this delay

Is longer than the tale thou dost excuse.[14]

35 Is thy news good, or bad? Answer to that.

Say either, and I'll stay the circumstance.[15]

Let me be satisfied, is't good or bad?

NURSE

Well, you have made a simple[16] choice. You know not

how to choose a man. Romeo? No, not he; though his face

40 be better than any man's, yet his leg excels all men's;

and for a hand, and a foot, and a body, though they

be not to be talked on,[17] yet they are past compare. He is

not the flower of courtesy, but, I'll warrant him,[18] as gentle

as a lamb. Go thy ways, wench;[19] serve God. What, have

45 you dined at home?

JULIET

No, no. But all this did I know before.

What says he of our marriage – what of that?

NURSE

Lord, how my head aches! What a head have I!

It beats as it would fall in twenty pieces.

My back –

[*JULIET rubs her back.*]

50   a' t'other side – ah, my back, my back!

Beshrew[20] your heart for sending me about,

To catch my death with jauncing[21] up and down.

JULIET

I'faith, I am sorry that thou art not well.

Sweet, sweet, sweet Nurse, tell me, what says my love?

NURSE

Your love says, like an honest gentleman, and a courteous,   55

and a kind, and a handsome, and, I warrant, a virtuous[22] –

where is your mother?

22. honest

JULIET

Where is my mother! Why, she is within.

Where should she be? How oddly thou repliest![23]

23. What a strange reply!

'Your love says, like an honest gentleman,   60

"Where is your mother?"'

NURSE

          O, God's lady[24] dear!

24. Mary, Mother of God

Are you so hot? Marry, come up, I trow.[25]

25. an expression of impatience

Is this the poultice[26] for my aching bones?

26. remedy (line 63: Is this the thanks I get for all my efforts?)

Henceforward[27] do your messages yourself.

27. From now on

JULIET

Here's such a coil![28] Come, what says Romeo?   65

28. fuss

NURSE

Have you got leave to go to shrift today?

JULIET

I have.

NURSE

Then hie[29] you hence to Friar Laurence's cell.

29. hurry

There stays a husband to make you a wife.

Now comes the wanton[30] blood up in your cheeks.   70

30. playful

They'll be in scarlet straight[31] at any news.

31. You'll blush immediately

Hie you to church. I must[32] another way,

32. I must go

To fetch a ladder, by the which your love

Must climb a bird's nest soon, when it is dark.

I am the drudge, and toil in your delight,[33]   75

33. I am doing all of the hard work for you

But you shall bear the burden soon at night.[34]

34. But you will pay the price tonight. (The Nurse is being bawdy.)

Go, I'll to dinner. Hie you to the cell.[35]

35. Hurry to Friar Laurence's cell.

JULIET

Hie to high fortune! Honest Nurse, farewell!

Exeunt.

Overview of Act 2, Scene 5

- Juliet is becoming increasingly impatient at the beginning of this scene. The Nurse has been gone for three hours.
- When the Nurse returns, she tells Juliet that she is tired and is not forthcoming with news from Romeo.
- Juliet becomes more even more exasperated with the Nurse and tries to elicit (find out) the information from her.
- However, the Nurse soon reveals the good news to Juliet: that she will find Romeo waiting to marry her at Friar Laurence's cell.
- Juliet is overjoyed at the news. The Nurse informs her that she must go somewhere else to procure a ladder, which Romeo will use to reach her room later that night.

A. REVIEWING

1. How is Juliet feeling at the beginning of the scene? Write out the lines that tell us this.
2. What news does the Nurse tell Juliet?
3. How does Juliet react to the news?
4. How would you describe the relationship between Juliet and the Nurse in this scene?

B. CREATING

Juliet's Diary ⎰P⎱

Imagine that you are Juliet. Write a brief diary entry outlining your thoughts and feelings about the news that the Nurse has just told you. Turn to **page 44** of your portfolio to complete this task.

ACT 2, SCENE 6

Setting: Verona; Friar Laurence's cell.

In this **scene**, you will:

- Gain an insight into the **theme of love**.

Action – What Happens?

Romeo and Juliet meet at Friar Laurence's cell to get married. Friar Laurence warns them about loving too intensely. Note that we do not witness the actual marriage ceremony – it happens off-stage at the end of the scene.

Useful Words

to chide – to reprimand (give out to)

loathsome – hateful/disgusting

gossamer – cobwebs

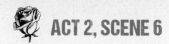

Enter FRIAR LAURENCE and ROMEO.

FRIAR LAURENCE

So smile the heavens upon this holy act,

That after-hours with sorrow chide us not![1]

ROMEO

Amen, amen! But come what sorrow can,

It cannot countervail[2] the exchange of joy

5   That one short minute gives me in her sight.

Do thou but close[3] our hands with holy words,

Then love-devouring death do what he dare –

It is enough I may but call her mine.

FRIAR LAURENCE

These violent[4] delights have violent ends,

10   And in their triumph die,[5] like fire and powder,[6]

Which as they kiss consume.[7] The sweetest honey

Is loathsome in his own deliciousness

And in the taste confounds the appetite.[8]

Therefore love moderately. Long love doth so.[9]

15   Too swift arrives as tardy as too slow.

Enter JULIET somewhat fast.
She embraces ROMEO.

Here comes the lady. O, so light a foot

Will ne'er wear out the everlasting flint.[10]

A lover may bestride the gossamers

That idles in the wanton summer air,[11]

20   And yet not fall, so light is vanity.

JULIET

Good even to my ghostly[12] confessor.

FRIAR LAURENCE

Romeo shall thank thee, daughter, for us both.

JULIET

As much to him, else is his thanks too much.

---

1. (lines 1–2) May heaven bless this marriage and may we not be punished for it later on.

2. outweigh

3. join

4. sudden

5. And are destroyed at their peak
6. gunpowder
7. Which destroy themselves when they meet

8. (lines 11–13) The sweetest honey is sickening when you have too much, and it ruins the appetite. (Friar Laurence is saying that too much of a good thing is bad.)
9. (Friar Laurence is warning Romeo and Juliet not to love each other too intensely.)

10. stones

11. (lines 18–19) A lover may walk on cobwebs that sway in the playful summer breeze

12. spiritual/holy

ROMEO

Ah Juliet, if the measure[13] of thy joy

Be heaped[14] like mine, and that thy skill be more   25

To blazon[15] it, then sweeten with thy breath

This neighbour air, and let rich music's tongue

Unfold the imagined happiness that both

Receive in either by this dear encounter.[16]

JULIET

Conceit, more rich in matter than in words,   30

Brags of his substance, not of ornament.

They are but beggars that can count their worth,

But my true love is grown to such excess

I cannot sum up some of half my wealth.[17]

FRIAR LAURENCE

Come, come with me, and we will make short work,   35

For, by your leaves, you shall not stay alone

Till holy church incorporate two in one.[18]

Exeunt.

13. amount

14. great

15. express

16. (lines 26–29) If you are as happy as I am and can express it, let me hear your sweet voice describe how you feel at this moment.

17. (lines 30–34) I have so much love that I cannot express it. Those who can count their wealth (i.e. love) are poor (beggars). I have so much love I cannot possibly count it.

18. join your hands in marriage

Overview of Act 2, Scene 6

- In this scene, Romeo and Juliet meet at Friar Laurence's cell to get married.
- Before Juliet arrives, Friar Laurence is apprehensive (worried/uneasy) and prays that heaven will bless Romeo and Juliet's holy marriage and not punish the couple in the future by bringing them sorrow:

  > *So smile the heavens upon this holy act,*
  >
  > *That after-hours with sorrow chide us not!* (lines 1–2)

- Romeo answers by saying that whatever happens in the future, it cannot outweigh the joy that even one minute with Juliet gives him. He says, ominously, that once he marries her, let 'love-devouring death do what he dare' (line 7).
- Friar Laurence warns Romeo about loving too intensely and tells him that 'these violent delights have violent ends' (line 9), meaning that sudden, passionate love can end as suddenly as it begins.
- When Juliet enters, Romeo asks her to express her love. Juliet replies that she cannot adequately express her love, because she loves him too much:

  > *But my true love is grown to such excess*
  >
  > *I cannot sum up some of half my wealth.* (lines 33–34)

- The scene ends with Friar Laurence leading Romeo and Juliet away to get married.

A. REVIEWING

1. Why is Friar Laurence worried at the beginning of the scene?
2. Do you think he is right to be worried?
3. Pick out the lines that tell us that too much of a good thing may be bad.

B. REFLECTING

Looking at Images

Look at the images of Romeo and Juliet in Act 1, Scene 5, Act 2, Scene 2 and Act 2, Scene 6 of this book. Which image corresponds to your idea of what Romeo and Juliet should look like? Write a paragraph discussing your chosen image (or images).

C. LOOKING BACK AT ACT 2

1. Overview P

Pair Activity

With your partner, turn to **page 4** of your portfolio and write one sentence or phrase in the box for each scene in Act 2. This sentence or phrase should sum up the main action in the scene. For example, in the box for Act 2, Scene 2, you might say: 'The Balcony Scene – Romeo and Juliet exchange vows of love and decide to get married'.

2. What If…?

Pair Activity

What if Romeo and Juliet had **mobile phones** and had continued their conversation after they said goodnight to one another in the Balcony Scene? Write a **text message conversation** that might have taken place at the end of **Act 2, Scene 2**. Write it in modern English. Feel free to use 'textspeak' if you feel it would make it more realistic!

A street in Verona

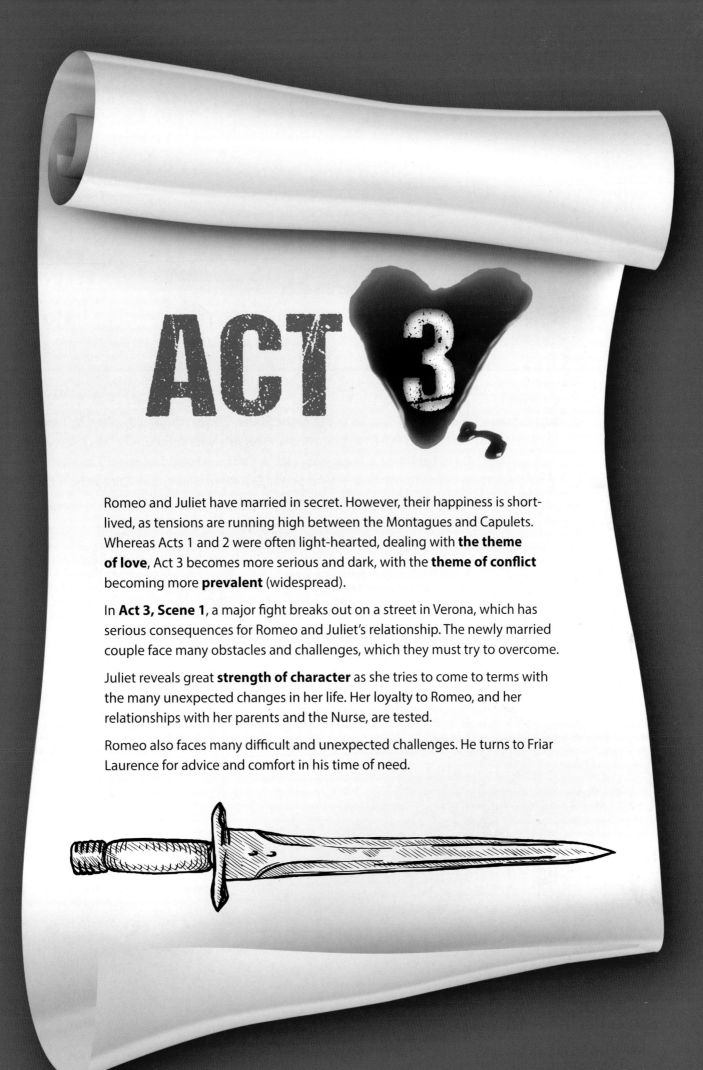

ACT 3

Romeo and Juliet have married in secret. However, their happiness is short-lived, as tensions are running high between the Montagues and Capulets. Whereas Acts 1 and 2 were often light-hearted, dealing with **the theme of love**, Act 3 becomes more serious and dark, with the **theme of conflict** becoming more **prevalent** (widespread).

In **Act 3, Scene 1**, a major fight breaks out on a street in Verona, which has serious consequences for Romeo and Juliet's relationship. The newly married couple face many obstacles and challenges, which they must try to overcome.

Juliet reveals great **strength of character** as she tries to come to terms with the many unexpected changes in her life. Her loyalty to Romeo, and her relationships with her parents and the Nurse, are tested.

Romeo also faces many difficult and unexpected challenges. He turns to Friar Laurence for advice and comfort in his time of need.

ACT 3, SCENE 1

Setting: Verona; a public place.

In this **scene**, you will:

- Find out more about the theme of **conflict**.
- Write a **news report** summarising the main action.
- Examine the **setting** of the scene.

Action – What Happens?

Act 3, Scene 1 is commonly known as the **Fight Scene**. Tybalt, who was insulted by Romeo's appearance at the Capulet feast, has come looking for revenge. Romeo, who has just married Juliet, is unwilling to fight Tybalt. The events in this scene will have devastating and far-reaching consequences for all involved – especially for Romeo and Juliet. This scene is the **turning point** of the play.

Useful Words

grievance – problem/insult

submission – surrender

to slay – to kill someone violently (past tense: he **slew**)

Enter MERCUTIO, BENVOLIO, PAGE, and SERVANTS.

BENVOLIO

I pray thee, good Mercutio, let's retire.[1]
The day is hot, the Capels abroad,[2]
And if we meet we shall not scape[3] a brawl,
For now, these hot days, is the mad blood stirring.

MERCUTIO

Thou art like one of those fellows that, when he enters   5
the confines of a tavern, claps me[4] his sword upon the
table and says 'God send me no need of thee', and by the
operation of the second cup draws him on the drawer,[5]
when indeed there is no need.

BENVOLIO

Am I like such a fellow?   10

MERCUTIO

Come, come, thou art as hot a jack[6] in thy mood as
any in Italy, and as soon moved[7] to be moody,[8] and as
soon moody to be[9] moved.

BENVOLIO

And what to?

MERCUTIO

Nay, an[10] there were two such, we should have none   15
shortly, for one would kill the other. Thou – why, thou wilt
quarrel with a man that hath a hair more or a hair less in
his beard than thou hast. Thou wilt quarrel with a man
for cracking nuts, having no other reason but because
thou hast hazel eyes. What eye but such an eye would   20
spy out such a quarrel? Thy head is as full of quarrels as
an egg is full of meat,[11] and yet thy head hath been beaten
as addle as an egg[12] for quarrelling. Thou hast quarrelled
with a man for coughing in the street, because he hath
wakened thy dog that hath lain asleep in the sun. Didst   25
thou not fall out with a tailor for wearing his new doublet[13]
before Easter; with another, for tying his new shoes
with old riband? And yet thou wilt tutor me from quarrelling![14]

1. leave
2. Capulets are around
3. escape
4. puts
5. (lines 7–8) when the second drink takes effect, draws his sword on the bartender
6. rogue
7. provoked
8. angry
9. at being
10. if
11. food
12. rotten/confused
13. padded jacket
14. (lines 23—28: Mercutio is joking with Benvolio, whom we know is not at all quarrelsome and tries to avoid conflict.)

15. If I were as inclined

16. (lines 29–30) If I were as quarrelsome as you, I would be dead within an hour and a quarter.

17. Foolish!

BENVOLIO

An I were so apt[15] to quarrel as thou art, any man should

30   buy the fee simple of my life for an hour and a quarter.[16]

MERCUTIO

The fee-simple? O simple![17]

BENVOLIO

By my head, here come the Capulets.

MERCUTIO

By my heel, I care not.

Enter TYBALT and OTHERS.

TYBALT

Follow me close, for I will speak to them.

35   Gentlemen, good e'en. A word with one of you.

MERCUTIO

And but one word with one of us? Couple it with

something: make it a word and a blow.[18]

18. strike (Mercutio is provoking Tybalt.)

TYBALT

You shall find me apt enough to that, sir, an you will give

me occasion.[19]

19. You will find me willing to do that, if you give me a reason.

MERCUTIO

40   Could you not take some occasion without giving?

TYBALT

Mercutio, thou consortest with Romeo.[20]

20. you are Romeo's companion

MERCUTIO

'Consort'? What, dost thou make us minstrels?[21] An thou

make minstrels of us, look to hear nothing but discords.[22]

[*touching his rapier*] Here's my fiddlestick; here's that shall

45   make you dance. Zounds[23] – 'consort'!

21. musicians

22. dissonance/disagreement

23. By God's wounds

BENVOLIO

We talk here in the public haunt of men.

Either withdraw unto some private place,

Or reason coldly of your grievances,[24]

Or else depart. Here all eyes gaze on us.

24. calmly discuss your differences

MERCUTIO

Men's eyes were made to look, and let them gaze.   50

I will not budge for no man's pleasure, I.

Enter ROMEO.

TYBALT

Well, peace be with you, sir. Here comes my man.[25]

25. the person I am looking for (Mercutio deliberately misinterprets this as Tybalt calling Romeo his servant – his 'man'.)

MERCUTIO

But I'll be hanged,[26] sir, if he wear your livery.[27]

Marry,[28] go before to field, he'll be your follower.

Your worship in that sense may call him 'man.'   55

26. damned
27. servant's uniform
28. By Mary (an oath)

TYBALT

Romeo, the love I bear thee can afford thee

No better term than this: thou art a villain.[29]

29. rogue

ROMEO

Tybalt, the reason that I have to love thee

Doth much excuse the appertaining[30] rage

To such a greeting. Villain am I none.   60

Therefore, farewell. I see thou knowest me not.

30. usual/accompanying

TYBALT

Boy, this shall not excuse the injuries[31]

That thou hast done me. Therefore turn and draw.

31. wrongs

ROMEO

I do protest, I never injured thee,

But love thee better than thou canst devise,[32]   65

Till thou shalt know the reason of my love.

And so, good Capulet – which name I tender

As dearly as mine own – be satisfied.

32. realise/understand

MERCUTIO

[*drawing*] O calm, dishonourable, vile submission![33]

33. surrender

34. (i.e. king of cats)

35. That I mean to take
36. thrash
37. scabbard/cover

38. sword

39. lunge/forward thrust

40. fighting

70   *Alla stoccata* carries it away.

Tybalt, you ratcatcher,[34] will you walk?

TYBALT

What wouldst thou have with me?

MERCUTIO

Good King of Cats, nothing but one of your nine lives.

That I mean to make bold withal,[35] and, as you shall use

75   me hereafter, dry-beat[36] the rest of the eight. Will you pluck

your sword out of his pilcher[37] by the ears? Make haste, lest

mine be about your ears ere it be out.

TYBALT

[*drawing*] I am for you.

ROMEO

Gentle Mercutio, put thy rapier[38] up.

MERCUTIO

80   Come, sir, your *passado*.[39]

They fight.

ROMEO

[*drawing*] Draw, Benvolio. Beat down their weapons.

Gentlemen, for shame forbear this outrage!

Tybalt, Mercutio, the Prince expressly hath

Forbid this bandying[40] in Verona streets.

85   Hold, Tybalt! Good Mercutio!

ROMEO beats down their points and rushes between them.

TYBALT, under ROMEO's arm, thrusts MERCUTIO in.

A FOLLOWER

Away, Tybalt!

Exit TYBALT with his followers.

'Hold, Tybalt! Good Mercutio!'

(Romeo, Act 3, Scene 1, line 85)

41. finished
42. no injuries

43. (i.e. an injury from Tybalt, 'King of Cats')
44. doctor

45. dead/serious (This is a pun, which shows that Mercutio is a joker to the end.)
46. done for
47. A curse on the houses of Capulet and Montague.

48. show-off/egotist

49. (meaning that he is all style, but has no real flair)

50. relative (Mercutio is related to Prince Escalus.)

51. fatal wound

MERCUTIO

I am hurt.

A plague o' both your houses! I am sped.[41]

Is he gone and hath nothing?[42]

BENVOLIO

90   What, art thou hurt?

MERCUTIO

Ay, ay, a scratch,[43] a scratch; marry, 'tis enough.

Where is my page? Go, villain. Fetch a surgeon.[44]

Exit PAGE.

ROMEO

Courage, man. The hurt cannot be much.

MERCUTIO

No, 'tis not so deep as a well, nor so wide as a church door.

95   But 'tis enough. 'Twill serve. Ask for me tomorrow, and

you shall find me a grave man.[45] I am peppered,[46] I warrant,

for this world. A plague o' both your houses![47] Zounds,

a dog, a rat, a mouse, a cat, to scratch a man to death!

A braggart,[48] a rogue, a villain, that fights by the book of

100   arithmetic![49] Why the devil came you between us? I was

hurt under your arm.

ROMEO

I thought all for the best.

MERCUTIO

Help me into some house, Benvolio,

Or I shall faint. A plague o' both your houses!

105   They have made worms' meat of me.

I have it, and soundly too. Your houses!

Exeunt all but ROMEO.

ROMEO

This gentleman, the Prince's near ally,[50]

My very friend, hath got this mortal hurt[51]

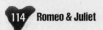

In my behalf, my reputation stained

With Tybalt's slander – Tybalt, that an hour   110

Hath been my cousin. O sweet Juliet,

Thy beauty hath made me effeminate[52]

And in my temper softened valour's steel![53]

Enter BENVOLIO.

BENVOLIO

O Romeo, Romeo, brave Mercutio is dead!

That gallant[54] spirit hath aspired[55] the clouds,   115

Which too untimely[56] here did scorn the earth.

ROMEO

This day's black fate on more days doth depend.

This but begins the woe others must end.[57]

Enter TYBALT.

BENVOLIO

Here comes the furious Tybalt back again.

ROMEO

Alive, in triumph, and Mercutio slain?[58]   120

Away to heaven, respective lenity,[59]

And fire-eyed fury be my conduct[60] now!

Now, Tybalt, take the 'villain' back again

That late thou gavest me,[61] for Mercutio's soul

Is but a little way above our heads,   125

Staying for thine to keep him company.[62]

Either thou, or I, or both, must go with him.

TYBALT

Thou, wretched[63] boy, that didst consort him here,

Shalt with him hence.

ROMEO

        This shall determine that.[64]

They fight. TYBALT falls and dies.

---

52. unmanly

53. lessened my bravery

54. brave/heroic
55. risen up to
56. prematurely

57. Today's events will have repercussions in the coming days.

58. killed

59. respectful mercy (Romeo is disregarding the Prince's order not to fight.)
60. guide

61. That you recently called me

62. Waiting for your soul to keep him company

63. vile/unfortunate

64. This sword shall decide that.

65. up in arms/agitated

66. startled
67. sentence you to death

BENVOLIO

130 Romeo, away, be gone!

The citizens are up,[65] and Tybalt slain.

Stand not amazed.[66] The Prince will doom thee death,[67]

If thou art taken. Hence, be gone, away!

ROMEO

O, I am fortune's fool!

BENVOLIO

Why dost thou stay?

Exit ROMEO.

Enter CITIZENS.

CITIZEN

135 Which way ran he that killed Mercutio?

Tybalt, that murderer, which way ran he?

BENVOLIO

There lies that Tybalt.

CITIZEN

[*to TYBALT*] Up, sir, go with me.

I charge thee in the Prince's name, obey.

Enter PRINCE, MONTAGUE, CAPULET, their WIVES and all.

PRINCE

68. fight

Where are the vile beginners of this fray?[68]

BENVOLIO

69. reveal

140 O noble Prince, I can discover[69] all

The unlucky manage of this fatal brawl.

70. killed

There lies the man, slain[70] by young Romeo,

71. killed

That slew[71] thy kinsman, brave Mercutio.

LADY CAPULET

Tybalt, my cousin! O my brother's child!

145 O Prince! O cousin! Husband! O, the blood is spilled

Of my dear kinsman! Prince, as thou art true,

For blood of ours, shed blood of Montague.

O cousin, cousin!

PRINCE

Benvolio, who began this bloody fray?

BENVOLIO

Tybalt, here slain,[72] whom Romeo's hand did slay.	150
Romeo, that spoke him fair, bid[73] him bethink	
How nice[74] the quarrel was, and urged withal	
Your high displeasure.[75] All this – utterèd	
With gentle breath, calm look, knees humbly bowed –	
Could not take truce[76] with the unruly spleen[77]	155
Of Tybalt deaf to peace, but that he tilts	
With piercing steel at bold Mercutio's breast,	
Who, all as hot, turns deadly point to point,	
And, with a martial scorn, with one hand beats	
Cold death aside, and with the other sends	160
It back to Tybalt, whose dexterity[78]	
Retorts it. Romeo, he cries aloud,	
'Hold, friends! Friends, part!' and, swifter than his tongue,	
His agile arm beats down their fatal points,	
And 'twixt[79] them rushes, underneath whose[80] arm	165
An envious[81] thrust from Tybalt hit the life	
Of stout[82] Mercutio, and then Tybalt fled,	
But by and by comes back to Romeo,	
Who had but newly entertained[83] revenge,	
And to't they go like lightning; for ere[84] I	170
Could draw to part them was stout Tybalt slain,	
And as he fell did Romeo turn and fly.	
This is the truth, or let Benvolio die.	

LADY CAPULET

He is a kinsman to the Montague.	
Affection makes him false.[85] He speaks not true.	175
Some twenty of them fought in this black strife,	
And all those twenty could but kill one life.	
I beg for justice, which thou, Prince, must give.	
Romeo slew Tybalt; Romeo must not live.	

72. killed

73. asked

74. insignificant

75. disapproval

76. calm
77. uncontrollable anger

78. skill

79. between
80. (i.e. Romeo's)
81. A spiteful

82. brave

83. had only just thought of

84. before

85. His friendship with Romeo makes him unreliable/biased.

86. Mercutio's

87. offence/crime

88. relative

89. punish

90. compensate for

91. Showing mercy to those who have committed murder only results in more killing.

PRINCE

180 Romeo slew him, he slew Mercutio.

Who now the price of his[86] dear blood doth owe?

MONTAGUE

Not Romeo, Prince. He was Mercutio's friend.

His fault[87] concludes but what the law should end,

The life of Tybalt.

PRINCE

And for that offence

185 Immediately we do exile him hence.

I have an interest in your hate's proceeding;

My blood[88] for your rude brawls doth lie a-bleeding;

But I'll amerce[89] you with so strong a fine

That you shall all repent the loss of mine.

190 I will be deaf to pleading and excuses.

Nor tears nor prayers shall purchase out[90] abuses.

Therefore use none. Let Romeo hence in haste,

Else, when he is found, that hour is his last.

Bear hence this body, and attend our will.

195 Mercy but murders, pardoning those that kill.[91]

Exeunt.

OVERVIEW OF ACT 3, SCENE 1
KEY SCENE OF CONFLICT

- At the beginning of the scene, tensions are running high. Benvolio thinks that they should leave and warns Mercutio about the risk of a quarrel if they meet the Capulets. Benvolio says:

  I pray thee, good Mercutio, let's retire.
  The day is hot, the Capels abroad,
  And if we meet we shall not scape a brawl,
  For now, these hot days, is the mad blood stirring. (lines 1–4)

- Tybalt arrives, looking for Romeo. He has sent him a challenge (an invitation to fight).

- Mercutio becomes argumentative, while Benvolio tries to keep the peace. Benvolio thinks that it would be better to talk things through:

  We talk here in the public haunt of men.
  Either withdraw unto some private place,
  Or reason coldly of your grievances,
  Or else depart. Here all eyes gaze on us. (lines 46–49)

- Meanwhile, Romeo arrives and Tybalt tries to provoke him to fight by calling him 'a villain' (line 57).

- However, Romeo, who has just married Juliet, has no intention of fighting and simply says, 'Villain am I none' (line 60).

- Mercutio is outraged at what he calls Romeo's 'dishonourable, vile submission' (line 69) and takes it upon himself to fight on Romeo's behalf.

- Tybalt and Mercutio fight and Romeo tries to get between them to break it up. As he does so, Tybalt strikes Mercutio under Romeo's arm and fatally wounds him.

- Mercutio curses the Capulets and Montagues and dies:

    A plague o' both your houses!

    They have made worms' meat of me. (lines 104–105)

- Romeo, realising his friend Mercutio died trying to defend his honour, approaches Tybalt saying:

    Now, Tybalt, take the 'villain' back again

    That late thou gavest me (lines 123–124)

- They fight and Romeo kills Tybalt.

- Benvolio, remembering the Prince's earlier warning, urges Romeo to flee:

    Stand not amazed. The Prince will doom thee death,

    If thou art taken. Hence, be gone, away! (lines 132–133)

- Romeo is immediately aware of the **magnitude** (greatness/extent) of his crime. He says, 'O, I am fortune's fool' (line 134), conveying regret that he is a victim of fate. At the beginning of the scene, he had just married Juliet and was unwilling to fight, but by the end of the scene, he has become embroiled (involved) in the conflict and is guilty of killing Tybalt.

- When Prince Escalus arrives, Benvolio recounts what happened. As punishment for Tybalt's death, the Prince decides to 'exile him hence' (line 185), which means that Romeo is now banished from Verona. If found in Verona, he will be put to death:

    Let Romeo hence in haste,

    Else, when he is found, that hour is his last. (lines 192–193)

- In the last line of the scene, the Prince claims that 'Mercy but murders, pardoning those that kill' (line 195), suggesting that not punishing those who kill may incite/lead to further killings.

A. REVIEWING

1. Why does Benvolio want to leave at the start of the scene?

2. When Tybalt insults Romeo, Romeo refuses to fight him. **Paraphrase** (write in your own words) what he says.

3. Why is Romeo so reluctant to fight Tybalt at this stage?

4. Why does Mercutio get involved in the fight? Do you think he is brave or foolish to do so?

5. Why does Romeo change his mind about fighting Tybalt?

6. What do you think Romeo means by 'O, I am fortune's fool' (line 134)? Do you feel sorry for him at this point?

B. EXPLORING

1. Who Killed Whom? |P|

Turn to **page 46** of your portfolio and complete the activity on the **main stages** of the fight scene.

2. Characters |P|

Pair Activity

With your partner, fill in the grid about the characters on **page 48** of the portfolio. Then, discuss who you both feel is **responsible** for starting the fight.

3. Performing a Tableau

What is a tableau?

A **tableau** (freeze-frame) involves representing a group of characters in a still scene. The aim of a tableau is to capture a specific moment from a scene, as if the action has been paused or is frozen in time. The actions and facial expressions of the characters are held for a time.

Group Activity

In groups of four, choose one moment from the scene and create a tableau. Can your classmates guess which part of the scene you have chosen?

4. Looking at Setting

Picture A: From *Romeo and Juliet* (1968)

Picture B: From *Romeo and Juliet* (1996)

(a) Examine **Picture A** and **Picture B** above, which are still images taken from two film versions of *Romeo and Juliet*.

(b) Briefly compare both settings.

(c) Which setting do you like best? Explain your answer.

(d) What part of the scene is each still image depicting in your opinion?

C. CREATING

The *Verona Times* ⫼P⫼

Write a front-page news story for the serious newspaper, the *Verona Times*, reporting on the events that took place in this scene. Turn to **page 49** of your portfolio to complete this task.

D. REFLECTING

1. My Reflection on Act 3, Scene 1 – a Key Scene ⫼P⫼

Turn to **page 51** of your portfolio and complete the reflection on this scene.

2. Key Quotes ⫼P⫼

Turn to **page 52** of your portfolio. Write out three quotes that you think are important in this scene and say what you think they might mean.

3. Character File ⫼P⫼

Turn to the Character File section of your portfolio and continue recording your impressions of **(a) Romeo (page 86)**, **(b) Tybalt (page 96)** and **(c) Mercutio (page 103)** based on this scene.

ACT 3, SCENE 2

Setting: Verona; Capulet's orchard.

In this **scene**, you will:

- Find out more about the **character of Juliet**.
- Explore aspects of **Juliet's language**.
- Learn about **oxymorons** and **dramatic irony**.

Action – What Happens?

At the beginning of this scene, Juliet is waiting for nightfall, when Romeo will join her for their wedding night. She is full of excitement and anticipation. However, the Nurse soon interrupts Juliet's reverie (daydream) by bringing news of Tybalt's death and Romeo's banishment. At first, Juliet thinks that the Nurse is weeping over Romeo's death. When it later emerges that Romeo is responsible for Tybalt's death, Juliet experiences a range of conflicting emotions.

Useful Words

fiend – devil   **beguiled** – tricked/deceived

Enter JULIET alone.

JULIET

Gallop apace,[1] you fiery-footed steeds,[2]

Towards Phoebus' lodging.[3] Such a waggoner[4]

As Phaeton[5] would whip you to the west,

And bring in cloudy night immediately

Spread thy close[6] curtain, love-performing night!   5

That runaway's eyes may wink,[7] and Romeo

Leap to these arms, untalked of and unseen.

Lovers can see to do their amorous rites

By their own beauties;[8] or, if love be blind,

It best agrees with[9] night. Come, civil night,   10

Thou sober-suited matron, all in black,

And learn me how to lose a winning match,[10]

Played for a pair of stainless maidenhoods.[11]

Hood my unmanned blood,[12] bating in my cheeks,

With thy black mantle[13] till strange[14] love grown bold   15

Think true love acted simple modesty.

Come, night. Come, Romeo. Come, thou day in night,

For thou wilt lie upon the wings of night

Whiter than new snow upon a raven's back.

Come, gentle night. Come, loving, black-browed night,   20

Give me my Romeo, and when I shall die,

Take him and cut him out in little stars,

And he will make the face of heaven so fine

That all the world will be in love with night,

And pay no worship to the garish[15] sun.   25

O, I have bought the mansion of a love,

But not possessed it, and though I am sold,

Not yet enjoyed. So tedious is this day

As is the night before some festival

To an impatient child that hath new robes[16]   30

And may not wear them.

Enter NURSE, wringing her hands, with the ladder of cords.

                    O, here comes my Nurse,

And she brings news, and every tongue that speaks

But Romeo's name speaks heavenly eloquence.

Now, Nurse, what news? What hast thou there the cords

That Romeo bade thee fetch?

1. quickly
2. horses
3. Phoebus's home (Juliet is wishing that the horses belonging to the Greek sun god, Phoebus Apollo, will quickly take the sun to the west, so night will fall.)
4. driver
5. (Phaeton, the son of Apollo, once took charge of steering his father's chariot across the sky and nearly crashed it into Earth. Jupiter struck him down, killing him.)
6. covering
7. (The meaning of this line is unclear. One possible meaning is that Juliet wants the sun to close its eyes so that night will fall.)
8. (lines 8–9) Lovers' beauty gives them all the light they need to perform their loving acts
9. suits
10. teach me how to win Romeo over by surrendering to him
11. innocent young lovers
12. Hide my blushes
13. cloak
14. shy
15. bright
16. clothes

NURSE

35　　　　　　　Ay, ay, the cords.

[*She throws them down.*]

JULIET

Ah me! What news? Why dost thou wring thy hands?

NURSE

Ah weraday![17] He's dead, he's dead, he's dead!

We are undone, lady, we are undone![18]

Alack the day! He's gone, he's killed, he's dead!

JULIET

Can heaven be so envious?[19]

NURSE

40　　　　　　　Romeo can,

Though heaven cannot. O Romeo, Romeo,

Who ever would have thought it? Romeo!

JULIET

What devil art thou that dost torment me thus?

This torture should be roared in dismal hell.

45　Hath Romeo slain himself? Say thou but 'Ay,'

And that bare vowel 'I' shall poison more

Than the death-darting eye of cockatrice.[20]

I am not I, if there be such an 'Ay',

Or those eyes shut that make thee answer 'Ay'.

50　If he be slain, say 'Ay'; or if not, 'No'.

Brief sounds determine of my weal or woe.[21]

NURSE

I saw the wound, I saw it with mine eyes,

God save the mark, here on his manly breast –

A piteous corpse, a bloody piteous corpse –

55　Pale, pale as ashes, all bedaubed[22] in blood,

All in gore[23] blood. I swounded[24] at the sight.

JULIET

O, break, my heart, poor bankrupt, break at once!

To prison, eyes; ne'er look on liberty!

17. Alas! (an exclamation used to express grief or pity)

18. ruined/destroyed

19. spiteful

20. (a mythical serpent – half snake, half cockerel – that kills by just looking)

21. happiness or sadness

22. covered

23. gory

24. fainted

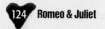

Vile earth,[25] to earth resign; end motion here,[26]
And thou and Romeo press one heavy bier![27]

60

NURSE

O Tybalt, Tybalt, the best friend I had!
O courteous Tybalt, honest[28] gentleman,
That ever I should live to see thee dead!

JULIET

What storm is this that blows so contrary?[29]
Is Romeo slaughtered, and is Tybalt dead?

65

My dearest cousin, and my dearer lord?
Then, dreadful trumpet, sound the general doom![30]
For who is living if those two are gone?

NURSE

Tybalt is gone, and Romeo banishèd;
Romeo, that killed him, he is banishèd.

70

JULIET

O God, did Romeo's hand shed Tybalt's blood?

NURSE

It did, it did! Alas the day, it did!

JULIET

O serpent heart, hid with[31] a flowering[32] face!
Did ever dragon keep[33] so fair a cave?
Beautiful tyrant,[34] fiend angelical![35]

75

Dove-feathered raven,[36] wolvish-ravening lamb![37]
Despisèd substance of divinest show!
Just opposite to what thou justly seemest;
A damnèd saint, an honourable villain.
O, nature, what hadst thou to do in hell

80

When thou didst bower the spirit of a fiend[38]
In mortal paradise of such sweet flesh?[39]
Was ever book containing such vile matter
So fairly bound? O, that deceit should dwell
In such a gorgeous palace!

25. body
26. stop all feeling
27. you and Romeo will lie together in death

28. honourable

29. What are these contradictory reports?

30. end of the world

31. by
32. beautiful
33. guard

34. oppressor
35. devil disguised as an angel
36. White-coloured raven (A raven is usually black.)
37. wolf-like lamb

38. devil

39. (lines 80—82) Nature, what were you doing in hell, when you enclosed a demon in such a beautiful body?

40. liars

41. deceivers
42. worthless
43. cheats
44. alcohol

NURSE

85   There's no trust,

No faith, no honesty in men; all perjured,[40]

All forsworn,[41] all naught,[42] all dissemblers.[43]

Ah, where's my man? Give me some aqua vitae[44]

These griefs, these woes, these sorrows make me old.

Shame come to Romeo!

JULIET

90   Blistered be thy tongue

For such a wish! He was not born to shame.

Upon his brow shame is ashamed to sit,

For 'tis a throne where honour may be crowned

Sole monarch of the universal earth.

45. criticise

95   O, what a beast was I to chide at[45] him!

NURSE

Will you speak well of him that killed your cousin?

JULIET

Shall I speak ill of him that is my husband?

46. praise you

Ah, poor my lord, what tongue shall smooth thy name,[46]

47. destroyed

When I, thy three-hours wife, have mangled[47] it?

48. why

100   But, wherefore,[48] villain, didst thou kill my cousin?

That villain cousin would have killed my husband.

49. go back to where you came from

Back, foolish tears, back to your native spring![49]

Your tributary drops belong to woe,

50. (lines 103—104) Tears are for sorrow, and you are mistakenly shedding tears that are not necessary at this time.

Which you, mistaking, offer up to joy.[50]

105   My husband lives, that Tybalt would have slain;

And Tybalt's dead, that would have slain my husband.

All this is comfort. Wherefore weep I then?

Some word there was, worser than Tybalt's death,

51. I would gladly forget it

That murdered me. I would forget it fain;[51]

110   But O, it presses to my memory,

Like damnèd guilty deeds to sinners' minds!

'Tybalt is dead, and Romeo banishèd!'

That 'banishèd,' that one word 'banishèd,'

Hath slain ten thousand Tybalts. Tybalt's death

115   Was woe enough, if it had ended there;

52. company

Or, if sour woe delights in fellowship,[52]

53. must be accompanied by

And needly will be ranked with[53] other griefs,

Why followed not, when she said 'Tybalt's dead',

'Thy father', or 'thy mother', nay, or both,

Which modern lamentation might have moved?[54]　　　　120

But with a rearward[55] following Tybalt's death,

'Romeo is banishèd!' – to speak that word

Is father, mother, Tybalt, Romeo, Juliet,

All slain, all dead. 'Romeo is banishèd!' –

There is no end, no limit, measure, bound　　　　125

In that word's death. No words can that woe sound.[56]

Where is my father and my mother, Nurse?

NURSE

Weeping and wailing over Tybalt's corpse.

Will you go to them? I will bring you thither.[57]

JULIET

Wash they his wounds with tears? Mine shall be spent,　　　　130

When theirs are dry, for Romeo's banishment.

Take up those cords. Poor ropes, you are beguiled,[58]

Both you and I, for Romeo is exiled.

He made you for a highway to my bed,

But I, a maid, die maiden-widowèd.[59]　　　　135

Come, cords; come, Nurse; I'll to my wedding bed,

And death, not Romeo, take my maidenhead!

NURSE

Hie[60] to your chamber. I'll find Romeo

To comfort you. I wot[61] well where he is.

Hark ye,[62] your Romeo will be here at night.　　　　140

I'll to him. He is hid at Laurence' cell.

JULIET

O, find him! Give this ring to my true knight,

And bid him come to take his last farewell.

Exeunt.

54. Which would have produced a moderate amount of grief
55. final word

56. express that sorrow

57. there

58. cheated

59. a virgin-widow

60. hurry
61. know
62. Listen to me

OVERVIEW OF ACT 3, SCENE 2

- At the beginning of this scene, Juliet, alone on stage, is longing for nightfall, when Romeo will ascend the rope ladder to her chamber. She is both excited and nervous at this prospect.

- However, her excitement is short-lived, as the Nurse enters visibly distraught. The audience knows that the Nurse is upset over Tybalt's death, but it is some time before this information becomes apparent to Juliet.

- When the Nurse says, 'He's dead, he's dead, he's dead' (line 37), Juliet assumes she is talking about Romeo. Juliet asks, 'Hath Romeo slain himself?' (line 45). The Nurse's inability to articulate exactly what has happened causes Juliet to misinterpret the situation entirely. The audience knows exactly what is happening, but Juliet does not. This is known as **dramatic irony**.

- When it finally emerges that Romeo has killed Tybalt, Juliet is **incredulous** (in disbelief). She asks:

    O God, did Romeo's hand shed Tybalt's blood? (line 71)

- Juliet's language is **replete** (filled) with **oxymorons**, reflecting her feeling that she has been **duped** (tricked) by Romeo:

    O serpent heart, hid with a flowering face! (line 73)

- She believes she has been utterly deceived and that the 'spirit of a fiend [devil]' is hidden in Romeo's 'sweet flesh [body]' (lines 81–82).

- The Nurse joins in condemning Romeo:

    Shame come to Romeo! (line 90)

- Interestingly, Juliet, on hearing Romeo being criticised, jumps to his defence and **berates** (gives out to) the Nurse for speaking badly of him:

    Blistered be thy tongue

    For such a wish! He was not born to shame. (lines 90–91)

- She rebukes herself for not being loyal to her husband:

    Ah, poor my lord, what tongue shall smooth thy name,

    When I, thy three-hours wife, have mangled it? (lines 98–99)

- Juliet regains her **composure** (calm) and forces herself to reflect on the positive aspects of the situation. She displays immense maturity in this scene as she rationally **evaluates** the situation:

    Back, foolish tears, back to your native spring! (line 102)

- She realises that she has a lot to be thankful for: 'All this is comfort' (line 107). However, remembering that Romeo has been banished plunges her into further despair and she claims it is the equivalent of:

    … father, mother, Tybalt, Romeo, Juliet,

    All slain, all dead. (lines 123–124)

- At the end of the scene, the Nurse comforts Juliet by saying that she knows Romeo's whereabouts and will find him. Juliet gives the Nurse a ring for Romeo as a token of her love. This provides a slight glimmer of hope for Juliet at the end of an otherwise distressing scene.

A. REVIEWING

1. Describe Juliet's mood at the beginning of the scene.
2. How does Juliet react when she thinks that Romeo has taken his own life?
3. How does Juliet respond when the Nurse says, 'Will you speak well of him that killed your cousin' (line 96)?
4. How does Juliet react to the news that Romeo is banished?

B. EXPLORING

Juliet's Language /P\

Juliet's language reflects how confused she is in this scene. She uses **oxymorons** in her speech.

What is an oxymoron?

An oxymoron is a figure of speech that uses opposites to achieve a certain effect. Examples are 'loving hate' and 'cold fire'.

Keeping the definition of oxymoron in mind, turn to **page 53** of your portfolio and complete the activity on Juliet's language.

C. ORAL LANGUAGE

1. Performing 'Fiend Angelical' in Groups of Three

Group Activity

Characters: Juliet, an Angel, a Fiend (devil)

The **angel** writes down **three positive things** about Romeo, and the **fiend** writes down **three negative things** about him. These can be direct quotes or improvised statements based on the play so far. The **angel** and **fiend** sit at either side of Juliet and take turns saying positive and negative things about Romeo. Juliet, while listening, responds either verbally or non-verbally.

2. Discussing Dramatic Irony

Pair/Group Activity

What is dramatic irony?

Dramatic irony occurs when the audience or certain characters on stage have information that another character(s) does not have.

For example, in this scene, the Nurse enters and says, 'He's dead' (line 37). Juliet assumes that she is referring to Romeo. This **misapprehension** (misinterpretation) causes Juliet to experience a range of conflicting emotions.

Discuss:

(a) Why do you think Shakespeare uses the device of **dramatic irony** in this particular part of the play?

(b) Can you think of any film, television programme, or another play that has made use of **dramatic irony**? Describe the **scenario** and say whether you, as a viewer/audience member, thought that this was an effective device.

D. REFLECTING

Juliet's Character /P\

Pair Activity

Chart Juliet's **changing emotions** in this scene. Turn to **page 55** of your portfolio to help you with this task. Turn to the Character File section of your portfolio and continue recording your impressions of **Juliet (page 92)** when you are finished with the previous task.

ACT 3, SCENE 3

Setting: Verona; Friar Laurence's cell.

In this **scene**, you will:

- Learn more about the characters of **Friar Laurence** and **Romeo**.
- Explore Friar Laurence's **speech**.

Action – What Happens?

Romeo is waiting for news of the Prince's sentence. He is overwrought with emotion, and when he finds out that he has been banished, he is virtually inconsolable. However, Friar Laurence gives him advice and presents him with a plan of action to help deal with the situation. The Nurse's arrival with the ring from Juliet lessens Romeo's anguish.

Useful Words

overwrought – distraught/hysterical

adversity – suffering/misery

calamity – tragedy/misfortune

decreed – decided

Enter FRIAR LAURENCE.

FRIAR LAURENCE

Romeo, come forth. Come forth, thou fearful[1] man.

Affliction is enamoured of thy parts,[2]

And thou art wedded to calamity.[3]

Enter ROMEO.

ROMEO

Father, what news? What is the Prince's doom?[4]

What sorrow craves acquaintance at my hand,   5

That I yet know not?[5]

FRIAR LAURENCE

         Too familiar

Is my dear son with such sour company.

I bring thee tidings[6] of the Prince's doom.

ROMEO

What less than doomsday[7] is the Prince's doom?

FRIAR LAURENCE

A gentler judgement vanished[8] from his lips: 10

Not body's[9] death, but body's banishèd.

ROMEO

Ha, banishment? Be merciful, say 'death',

For exile hath more terror in his look,

Much more than death. Do not say 'banishment.'

FRIAR LAURENCE

Hence from Verona art thou banishèd.   15

Be patient,[10] for the world is broad and wide.

ROMEO

There is no world without[11] Verona walls,

But purgatory, torture, hell itself.

Hence banishèd is banished from the world,

And world's exile is death. Then 'banishèd'   20

Is death mistermed. Calling death 'banishèd'.[12]

1. full of fear
2. Misery seems to love you
3. misfortune follows you wherever you go
4. sentence/judgement
5. (lines 5—6) What is the bad news?
6. news
7. the end of the world
8. came
9. your
10. calm
11. outside
12. (lines 20—21) Banishment is the equivalent of death for me, as being banished from Verona is like being banished from the world.

Thou cuttest my head off with a golden axe,

And smilest upon the stroke that murders me.

FRIAR LAURENCE

O deadly[13] sin! O rude unthankfulness!

25 Thy fault our law calls death,[14] but the kind Prince,

Taking thy part, hath rushed[15] aside the law,

And turned that black word 'death' to banishment.[16]

This is dear mercy, and thou seest it not.

ROMEO

'Tis torture, and not mercy. Heaven is here,

30 Where Juliet lives, and every cat and dog

And little mouse, every unworthy thing,

Live here in heaven and may look on her,

But Romeo may not. More validity,[17]

More honourable state,[18] more courtship lives

35 In carrion flies[19] than Romeo. They may seize[20]

On the white wonder of dear Juliet's hand,

13. damnable

14. a capital offence (a crime punishable by death)

15. set

16. (lines 25–27) Generally, the penalty for your crime is death, but the Prince has shown you mercy by changing the sentence to banishment.

17. value

18. status

19. flies that hover around dead bodies

20. land

And steal immortal blessings from her lips,

Who, even in pure and vestal[21] modesty,

Still blush, as thinking their own kisses sin.

But Romeo may not, he is banishèd.   40

Flies may do this, but I from this must fly.

They are free men, but I am banishèd.

And sayest thou yet that exile is not death?

Hadst thou no poison mixed, no sharp-ground knife,

No sudden mean[22] of death, though ne'er so mean,[23]   45

But 'banishèd' to kill me? – 'Banishèd'?

O Friar! The damnèd use that word in hell.

Howling attends it.[24] How hast thou the heart,

Being a divine, a ghostly confessor,

A sin-absolver, and my friend professed,   50

To mangle[25] me with that word 'banishèd?'

FRIAR LAURENCE

Thou fond[26] mad man, hear me a little speak.

ROMEO

O, thou wilt speak again of banishment.

FRIAR LAURENCE

I'll give thee armour to keep off that word –

Adversity's sweet milk,[27] philosophy,   55

To comfort thee though thou art banishèd.

ROMEO

Yet 'banishèd'? Hang up philosophy!

Unless philosophy can make a Juliet,

Displant[28] a town, reverse a prince's doom,

It helps not, it prevails not. Talk no more.   60

FRIAR LAURENCE

O, then I see that madmen have no ears.

ROMEO

How should they, when that wise men have no eyes?

FRIAR LAURENCE

Let me dispute with thee of thy estate.[29]

21. virginal

22. method
23. no matter how ignoble/low

24. (because they are banished from heaven)

25. destroy

26. foolish

27. Something to help you cope with your suffering

28. Uproot

29. Let me talk to you about your situation/ predicament.

ROMEO

Thou canst not speak of that thou dost not feel.

65 Wert thou as young as I, Juliet thy love,

An hour but married, Tybalt murderèd,

Doting like me,[30] and like me banishèd,

Then mightst thou speak, then mightst thou tear thy hair,

And fall upon the ground, as I do now,

70 Taking the measure of an unmade grave.[31]

Knock.

FRIAR LAURENCE

Arise, one knocks. Good Romeo, hide thyself.

ROMEO

Not I, unless the breath of heartsick groans

Mist-like enfold me[32] from the search of eyes.

Knock.

FRIAR LAURENCE

Hark, how they knock! – Who's there? – Romeo, arise.

75 Thou wilt be taken – Stay a while! – Stand up.

Knock.

Run to my study. – By and by! – God's will,

What simpleness[33] is this! – I come, I come!

Knock.

Who knocks so hard? Whence[34] come you?

What's your will?

NURSE

80 Let me come in, and you shall know my errand.

I come from Lady Juliet.

FRIAR LAURENCE

Welcome, then.

---

30. In love like me

31. (Romeo falls on the ground, taking up the area his body would cover if he were dead.)

32. Hides me in its mist

33. foolishness

34. From where

Enter NURSE.

NURSE

O holy Friar! O, tell me, holy Friar,

Where is my lady's lord? Where's Romeo?

FRIAR LAURENCE

There on the ground, with his own tears made drunk.

NURSE

O, he is even in my mistress' case,[35]   85

Just in her case! O woeful sympathy,

Piteous predicament! Even so lies she,

Blubbering and weeping, weeping and blubbering.

Stand up, stand up, stand, an[36] you be a man.

For Juliet's sake, for her sake, rise and stand.   90

Why should you fall into so deep an O?[37]

ROMEO

Nurse.

NURSE

   Ah sir, ah sir, death's the end of all.[38]

ROMEO

Spakest thou of Juliet? How is it with her?

Doth she not think me an old murderer,

Now I have stained the childhood of our joy   95

With blood removed but little from her own?[39]

Where is she? And how doth she? And what says

My concealed lady[40] to our cancelled[41] love?

NURSE

O, she says nothing, sir, but weeps and weeps,

And now falls on her bed; and then starts up,   100

And Tybalt calls, and then on Romeo cries,

And then down falls again.

ROMEO

   As if that name,

Shot from the deadly level[42] of a gun,

35. he is exactly the same as Juliet

36. if

37. a groaning

38. (This is a saying to help Romeo to feel better.)

39. the blood of her relative

40. secret love
41. terminated

42. aim

43. my body

44. despised place

45. shape/body

46. Improper
47. in what looks like a man
48. unnatural
49. for seeming to be both (i.e. man and animal)

50. I thought your personality was more balanced.

Did murder her as that name's cursèd hand

105 Murdered her kinsman. O tell me, Friar, tell me,

In what vile part of this anatomy[43]

Doth my name lodge? Tell me, that I may sack

The hateful mansion.[44]

He offers to stab himself, and the NURSE snatches the dagger away.

FRIAR LAURENCE

       Hold thy desperate hand.

Art thou a man? Thy form[45] cries out thou art.

110 Thy tears are womanish, thy wild acts denote

The unreasonable fury of a beast.

Unseemly[46] woman in a seeming man,[47]

And ill-beseeming[48] beast in seeming both![49]

Thou hast amazed me. By my holy order,

115 I thought thy disposition better tempered.[50]

Hast thou slain Tybalt? Wilt thou slay thyself,

And slay thy lady that in thy life lives

By doing damnèd[51] hate upon thyself?

Why railest thou on thy birth, the heaven, and earth[52]

Since birth, and heaven,[53] and earth,[54] all three do meet   120

In thee at once, which thou at once wouldst lose?

Fie, fie, thou shamest[55] thy shape,[56] thy love, thy wit,[57]

Which, like a usurer,[58] aboundest in all,

And usest none in that true use indeed

Which should bedeck thy shape, thy love, thy wit.   125

Thy noble shape is but a form of wax,

Digressing from the valour of a man;[59]

Thy dear love sworn but hollow perjury,[60]

Killing that love which thou hast vowed to cherish;[61]

Thy wit,[62] that ornament[63] to shape and love,   130

Misshapen in the conduct of them both,

Like powder[64] in a skilless soldier's flask,

To set afire by thine own ignorance,

And thou dismembered with thine own defence.[65]

What, rouse thee, man! Thy Juliet is alive,   135

For whose dear sake thou wast but lately dead:

There art thou happy. Tybalt would kill thee,

But thou slewest[66] Tybalt: there art thou happy.[67]

The law that threatened death becomes thy friend,

And turns it to exile: there art thou happy.   140

A pack of blessings light upon thy back,

Happiness courts thee in her best array,

But, like a mishavèd and sullen wench,[68]

Thou poutest upon thy fortune and thy love.

Take heed,[69] take heed, for such die miserable.   145

Go, get thee to thy love, as was decreed,[70]

Ascend her chamber, hence and comfort her.

But look thou stay not till the Watch be set,[71]

For then thou canst not pass to Mantua,

Where thou shalt live till we can find a time   150

To blaze[72] your marriage, reconcile your friends,

Beg pardon of the Prince, and call thee back

With twenty hundred thousand times more joy

Than thou wentest forth in lamentation.[73]

Go before, Nurse. Commend me to thy lady,   155

And bid her hasten[74] all the house to bed,

Which heavy sorrow makes them apt unto.[75]

Romeo is coming.

---

51. sinful (by committing suicide)

52. Why are you condemning your birth, soul and body

53. soul

54. body

55. disgrace

56. body

57. intelligence

58. moneylender (Just like a usurer, who has plenty of money, Romeo has many natural gifts, which he is not using properly.)

59. (lines 126–127) Your body is just a hollow shell if it lacks the courage of a man

60. lies

61. (lines 128–129) Your marriage vows were lies if you are now going to kill yourself and the love that you vowed to cherish

62. intelligence

63. necessary addition

64. gunpowder

65. (lines 133–134) You are destroyed by your own weapons, because of your ignorance and your inability to think things through.

66. killed

67. fortunate

68. badly behaved, sulky girl

69. notice

70. decided

71. guards take up their positions (i.e. at the city gates)

72. announce

73. sorrow

74. hurry

75. makes them liable/likely to do

NURSE

O Lord, I could have stayed here all the night

160 To hear good counsel![76] O, what learning is!

My lord, I'll tell my lady you will come.

ROMEO

Do so, and bid my sweet prepare to chide.[77]

NURSE

Here, sir, a ring she bid me give you, sir.

Hie you, make haste, for it grows[78] very late.

ROMEO

165 How well my comfort is revived by this.

Exit NURSE.

FRIAR LAURENCE

Go hence, good night, and here stands all your state.[79]

Either be gone before the Watch be set,

Or by the break of day disguised from hence.

Sojourn[80] in Mantua. I'll find out your man,[81]

170 And he shall signify from time to time

Every good hap to you that chances here.[82]

Give me thy hand. 'Tis late. Farewell. Good night.

ROMEO

But that a joy past joy calls out on me,

It were a grief so brief to part with thee.[83]

175 Farewell.

Exeunt.

Side notes:

76. advice

77. tell my love to get ready to give out to me

78. it is getting

79. everything depends on this

80. Stay a while
81. servant

82. (lines 170–171) He will let you know everything that happens.

83. (lines 173–174) Only for the fact that my love is waiting for me, I would be sorry to leave you so soon.

OVERVIEW OF ACT 3, SCENE 3

- This scene closely mirrors the previous scene, in which a distraught Juliet received help from the Nurse. In this scene, Romeo receives similar emotional and practical help from Friar Laurence.
- At the beginning of the scene, Romeo is in Friar Laurence's cell while he awaits news of the Prince's judgement. When Friar Laurence informs him that he has been banished, he becomes hysterical and overwrought with emotion:

    Ha, banishment? Be merciful, say 'death' (line 12)

- Romeo claims that 'there is no world without Verona walls' (line 17), because Juliet is in Verona.
- The Nurse arrives at Friar Laurence's cell and witnesses Romeo's anguish. Friar Laurence informs her that Romeo is 'on the ground, with his own tears made drunk' (line 84).
- When the Nurse tells him that Juliet 'says nothing, sir, but weeps and weeps' (line 99), Romeo becomes desperate and attempts to stab himself.
- Friar Laurence uses his skills of persuasion and reassurance to help Romeo to see the positive side of the situation. He lists various reasons for Romeo to be grateful:

> *What, rouse thee, man! Thy Juliet is alive,*
>
> *For whose dear sake thou wast but lately dead:*
>
> *There art thou happy. Tybalt would kill thee,*
>
> *But thou slewest Tybalt: there art thou happy.*
>
> *The law that threatened death becomes thy friend,*
>
> *And turns it to exile: there art thou happy.* (lines 135–140)

- As well as offering Romeo spiritual guidance, Friar Laurence offers him practical advice. He tells him to go to Juliet as planned, and to leave either before the Watch (guards) come out, or before morning.
- Then, he must to go to Mantua for a time until Friar Laurence can announce the marriage and ask the Prince to pardon him. He will contact Romeo's servant (Balthasar), who will inform Romeo about everything that happens in Verona.
- The Nurse gives Romeo Juliet's ring, which cheers him up immediately:

> *How well my comfort is revived by this.* (line 165)

A. REVIEWING

1. How does Romeo react to the news of his banishment?
2. Friar Laurence lists many things for which Romeo should be grateful. Can you find examples?
3. Friar Laurence has formulated a plan. Write each step of the plan as a bullet point, with the relevant quote beside it.

B. ORAL LANGUAGE

Performing Friar Laurence's Speech to Romeo | P |

Group Activity

1. In three groups, read Friar Laurence's speech. Group One reads part one, Group Two reads part two, and Group Three reads part three.

Group One

Friar Laurence rebukes Romeo for not seeing how fortunate he is (lines 108–134).

(a) Take turns reading one line each, paying attention to the tone of voice.

(b) As a group, **summarise** your section. What are the main points Friar Laurence says to Romeo here?

Group Two

Friar Laurence outlines all of the things for which Romeo should be grateful (lines 135–145).

(a) Take turns reading one line each, paying attention to the tone of voice.

(b) As a group, **summarise** your section. What are the main points Friar Laurence says to Romeo here?

Group Three

Friar Laurence outlines his plan to help Romeo (lines 146–158).

(a) Take turns reading one line each, paying attention to the tone of voice.

(b) As a group, **summarise** your section. What are the main points Friar Laurence says to Romeo here?

2. Next, one person volunteers to pretend to be **Romeo** and sits in the middle of the room. A volunteer from each group pretends to be **Friar Laurence** and delivers the summary of his/her section of the speech to Romeo. Romeo can choose to be silent, or improvise!

3. Listen carefully to the summaries of each section and complete the task on **page 56** of your portfolio.

C. EXPLORING

Romeo's Language – Hyperbole |P|

Romeo's reaction to the news of his banishment is very dramatic. He uses hyperbole frequently in this scene.

> ### What is hyperbole?
> **Hyperbole** is the use of **exaggerated, over-the-top language** for a dramatic effect.

Turn to **page 57** of your portfolio and complete the activity on hyperbole in Romeo's language.

D. REFLECTING

Character File |P|

Turn to the Character File section of your portfolio and continue recording your impressions of **(a) Romeo (page 87)**, **(b)** the **Nurse (page 99)** and **(c) Friar Laurence (page 101)** based on this scene.

ACT 3, SCENE 4

Setting: Verona; the Capulet house.

In this **scene**, you will:

- Find out more about the theme of **marriage**.
- Focus on the **character of Capulet** and consider whether he is a good father.

Action – What Happens?

In this short scene, Lord Capulet makes a bold, spontaneous gesture to Paris by offering him Juliet's hand in marriage. Capulet is confident that Juliet will obey his wishes. He sets the wedding day for three days' time – Thursday.

Useful Words

tender – offer

heaviness – sadness/sorrow

mewed up – shut in/locked up

Enter CAPULET, his WIFE, and PARIS.

CAPULET

Things have fallen out, sir, so unluckily,

That we have had no time to move[1] our daughter.

Look you, she loved her kinsman Tybalt dearly,

And so did I. Well, we were born to die.

5 'Tis very late. She'll not come down tonight.

I promise you, but for your company

I would have been abed an hour ago.

PARIS

These times of woe afford no time to woo.

Madam, good night. Commend me to your daughter.

LADY CAPULET

10 I will, and know her mind[2] early tomorrow.

Tonight she's mewed up to her heaviness.[3]

PARIS offers to go in and CAPULET calls him again.

CAPULET

Sir Paris, I will make a desperate tender[4]

Of my child's love. I think she will be ruled

In all respects by me. Nay, more, I doubt it not.

15 Wife, go you to her ere[5] you go to bed.

Acquaint her here of[6] my son Paris' love,[7]

And bid her – mark you me? – on Wednesday next –

But soft[8] – what day is this?

PARIS

　　　　　　Monday, my lord.

CAPULET

Monday. Ha, ha! Well, Wednesday is too soon.

20 A'[9] Thursday let it be. A' Thursday, tell her,

She shall be married to this noble earl.

Will you be ready? Do you like this haste?

We'll keep no great ado[10] – a friend or two.

For hark you, Tybalt being slain so late,[11]

25 It may be thought we held him carelessly,[12]

Being our kinsman, if we revel much.[13]

---

1. persuade

2. find out what she is thinking

3. shut in with her sadness

4. an impulsive offer

5. before

6. Inform her about
7. (Already, Capulet seems to consider Paris to be his son-in-law.)

8. wait

9. On

10. There will be no great fuss

11. recently

12. we had little regard for him

13. have a big celebration

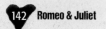

Therefore we'll have some half a dozen friends,
And there an end. But what say you to Thursday?

PARIS

My lord, I would[14] that Thursday were tomorrow.

14. I wish

CAPULET

Well get you gone. A' Thursday be it, then.   30
Go you to Juliet ere you go to bed.
Prepare her, wife, against[15] this wedding-day. –   15. for
Farewell, my lord. – Light to my chamber, ho! –
Afore me,[16] it is so very late that we   16. Indeed
May call it early by and by. Good night.   35

Exeunt.

OVERVIEW OF ACT 3, SCENE 4

- In this scene, Capulet makes a 'desperate tender' (bold offer) (line 12) of Juliet's hand in marriage to Paris. Capulet is confident that Juliet will obey him:

  I think she will be ruled

  In all respects by me. Nay, more, I doubt it not. (lines 13–14)

- Paris, overjoyed by this news, says:

  My lord, I would that Thursday were tomorrow. (line 29)

- The wedding is to take place in three days' time. (It is Monday and the wedding is due to take place on Thursday.)

- Juliet, who is 'mewed up to her heaviness' (shut up in her room because she is grieving) (line 11), is completely unaware that her father is making such plans for her future. These plans will have **detrimental** (dangerous) consequences for Romeo and Juliet.

- Capulet asks his wife to go to Juliet before she goes to bed and inform her of her proposed marriage to Paris.

A. REVIEWING

1. What do you think Paris might mean when he says, 'These times of woe afford no time to woo' (line 8)?

2. What plan does Capulet make for Juliet?

3. Why does Capulet want to make the wedding a low-key affair?

4. What is your opinion of **Paris** in this scene?

B. ORAL LANGUAGE

Discussing the Scene

Pair Activity

1. What **kind of father** is Capulet, in your opinion? Give reasons for your answer.

2. What **problems** can you foresee for Romeo and Juliet following this scene?

3. Can you find any examples of **dramatic irony** (when the audience knows something that a character does not) in this scene?

ACT 3, SCENE 5

Setting: Verona; the Capulet house; Juliet's chamber.

In this **scene**, you will:

- Find out more about the **characters of Juliet and Capulet**.
- Explore aspects of **Capulet's language and imagery**.

Action – What Happens?

Dawn is approaching and Romeo and Juliet must say farewell to each other. At the beginning of the scene, Juliet is reluctant to say goodbye to Romeo. She comes to her senses when she realises that he is in danger. In the second part of the scene, Juliet's mother comes to tell her of her proposed marriage to Paris. Juliet is overwhelmed by this news and informs her mother that she will not marry Paris.

Capulet arrives and Juliet tells him of her decision. Capulet is outraged and threatens to disown Juliet if she goes against his wishes. The scene ends with the Nurse also telling Juliet that she should marry Paris. At this stage, Juliet feels isolated from those closest to her and decides to consult Friar Laurence.

Useful Words

envious – spiteful

discourses – conversations

beseech – beg/ask

fickle – changeable

ACT 3, SCENE 5

1. That you heard
2. that

3. messenger of the morning
4. spiteful
5. parting
6. The stars
7. cheerful

8. breathes out (Meteors were thought to be formed by impure vapours from Earth that were lit up by the sun. They were considered to be bad omens [signs].)

Enter ROMEO and JULIET aloft, at the window.

JULIET

Wilt thou be gone? It is not yet near day.

It was the nightingale, and not the lark,

That pierced the fearful hollow of thine ear.[1]

Nightly she sings on yon[2] pomegranate tree.

5   Believe me, love, it was the nightingale.

ROMEO

It was the lark, the herald of the morn,[3]

No nightingale. Look, love, what envious[4] streaks

Do lace the severing[5] clouds in yonder east.

Night's candles[6] are burnt out, and jocund[7] day

10   Stands tiptoe on the misty mountain tops.

I must be gone and live, or stay and die.

JULIET

Yon light is not daylight; I know it, I.

It is some meteor that the sun exhales,[8]

To be to thee this night a torch-bearer,

15   And light thee on thy way to Mantua.

Therefore stay yet. Thou need'st not to be gone.

ROMEO

Let me be ta'en,[9] let me be put to death;

I am content, so[10] thou wilt have it so.

I'll say yon grey[11] is not the morning's eye,

'Tis but the pale reflex of Cynthia's brow;[12]   20

Nor that is not the lark, whose notes do beat

The vaulty heaven so high above our heads.

I have more care[13] to stay than will to go.

Come, death, and welcome! Juliet wills it so.

How is't, my soul? Let's talk. It is not day.   25

JULIET

It is, it is. Hie hence,[14] be gone, away!

It is the lark that sings so out of tune,

Straining harsh discords and unpleasing sharps.[15]

Some say the lark makes sweet division;[16]

This doth not so, for she divideth[17] us.   30

Some say the lark and loathèd toad changed[18] eyes

O, now I would they had changed voices too,

Since arm from arm that voice doth us affray,[19]

Hunting thee hence with hunt's-up[20] to the day.

O, now be gone! More light and light it grows.   35

ROMEO

More light and light, more dark and dark our woes.

Enter NURSE hastily.

NURSE

Madam!

JULIET

Nurse?

NURSE

Your lady mother is coming to your chamber:

The day is broke; be wary, look about.   40

Exit NURSE.

JULIET

Then, window, let day in, and let life out.

9.	captured
10.	as long as
11.	that grey light
12.	reflection of the moon (Cynthia was the goddess of the moon.)
13.	desire
14.	Hurry away from here
15.	very high, unpleasant notes
16.	music
17.	separates
18.	exchanged
19.	frighten
20.	morning call

ROMEO

Farewell, farewell! One kiss, and I'll descend.

[*He lets down the ladder of cords and goes down.*]

JULIET

Art thou gone so, love, lord, ay husband, friend?

I must hear from thee every day in the hour,

For in a minute there are many days.   45

O, by this count I shall be much in years

Ere I again behold my Romeo.

ROMEO

Farewell!

I will omit no opportunity

That may convey my greetings, love, to thee.   50

JULIET

O, think'st thou we shall ever meet again?

ROMEO

I doubt it not, and all these woes shall serve

For sweet discourses[21] in our times to come.

21. conversations

JULIET

O God, I have an ill-divining soul![22]

Methinks[23] I see thee, now thou art so low,   55

As one dead in the bottom of a tomb.

Either my eyesight fails, or thou look'st pale.[24]

22. I have a very bad feeling
23. I think
24. (Juliet has an unsettling premonition of Romeo lying dead in a tomb.)

ROMEO

And trust me, love, in my eye so do you.

Dry sorrow drinks our blood.[25] Adieu! Adieu![26]

Exit.

25. (A sigh was thought to use up a drop of blood; therefore the lovers' sadness at separating has made them very pale.)
26. Goodbye!

JULIET

O fortune, fortune! All men call thee fickle.[27]   60

If thou art fickle, what dost thou with him

That is renowned for faith?[28] Be fickle, fortune,

For then, I hope, thou wilt not keep him long,

But send him back.[29]

27. changeable/unpredictable
28. known for his faithfulness
29. (Juliet wants fortune [fate] to be changeable, so that her bad luck at Romeo's departure may be reversed by his return to her.)

LADY CAPULET [*within*]
        Ho, daughter, are you up?

JULIET

65 Who is't that calls? It is my lady mother.

Is she not down so late, or up so early?

What unaccustomed cause procures her hither?[30]

Enter LADY CAPULET.

LADY CAPULET

Why, how now, Juliet?

JULIET

        Madam, I am not well.

LADY CAPULET

Evermore[31] weeping for your cousin's death?

70 What, wilt thou wash him from his grave with tears?

An if thou couldst, thou couldst not make him live,

Therefore, have done.[32] Some grief shows much of love,

But much of grief shows still some want of wit.[33]

JULIET

Yet let me weep for such a feeling[34] loss.

LADY CAPULET

75 So shall you feel the loss, but not the friend[35]

Which you weep for.

JULIET

        Feeling so the loss,

I cannot choose but ever weep the friend.[36]

LADY CAPULET

Well, girl, thou weepest not so much for his death,

As that the villain lives which slaughtered him.

JULIET

What villain, madam?

30. What unusual reason brings her here?

31. Still

32. stop crying

33. (lines 72–73) Showing a little grief shows a lot of love, but showing a lot of grief is foolish.

34. profound

35. relative

36. lover

LADY CAPULET

That same villain Romeo.   80

JULIET

[*aside*] Villain and he be many miles asunder.[37]

[*to her mother*] God pardon him – I do, with all my heart.

And yet no man like he doth grieve my heart.[38]

LADY CAPULET

That is because the traitor murderer lives.

JULIET

Ay, madam, from the reach of these my hands.   85

Would none but I might venge my cousin's death!

LADY CAPULET

We will have vengeance for it, fear thou not.

Then weep no more. I'll send to one[39] in Mantua,

Where that same banished runagate[40] doth live,

Shall give him such an unaccustomed dram[41]   90

That he shall soon keep Tybalt company;

And then, I hope, thou wilt be satisfied.

JULIET

Indeed, I never shall be satisfied

With Romeo, till I behold[42] him – dead –

Is my poor heart so for a kinsman vexed.[43]   95

Madam, if you could find out but a man

To bear[44] a poison, I would temper[45] it,

That Romeo should, upon receipt thereof,

Soon sleep in quiet. O, how my heart abhors[46]

To hear him named, and cannot come to him   100

To wreak[47] the love I bore my cousin Tybalt

Upon his body that hath slaughtered him!

LADY CAPULET

Find thou the means, and I'll find such a man.

But now I'll tell thee joyful tidings,[48] girl.

JULIET

And joy comes well in such a needy time.   105

What are they, I beseech[49] your ladyship?

37. He is very far from being a villain.

38. (This line can be interpreted in two ways: No one angers her so much, or no one upsets her so much.)

39. someone

40. fugitive

41. strange poison

42. see

43. upset

44. carry
45. mix

46. hates

47. unleash

48. great news

49. beg/ask

LADY CAPULET

Well, well, thou hast a careful[50] father, child;

One who, to put thee from thy heaviness,

Hath sorted out a sudden day of joy

110 That thou expects not, nor I looked not for.

JULIET

Madam, in happy time.[51] What day is that?

LADY CAPULET

Marry,[52] my child, early next Thursday morn,

The gallant, young, and noble gentleman,

The County[53] Paris, at Saint Peter's Church

115 Shall happily make thee there a joyful bride.

JULIET

Now, by Saint Peter's Church, and Peter too,

He shall not make me there a joyful bride.

I wonder at this haste,[54] that I must wed

Ere[55] he that should be husband comes to woo.

120 I pray you, tell my lord and father, madam,

I will not marry yet; and when I do, I swear

It shall be Romeo – whom you know I hate –

Rather than Paris. These are news indeed!

LADY CAPULET

Here comes your father. Tell him so yourself,

125 And see how he will take it at your hands.

Enter CAPULET and NURSE.

CAPULET

When the sun sets, the air doth drizzle dew,

But for the sunset of my brother's son

It rains downright.

How now, a conduit,[56] girl? What, still in tears?

130 Evermore showering? In one little body

Thou counterfeit'st a bark,[57] a sea, a wind.

For still thy eyes – which I may call the sea –

Do ebb and flow with tears. The bark thy body is,

Sailing in this salt flood; the winds, thy sighs,

50. caring

51. at such a fortunate time

52. ('Marry' has two meanings here: the first is 'by Mary', which means 'well', and the second relates to the purpose of Lady Capulet's conversation with Juliet — her expected marriage to Paris.)

53. Count

54. I am astonished at this speed

55. Before

56. a fountain/water-pipe (Capulet assumes that Juliet is crying over Tybalt's death, but she is upset at the news that she is expected to marry Paris.)

57. You resemble a ship (i.e. 'bark')

Who,[58] raging with thy tears and they with them,   135

Without a sudden calm, will overset[59]

Thy tempest-tossèd[60] body. How now, wife,

Have you delivered to her our decree?[61]

LADY CAPULET

Ay, sir, but she will none,[62] she gives you thanks.

I would[63] the fool were married to her grave.   140

CAPULET

Soft, take me with you, take me with you, wife.[64]

How, will she none? Doth she not give us thanks?

Is she not proud?[65] Doth she not count her blest,

Unworthy as she is, that we have wrought[66]

So worthy a gentleman to be her bride?[67]   145

JULIET

Not proud you have, but thankful that you have.

Proud can I never be of what I hate,

But thankful even for hate[68] that is meant love.[69]

CAPULET

How, how, how, how – chopped-logic?[70] What is this?

'Proud,' and 'I thank you', and 'I thank you not',   150

And yet 'not proud', mistress minion,[71] you,

Thank me no thankings, nor proud me no prouds,

58. Which

59. capsize

60. storm-tossed

61. decision

62. not agree

63. wish

64. Hold on, let me understand what you're saying

65. gratified

66. arranged

67. bridegroom

68. something hateful
69. as a loving gesture

70. nonsense

71. spoiled brat

72. prepare
73. for

74. there

75. pale carcass (rotten thing)
76. good-for-nothing
77. coward

78. (It seems that Lady Capulet is astonished by her husband's over-the-top reaction.)

79. beg

80. worthless, good-for-nothing person

81. berate (give out to her)

82. be quiet

83. Chatter

84. For God's sake!

But fettle[72] your fine joints 'gainst[73] Thursday next
To go with Paris to Saint Peter's Church,
155   Or I will drag thee on a hurdle thither.[74]
Out, you green-sickness carrion![75] Out, you baggage,[76]
You tallow-face![77]

LADY CAPULET

       Fie, fie, what, are you mad?[78]

JULIET

Good father, I beseech[79] you on my knees,
Hear me with patience but to speak a word.

CAPULET

160   Hang thee, young baggage, disobedient wretch!
I tell thee what: get thee to church a' Thursday,
Or never after look me in the face.
Speak not, reply not, do not answer me!

JULIET rises.

My fingers itch. Wife, we scarce thought us blest
165   That God had lent us but this only child,
But now I see this one is one too much,
And that we have a curse in having her.
Out on her, hilding![80]

NURSE

       God in heaven bless her!
You are to blame, my lord, to rate[81] her so.

CAPULET

170   And why, my lady wisdom? Hold your tongue,[82]
Good Prudence. Smatter[83] with your gossips, go!

NURSE

I speak no treason.

CAPULET

       O, God-i'-good-e'en![84]

NURSE

May not one speak?

CAPULET

Peace, you mumbling fool,

Utter your gravity[85] o'er a gossip's bowl,[86]

For here we need it not.

LADY CAPULET

You are too hot.[87]   175

CAPULET

God's bread,[88] it makes me mad.

Day, night, work, play,

Alone, in company, still[89] my care hath been

To have her matched;[90] and having now provided

A gentleman of noble parentage,   180

Of fair demesnes,[91] youthful, and nobly lined,[92]

Stuffed, as they say, with honourable parts,

Proportioned as one's thought would wish a man –

And then to have a wretched puling[93] fool,

A whining mammet,[94] in her fortune's tender,[95]   185

To answer 'I'll not wed, I cannot love;

I am too young, I pray you, pardon me'!

But, an you will not wed, I'll pardon you!

Graze[96] where you will, you shall not house with me.

Look to't, think on't. I do not use to jest.[97]   190

Thursday is near. Lay hand on heart. Advise.

An you be mine, I'll give you to my friend.[98]

An you be not, hang, beg, starve, die in the streets,

For, by my soul, I'll ne'er acknowledge thee,

Nor what is mine shall never do thee good.   195

Trust to't. Bethink you. I'll not be forsworn.[99]

Exit.

JULIET

Is there no pity sitting in the clouds

That sees into the bottom of my grief?

O sweet my mother, cast me not away!

Delay this marriage for a month, a week;   200

---

85. wisdom
86. drinking bowl

87. angry/rash

88. The holy bread served at Mass (This is an oath.)

89. always
90. married

91. lands
92. descended

93. whinging

94. puppet
95. when given a golden opportunity

96. Eat

97. I am serious

98. If you are my daughter, you will accept the husband I have chosen for you.

99. I will not go back on my word.

Or if you do not, make the bridal bed
In that dim monument[100] where Tybalt lies.

LADY CAPULET

Talk not to me, for I'll not speak a word.
Do as thou wilt, for I have done with thee.

Exit.

JULIET

205 O, God – O Nurse, how shall this be prevented?
My husband is on earth,[101] my faith[102] in heaven.
How shall that faith return again to earth[103]
Unless that husband send it me from heaven
By leaving earth?[104] Comfort me, counsel[105] me.

210 Alack, alack, that heaven should practise stratagems[106]
Upon so soft a subject[107] as myself!
What sayst thou? Hast thou not a word of joy?
Some comfort, Nurse.

NURSE

Faith, here it is: Romeo
Is banished, and all the world to nothing[108]

215 That he dares ne'er come back to challenge you,
Or if he do, it needs must be by stealth.[109]
Then, since the case so stands as now it doth,
I think it best you married with the County.

100. tomb

101. alive
102. marriage vows made
103. How can I marry again

104. dying
105. advise
106. should play tricks

107. such a weak victim

108. and you can be very certain

109. in secret

O, he's a lovely gentleman!

Romeo's a dishclout[110] to him. An eagle, madam,   220

Hath not so green, so quick, so fair an eye

As Paris hath. Beshrew[111] my very heart,

I think you are happy in this second match,

For it excels your first; or if it did not,

Your first is dead, or 'twere as good he were,   225

As living here and you no use of him.[112]

JULIET

Speakest thou from thy heart?

NURSE

And from my soul, too, else beshrew them both.

JULIET

Amen.

NURSE

What?   230

JULIET

Well, thou hast comforted me marvellous much.[113]

Go in; and tell my lady I am gone,

Having displeased my father, to Laurence' cell,

To make confession and to be absolved.[114]

NURSE

Marry, I will; and this is wisely done.   235

Exit.

JULIET

Ancient damnation![115] O most wicked fiend![116]

Is it more sin to wish me thus forsworn,

Or to dispraise my lord with that same tongue

Which she hath praised him with above compare

So many thousand times?[117] Go, counsellor!   240

Thou and my bosom henceforth shall be twain.[118]

I'll to the friar, to know his remedy.

If all else fail, myself have power to die.

Exit.

---

110. dishcloth

111. Curse

112. Living on Earth and you not being able to see him

113. You have been a great help. (Juliet is being sarcastic.)

114. forgiven

115. Damnable woman!
116. devil

117. (lines 237–240) Which is worse — to urge me to break my marriage vows, or to criticise my husband, whom she used to praise so highly all the time?)

118. From now on, I will confide in you no more. (twain = divided)

Overview of Act 3, Scene 5

Part 1 — Romeo and Juliet say farewell.

- Dawn is breaking and Romeo realises that he must leave Juliet or risk getting caught. Juliet playfully protests, claiming that Romeo has heard the bird of the night, the nightingale, rather than the lark, which is 'the herald of the morn' (Romeo, line 6).

- Romeo says that he would gladly risk being captured, if it is Juliet's wish that he should stay:

   Let me be ta'en, let me be put to death;

   I am content, so thou wilt have it so. (lines 17–18)

- However, Juliet soon comes to her senses and urges Romeo to leave:

   O, now be gone! More light and light it grows. (line 35)

- The Nurse enters and warns Juliet that her mother is approaching. Romeo and Juliet say their final farewell:

   O, thinkst thou we shall ever meet again? (Juliet, line 51)

- Before Romeo leaves, Juliet informs him that she has a premonition (strong feeling/warning) of his death:

   O God, I have an ill-divining soul!

   Methinks I see thee, now thou art so low,

   As one dead in the bottom of a tomb. (lines 54–56)

- This is the last time that the two lovers will be together alive, so these lines are eerily significant. They create an ominous sense of foreboding and remind us that tragedy is in store for both Romeo and Juliet.

Part 2 — Juliet quarrels with her parents.

- In the second part of the scene, Lady Capulet informs Juliet of her expected marriage to Count Paris. Lady Capulet is convinced that Juliet will be overjoyed at the news:

   Marry, my child, early next Thursday morn,

   The gallant, young, and noble gentleman,

   The County Paris, at Saint Peter's Church

   Shall happily make thee there a joyful bride. (lines 112–115)

- However, Juliet is outraged and astonished by how quickly this marriage has been arranged:

   Now, by Saint Peter's Church, and Peter too,

   He shall not make me there a joyful bride.

   I wonder at this haste, that I must wed

   Ere he that should be husband comes to woo. (lines 116–119)

- Capulet is **incensed** (angry) that Juliet has refused to marry Paris. He proceeds to unleash a shocking **tirade** (a long, angry speech) of abuse at his daughter. He considers Juliet to be selfish in refusing to marry Paris, whom he **deems** (considers to be) an excellent match for his daughter.

- Juliet begs her father to listen to her. She kneels before him and pleads:

   Good father, I beseech you on my knees,

   Hear me with patience but to speak a word. (lines 158–159)

- Capulet flatly refuses to listen to Juliet, saying, 'Speak not, reply not, do not answer me' (line 163), and threatens to disown her if she continues to refuse to wed Paris:

   ... hang, beg, starve, die in the streets,

   For, by my soul, I'll ne'er acknowledge thee (lines 193–194)

- Juliet appeals to her mother to delay the marriage, claiming:

  Or if you do not, make the bridal bed

  In that dim monument where Tybalt lies. (lines 201–202)

- Lady Capulet does not take her daughter's side. Instead, she tells Juliet:

  Do as thou wilt, for I have done with thee. (line 204)

- When Lady Capulet leaves, Juliet turns to the Nurse for help. However, she does not get the comfort she so desperately requires from the Nurse. The Nurse wants what is best for Juliet and suggests that Paris would be a superior match for her. Juliet pretends that she has seen sense, but when the Nurse leaves, we see how Juliet truly feels – betrayed and abandoned by her only confidante.

- At the end of the scene, Juliet decides to seek Friar Laurence's help. It seems that he is her final hope. She says **ominously**:

  I'll to the friar, to know his remedy.

  If all else fail, myself have power to die. (lines 242–243)

- It appears that Juliet would rather die than go through with the marriage to Paris.

- At the end of the scene, Juliet is isolated and abandoned. Romeo has gone to Mantua, her parents are forcing her to marry against her will and even her trustworthy Nurse has seemingly abandoned her. This is an important scene for assessing the character of Juliet.

A. REVIEWING

1. What is Juliet's premonition?
2. How does Juliet react to the news that she is to marry Paris?
3. What is Capulet's response to Juliet's refusal to marry Paris?
4. What advice does the Nurse offer Juliet at the end of the scene?

B. EXPLORING

1. Double Meanings in Juliet's Speech |P|

Juliet's answers to her mother in this scene are vague and full of double meanings. Turn to **page 58** of your portfolio and complete the activity on double meanings in Juliet's speech.

2. Capulet's Description of Juliet as a Ship in a Storm |P|

Turn to **page 59** of your portfolio and complete the activity on Capulet's description of Juliet in her upset state.

3. Capulet's Language |P|

Pair Activity

(a) Look over Capulet's speech in lines 176–196. With your partner, paraphrase his main points. Turn to **page 60** of your portfolio to complete this task.

(b) Look back over the entire scene and find five examples of offensive things that Capulet says to Juliet. Put them in order, starting with the most offensive.

(c) Discuss your impression of Capulet in this scene and say whether you can understand why he behaves the way he does. Can his words/actions be justified in any way?

C. ORAL LANGUAGE

1. Performing Juliet's Isolation in Groups of Six

Group Activity

Characters: Juliet, Romeo, Capulet, Lady Capulet, the Nurse

(a) At the beginning of the scene, Juliet is in the centre. Characters arrange themselves as physically close to Juliet as they think they are to her emotionally. For example, at the start of the scene, Romeo will be beside Juliet, the Nurse will be the next closest person, etc.

(b) Next, read your character's lines from the scene in order. If you think that Juliet welcomes your comment, take a step closer to her. If your comment is unwelcome or elicits (gets) a negative response from Juliet, take as many steps back as you feel appropriate.

(c) At the end of the scene, discuss the changes in the patterns with your group.

2. Imagery ⫽P⟍

Choose two important/memorable quotes from this scene. Turn to **page 61** of your portfolio and draw pictures to illustrate these quotes.

D. REFLECTING

1. My Reflection on Act 3, Scene 5 ⫽P⟍

Turn to **page 61** of your portfolio and complete the reflection on this scene.

2. Character File ⫽P⟍

Turn to the Character File section of your portfolio and continue recording your impressions of **(a) Juliet (page 93)** and **(b)** the **Nurse (page 99)** based on this scene.

E. CREATING

Writing a Prologue for Act 3 ⫽P⟍

Write a **prologue** for **Act 3** of the play. This should take the form of a **sonnet**, like the prologues that Shakespeare included in Acts 1 and 2.

Remember:

- A sonnet has 14 lines.
- Try to have ten syllables in each line.
- Try to have one main idea per quatrain (four lines).
- Try to have a kind of conclusion for the couplet (final two lines).
- The **rhyming scheme** is: ABAB/CDCD/EFEF/GG. Try to follow the rhyming scheme as closely as you can, but don't worry if doesn't work out exactly! (Find out more about how the rhyming scheme works on page 161.)
- Turn to **page 62** of your portfolio to help you with this task.

How the Rhyming Scheme Works:

- Look at the **prologue** to Act 1 or Act 2 to help you with this task.
- Read the **last** word in each line of the prologue.
- In the first line, place an 'A' beside the last word. If the last word of any of the lines that follow has the same sound (or rhymes with it), then place an 'A' beside it too.
- Read the **last** word of the second line. Is the sound of this word the same as the last word on the first line? If not, place a 'B' beside it.
- Read the **last** word of the third line. If the sound is the same as the last word of the first line, place an 'A' beside it. If it is the same as the last word of the second line, place a 'B' beside it. If it is a new sound, place a 'C' beside it.
- Continue on in this way until you reach the end of the sonnet.

F. LOOKING BACK AT ACT 3

1. Overview P

Pair Activity

With your partner, turn back to **page 4** of your portfolio and write one sentence or phrase in the box for each scene in Act 3. This sentence or phrase should sum up the main action in that scene. For example, in the box for Act 3, Scene 1, you might say: 'The Fight Scene – Tybalt kills Mercutio, and Romeo then kills Tybalt and is banished as a result'.

2. What if…?

Pair Activity

What if the Fight Scene (Act 3, Scene 1) on the streets of Verona were reported on **Twitter** as breaking news? Pretend you are an eyewitness and **tweet the action** as it unfolds. Your partner will write replies to your tweets. Write in modern English.

Remember – A Good Tweet Will:

- Be short and to the point (less than 140 characters).
- Be clearly written.
- Attract readers' attention by asking a question or revealing interesting news/facts.
- Use the hashtag symbol (#) in front of a key word or an important topic.

A monastery
in Verona

ACT 4

In the previous scene, Romeo and Juliet said farewell to each other. Romeo has now left for Mantua and will not appear again until Act 5.

Act 4 focuses on the **characters** of Juliet and Lord and Lady Capulet. Lord Capulet arranges for Juliet to marry Paris against her wishes. Juliet shows great **strength of character** in this act. She faces many new challenges, including how to deal with her arranged marriage to Paris and her growing isolation from her family. By the end of this act, Juliet considers a **drastic plan** in order to avoid marrying Paris and remain loyal and faithful to Romeo. Friar Laurence helps Juliet when it seems that all others – including her loyal Nurse – have abandoned her.

ACT 4, SCENE 1

Setting: Verona; Friar Laurence's cell.

In this **scene**, you will:

- List examples of Juliet's language and **assess her character**.
- **Analyse** the positive and negative aspects of Friar Laurence's plan.

Action – What Happens?

Juliet has come to Friar Laurence's cell to ask for his assistance. When she arrives, she meets Paris, who has come to arrange their wedding. The meeting between Juliet and Paris is tense and awkward. When Paris leaves, Juliet reveals her **anguish** (distress) to Friar Laurence, who devises a plan to help her avoid a marriage to Paris.

Useful Words

counsel – advice   **prorogue** – postpone

valour – bravery   **borne** – carried

bier – a frame upon which a coffin or corpse was carried to the grave

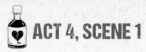

Enter FRIAR LAURENCE and PARIS.

FRIAR LAURENCE

On Thursday, sir? The time is very short.

PARIS

My father Capulet will have it so,

And I am nothing slow to slack his haste.[1]

FRIAR LAURENCE

You say you do not know the lady's mind?

Uneven is the course.[2] I like it not.   5

PARIS

Immoderately she weeps for Tybalt's death,

And therefore have I little talked of love,

For Venus[3] smiles not in a house of tears,

Now, sir, her father counts it dangerous

That she doth give her sorrow so much sway,[4]   10

And in his wisdom hastes[5] our marriage

To stop the inundation[6] of her tears.

Which, too much minded by herself alone,

May be put from her by society.[7]

Now do you know the reason of this haste.   15

FRIAR LAURENCE

[*aside*] I would[8] I knew not why it should be slowed.

[*to PARIS*] Look, sir, here comes the lady towards my cell.

Enter JULIET.

PARIS

Happily met, my lady and my wife!

JULIET

That may be, sir, when I may be a wife.

PARIS

That 'may be' must be, love, on Thursday next.   20

1. I am unwilling to argue with him to delay the marriage.

2. This is an unusual situation.

3. (the Roman goddess of love)

4. control

5. hurries

6. flow

7. (lines 13–14) Having somebody else's company might help her to stop brooding over things on her own.

8. wish

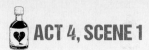

JULIET

What must be shall be.

FRIAR LAURENCE

That's a certain text.[9]

PARIS

Come you to make confession to this father?

JULIET

To answer that, I should confess to you.

PARIS

Do not deny to him that you love me.

JULIET

25   I will confess to you that I love him.

PARIS

So will ye, I am sure, that you love me.

JULIET

If I do so, it will be of more price,[10]

Being spoke behind your back, than to your face.

PARIS

Poor soul, thy face is much abused with tears.

JULIET

30   The tears have got small victory by that,

For it was bad enough before their spite.[11]

PARIS

Thou wrong'st it more than tears with that report.[12]

JULIET

That is no slander,[13] sir, which is a truth,

And what I spake,[14] I spake it to my face.

PARIS

35   Thy face is mine, and thou hast slandered it.

---

9. That's for sure.

10. value

11. injury/damage

12. You wrong your face more with such words.

13. lie

14. spoke

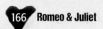

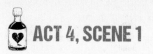

JULIET

It may be so, for it is not mine own.[15]

Are you at leisure, holy father, now,

Or shall I come to you at evening mass?

FRIAR LAURENCE

My leisure serves me, pensive[16] daughter, now.

My lord, we must entreat[17] the time alone.   40

PARIS

God shield[18] I should disturb devotion!

Juliet, on Thursday early will I rouse ye.[19]

[*kissing her*] Till then, adieu, and keep this holy kiss.

Exit PARIS.

JULIET

O, shut the door, and when thou hast done so,

Come weep with me, past hope, past cure, past help!   45

FRIAR LAURENCE

O Juliet, I already know thy grief.[20]

It strains me past the compass of my wits.[21]

I hear thou must, and nothing may prorogue[22] it,

On Thursday next be married to this County.[23]

JULIET

Tell me not, Friar, that thou hearest of this,   50

Unless thou tell me how I may prevent it.

If, in thy wisdom, thou canst give no help,

Do thou but call my resolution[24] wise,

[*She draws a knife.*]

And with this knife I'll help it presently.[25]

God joined my heart and Romeo's, thou our hands,[26]   55

And ere this hand, by thee to Romeo's sealed,

Shall be the label to another deed,

Or my true heart with treacherous revolt

Turn to another, this shall slay them both.[27]

Therefore, out of thy long-experienced time,   60

Give me some present counsel;[28] or behold,

'Twixt[29] my extremes[30] and me this bloody knife

15. (Juliet is saying that her face belongs to Romeo, but may also be suggesting that she is not revealing her true face by lying to Paris and evading his questions.)

16. sorrowful

17. request

18. forbid

19. wake you

20. dire situation
21. pushes me to the limit of my understanding (I am at my wits' end.)
22. delay

23. Count Paris

24. decision (i.e. to end her life)

25. I'll stab myself immediately

26. (in marriage)

27. (lines 56—59) Before my hand, which you joined in marriage, should be shamed in committing another crime (i.e. bigamy), or before I give my heart to another, this knife will kill both (i.e. my hand and my heart).
28. immediate advice
29. Between
30. extreme problems

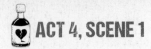

31. judge
32. concluding/coming to a judgement (Juliet is asking Friar Laurence for immediate advice, or she will kill herself.)
33. authority 34. learning
35. (lines 63–65) bringing an end to something, which neither your experience nor your learning could help me with
36. If you cannot offer me an immediate solution

37. Stop

38. requires as reckless/crazy an act

39. as the desperate situation we wish to prevent (Desperate times call for desperate measures.)

40. (lines 73–74) it is likely that you would be prepared to die to avoid the shameful situation
41. confronts

42. if you are really willing, I'll give you a solution

43. ask me to

44. in places where thieves are

45. (a building in a graveyard, in which corpses or bones were stacked in Elizabethan times)
46. Completely covered

47. stinking limbs
48. jawless

49. dread

50. pure

51. be sure

52. liquid that will spread throughout your body

53. immediately

54. fluid
55. (lines 96–97) your pulse will stop

Shall play the umpire,[31] arbitrating[32] that

Which the commission[33] of thy years and art[34]

65 Could to no issue of true honour bring.[35]

Be not so long to speak. I long to die

If what thou speak'st speak not of remedy.[36]

FRIAR LAURENCE

Hold,[37] daughter, I do spy a kind of hope

Which craves as desperate an execution[38]

70 As that is desperate which we would prevent.[39]

If, rather than to marry County Paris,

Thou hast the strength of will to slay thyself,

Then is it likely thou wilt undertake

A thing like death to chide away this shame,[40]

75 That cop'st with[41] death himself to 'scape from it,

And, if thou darest, I'll give thee remedy.[42]

JULIET

O, bid me[43] leap, rather than marry Paris,

From off the battlements of any tower,

Or walk in thievish ways,[44] or bid me lurk

80 Where serpents are. Chain me with roaring bears;

Or hide me nightly in a charnel-house,[45]

O'ercovered quite[46] with dead men's rattling bones,

With reeky shanks,[47] and yellow chapless[48] skulls;

Or bid me go into a new-made grave

85 And hide me with a dead man in his tomb –

Things that, to hear them told, have made me tremble –

And I will do it without fear or doubt,[49]

To live an unstained[50] wife to my sweet love.

FRIAR LAURENCE

Hold, then; go home, be merry, give consent

90 To marry Paris. Wednesday is tomorrow.

Tomorrow night look[51] that thou lie alone.

Let not thy Nurse lie with thee in thy chamber.

Take thou this vial, being then in bed,

And this distilling liquor[52] drink thou off,

95 When presently[53] through all thy veins shall run

A cold and drowsy humour;[54] for no pulse

Shall keep his native progress, but surcease.[55]

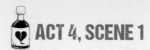

56. pale
57. lids

58. incapable of movement

No warmth, no breath, shall testify thou livest.

The roses in thy lips and cheeks shall fade

100   To wanny[56] ashes, thy eyes' windows[57] fall

Like death, when he shuts up the day of life.

Each part, deprived of supple government,[58]

Shall, stiff and stark and cold, appear like death;

And in this borrowed likeness of shrunk death

105   Thou shalt continue two-and-forty hours,

And then awake as from a pleasant sleep.

Now, when the bridegroom in the morning comes

To rouse thee from thy bed, there art thou dead.

Then, as the manner of our country is,

59. (a stretcher-like frame, on which a corpse was carried to a graveyard)
60. carried

61. family

62. in preparation for when you will wake

63. plan

110   In thy best robes, uncovered on the bier[59]

Thou shalt be borne[60] to that same ancient vault

Where all the kindred[61] of the Capulets lie.

In the mean time, against thou shalt awake,[62]

Shall Romeo by my letters know our drift,[63]

64. wait for

65. take you

115   And hither shall he come, and he and I

Will watch[64] thy waking, and that very night

Shall Romeo bear thee hence[65] to Mantua.

And this shall free thee from this present shame,

If no inconstant toy nor womanish fear

66. (lines 118–120) This plan will free you from the shame of marrying Paris, if you can stay focused and not allow fear to lessen your courage in seeing it through.

120   Abate thy valour in the acting it.[66]

JULIET

Give me, give me! O, tell me not of fear!

FRIAR LAURENCE

Hold, get you gone. Be strong and prosperous

67. (lines 122–123) Be strong, and good luck with the plan.

In this resolve.[67] I'll send a friar with speed

To Mantua with my letters to thy lord.

JULIET

125   Love give me strength and strength shall help afford.

Farewell, dear father.

Exeunt.

OVERVIEW OF ACT 4, SCENE 1

- At the beginning of this scene, Paris is arranging his upcoming wedding to Juliet with Friar Laurence. Friar Laurence expresses his surprise at how soon the wedding is due to take place:

    On Thursday, sir? The time is very short. (line 1)

- Paris explains that Juliet's father wishes to speed up the wedding to distract her from her supposed sorrow at Tybalt's death.

- Juliet has come to ask Friar Laurence for help and has a brief, awkward conversation with Paris about their **impending nuptials** (marriage that is due to take place). Juliet deliberately avoids responding directly to Paris when he mentions that they will be married on Thursday. She replies **cryptically** (mysteriously):

    What must be shall be. (line 21)

- When Paris leaves, Juliet is free to express her complete despair at the prospect of this second marriage. She says that she is 'past hope, past cure, past help!' (line 45). Her devotion to Romeo is so strong that she would rather kill herself than marry someone else. She takes out a knife, threatens to kill herself, and asks Friar Laurence for immediate advice:

    Give me some present counsel; or behold,

    'Twixt my extremes and me this bloody knife

    Shall play the umpire (lines 61–63)

- She also tells him that she will die if he cannot offer her an immediate solution:

    I long to die

    If what thou speak'st speak not of remedy. (lines 66–67)

The Plan

- The Friar realises that Juliet is willing to kill herself rather than marry Paris. Seeing how **volatile** (unpredictable) and upset she has become, he tries to offer her a solution:

    Hold, daughter, I do spy a kind of hope (line 68)

- The Friar devises a less-than-ideal, **impetuous** (not well thought-out) plan for Juliet. He instructs her to go home, pretend she is happy and agree to marry Paris. He gives her a potion, which he tells her to drink when she is alone in her room. This 'distilling liquor' (line 94) will cause her to appear to be dead. The next morning, her parents will think that she has died and will convey her 'uncovered on the bier' (line 110) to the 'ancient vault' (line 111) – the Capulet tomb.

- The effects of the potion will last for 42 hours, after which time Friar Laurence and Romeo – who will have been told of the plan in a letter – will wait in the tomb for Juliet to wake. Then, Romeo and Juliet will flee to Mantua together.

- Friar Laurence warns her that in order for the plan to be successful, it requires courage and determination.

- Juliet shows great **courage** and **strength of character** in this scene as she gladly accepts the potion:

    Give me, give me! O, tell me not of fear! (line 121)

- She is willing to do whatever it takes to stay loyal to Romeo:

    Love give me strength and strength shall help afford. (line 125)

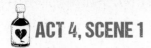

A. REVIEWING

1. Explain why Paris and Juliet have each come to see Friar Laurence.
2. Outline the **effects** that drinking the potion will have on Juliet. (Look over lines 94–106.)

B. EXPLORING

Things Juliet Would Rather Do than Marry Paris |P|

Turn to **page 63** of your portfolio and complete the activity on the things that Juliet says she would rather do than marry Paris.

C. ORAL LANGUAGE

Friar Laurence's Plan |P|

Pair Activity

Discuss Friar Laurence's plan (lines 89–120). Then, turn to **page 65** of your portfolio to complete the activity on Friar Laurence's plan.

D. REFLECTING

Character File |P|

Turn to the Character File section of your portfolio and continue recording your impressions of **(a) Juliet (page 94)** and **(b) Friar Laurence (page 101)** based on this scene.

ACT 4, SCENE 2

Setting: Verona; a hall in Capulet's house.

In this **scene**, you will:

- Identify the **change** in the relationship between Juliet and her father.

Action – What Happens?

As instructed by Friar Laurence, Juliet goes home and asks her parents for forgiveness. Capulet is so pleased with his daughter's change of heart that he brings forward the wedding day from Thursday to Wednesday. This will cause even more problems for Romeo and Juliet.

Useful Words

unfurnished – unprepared   **provision** – food and drink

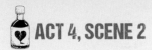
Enter CAPULET, LADY CAPULET, NURSE, and SERVINGMEN.

CAPULET
So many guests invite as here are writ.

Exit SERVANT.

Sirrah, go hire me twenty cunning[1] cooks.

SECOND SERVINGMAN
You shall have none ill, sir, for I'll try[2] if they can lick
their fingers.

CAPULET
5   How canst thou try them so?

SECOND SERVINGMAN
Marry,[3] sir, 'tis an ill[4] cook that cannot lick his own fingers,
therefore he that cannot lick his fingers goes not with me.

CAPULET
Go, be gone.

Exit SERVINGMAN.

We shall be much unfurnished[5] for this time.
10   [*to NURSE*] What, is my daughter gone to Friar Laurence?

NURSE
Ay, forsooth.[6]

CAPULET
Well, he may chance to do some good on her.
A peevish, self-willed harlotry it is.[7]

Enter JULIET.

NURSE
See where she comes from shrift[8] with merry look.

---

1. skilled

2. test

3. By Mary
4. a bad

5. unprepared

6. indeed

7. She is a stubborn, willful brat.

8. confession

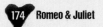

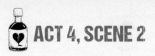

CAPULET

How now, my headstrong![9] Where have you been gadding?[10] 15

	9. stubborn girl
	10. wandering

JULIET

Where I have learned me to repent the sin

Of disobedient opposition

To you and your behests,[11] and am enjoined[12]

By holy Laurence to fall prostrate[13] here,

To beg your pardon. [*She kneels*.] Pardon, I beseech[14] you! 20

Henceforward I am ever ruled by you.[15]

11. commands
12. instructed
13. flat on the floor

14. beg

15. From now on I will obey you.

CAPULET

[*to NURSE*] Send for the County; go tell him of this.

I'll have this knot[16] knit up tomorrow morning.

16. marriage

JULIET

I met the youthful lord at Laurence' cell,

And gave him what becomèd[17] love I might, 25

Not stepping o'er the bounds of modesty.

17. acceptable

CAPULET

Why, I'm glad on't.[18] This is well. Stand up.

18. of it

JULIET rises.

This is as't should be. Let me see the County.

[*to NURSE*] Ay, marry, go, I say, and fetch him hither.

Now, afore God, this reverend holy friar, 30

All our whole city is much bound[19] to him.

19. obliged

JULIET

Nurse, will you go with me into my closet[20]

To help me sort such needful ornaments[21]

As you think fit to furnish[22] me tomorrow?

20. chamber/room

21. necessary clothing

22. dress

LADY CAPULET

No, not till Thursday. There is time enough. 35

CAPULET

Go, Nurse, go with her. We'll to[23] church tomorrow.

23. go to

Exeunt JULIET and NURSE.

24. food and drink

25. guarantee

26. dress

27. has returned

LADY CAPULET

We shall be short in our provision.[24]

'Tis now near night.

CAPULET

        Tush, I will stir about,

And all things shall be well, I warrant[25] thee, wife.

40   Go thou to Juliet, help to deck up[26] her.

I'll not to bed tonight. Let me alone.

I'll play the housewife for this once. What, ho!

They are all forth. Well, I will walk myself

To County Paris to prepare up him

45   Against tomorrow. My heart is wondrous light,

Since this same wayward girl is so reclaimed.[27]

Exeunt.

OVERVIEW OF ACT 4, SCENE 2

- In this short scene, Juliet arrives home and puts the first step of Friar Laurence's plan into action. She **reconciles** (makes up) **with** her father and tells him that she has been to see Friar Laurence, who has instructed her to obey her father's wishes:

  Pardon, I beseech you!

  Henceforward I am ever ruled by you. (lines 20–21)

- Capulet is so overjoyed at this news that he brings forward the day of the wedding.

- He says that the whole city of Verona is indebted to Friar Laurence for his help:

  All our whole city is much bound to him. (line 31)

- Lady Capulet is worried that they will not be ready for the wedding feast if the wedding is to be brought forward. However, Capulet, in a jovial mood, promises to take care of the arrangements himself. The scene ends with Capulet leaving to tell Paris the good news. Capulet says:

  My heart is wondrous light,

  Since this same wayward girl is so reclaimed. (lines 45–46)

- Bringing the wedding forward by a day will have a disastrous impact on Friar Laurence's plans for the lovers. Timing is a crucial factor in the success of the plan. The scene ends **ominously** (gloomily).

REVIEWING

1. What does Juliet say to her father when she returns from Friar Laurence's cell?
2. How does Capulet react to what Juliet says?

⚷ ACT 4, SCENE 3

Setting: Verona; Capulet's house, Juliet's chamber.

In this **scene**, you will:

- Identify Juliet's **fears** in her soliloquy.

Action – What Happens?

In this scene, Juliet prepares to take the potion. As instructed by Friar Laurence, she has ensured that she is alone in her chamber. This is a key scene for the character of Juliet, as it shows her unswerving loyalty and devotion to Romeo. She takes the potion despite her greatest fears and doubts.

Useful Words

attires – clothes/garments

behoveful – suitable/appropriate

orisons – prayers

conceit – image

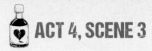
Enter JULIET and NURSE.

JULIET

Ay, those attires[1] are best. But, gentle Nurse,

I pray thee, leave me to myself tonight,

For I have need of many orisons[2]

To move the heavens to smile upon my state,[3]

Which, well thou know'st, is cross[4] and full of sin.   5

Enter LADY CAPULET.

LADY CAPULET

What, are you busy, ho? Need you my help?

JULIET

No, madam, we have culled[5] such necessaries

As are behoveful for our state tomorrow.[6]

So please you, let me now be left alone,

And let the Nurse this night sit up with you,   10

For, I am sure, you have your hands full all

In this so sudden business.

LADY CAPULET

       Good night.

Get thee to bed, and rest, for thou hast need.

Exeunt LADY CAPULET and NURSE.

1. clothes/garments

2. prayers

3. situation

4. unfortunate

5. chosen

6. everything we need for the ceremony

Mandrake

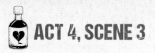

JULIET

Farewell. God knows when we shall meet again.

I have a faint cold fear thrills[7] through my veins   15   7. flows through

That almost freezes up the heat of life.

I'll call them back again to comfort me.

Nurse! – What should she do here?

My dismal scene I needs must act alone.[8]   8. I must face this dreadful situation alone.

Come, vial.[9]   20   9. (a glass bottle containing the potion)

What if this mixture do not work at all?

Shall I be married then tomorrow morning?

No, no, this[10] shall forbid it. Lie thou there.   10. (a knife)

[*She lays down a knife.*]

What if it be a poison which the friar

Subtly hath ministered[11] to have me dead,   25   11. created

Lest[12] in this marriage he should be dishonoured   12. In case

Because he married me before to Romeo?

I fear it is – and yet, methinks[13] it should not,   13. I think

For he hath still been tried a holy man.[14]   14. he has always proven himself to be a holy man

How if,[15] when I am laid into the tomb,   30   15. What if

I wake before the time that Romeo

Come to redeem[16] me? There's a fearful point!   16. save

Shall I not then be stifled[17] in the vault,   17. suffocated

To whose foul mouth no healthsome[18] air breathes in,   18. healthy

And there die strangled[19] ere my Romeo comes?   35   19. suffocated

Or, if I live, is it not very like,[20]   20. likely

The horrible conceit[21] of death and night,   21. image

Together with the terror of the place –

As[22] in a vault, an ancient receptacle   22. As it is

Where for this many hundred years the bones   40

Of all my buried ancestors are packed;

Where bloody Tybalt, yet but green in earth,[23]   23. recently dead

Lies festering in his shroud;[24] where, as they say,   24. (a cloth used to cover a corpse)

At some hours in the night spirits resort[25] –   25. haunt

Alack, alack, is it not like that I,   45

So early waking – what with loathsome smells,

And shrieks like mandrakes[26] torn out of the earth,   26. (The mandrake plant was thought to shriek when
                                                                                                pulled from the ground, causing the one who
                                                                                                pulled it to go mad.)

That living mortals, hearing them, run mad –

O, if I wake, shall I not be distraught,

Environèd with all these hideous fears,   50

And madly play with my forefathers' joints,

And pluck the mangled[27] Tybalt from his shroud,   27. rotting

ACT 4, SCENE 3

28. madness

29. stick

30. pierce

31. point of a sword

And, in this rage,[28] with some great kinsman's bone,

As with a club[29] dash out my desperate brains?

55 O look! Methinks I see my cousin's ghost

Seeking out Romeo that did spit[30] his body

Upon a rapier's point.[31] Stay, Tybalt, stay!

Romeo, Romeo, Romeo! Here's drink. I drink to thee.

She drinks from the vial and falls upon her bed within the curtains.

OVERVIEW OF ACT 4, SCENE 3
KEY SCENE

- At the beginning of the scene, Juliet makes sure that she is alone, so that she can take the potion as instructed by Friar Laurence. She tells the Nurse:

    I pray thee, leave me to myself tonight (line 2)

Juliet's Soliloquy

- Juliet's soliloquy (lines 14–58) is a powerful speech in which she outlines her many fears about taking the potion. She is **apprehensive** (uneasy/nervous) as she reflects on the **daunting** (frightening) task ahead. Initially, she questions the Friar's loyalty, but dismisses this idea quickly. She is also worried about waking too early and being smothered in the stifling tomb before Romeo comes to rescue her. As she outlines her many fears and doubts, her speech gathers **momentum** (force), finally **culminating** (ending) with her taking the potion:

    Romeo, Romeo, Romeo! Here's drink. I drink to thee. (line 58)

- Despite her worst fears, Juliet follows through with the plan in order to stay loyal to Romeo. This scene displays Juliet's **strength of character**. She is portrayed as a **realistic, three-dimensional** character with genuine fears, which she is willing to overcome for the sake of love.

A. REVIEWING

1. At the beginning of this scene, how does Juliet manage to arrange to be on her own?
2. Why does Juliet wish to call her mother and the Nurse back?
3. Why do you think she changes her mind about calling them back?
4. What does she suggest she will do if the potion does not work?

B. EXPLORING

Juliet's Soliloquy ⎮P⎮

Pair Activity

Read Juliet's soliloquy (lines 14–58) aloud in pairs. Focus on the appropriate tone to use throughout. Then, turn to **page 67** of your portfolio and complete the activity on the soliloquy.

C. REFLECTING

Character File ⎮P⎮

Turn to the Character File section of your portfolio and continue recording your impressions of **Juliet (page 95)** based on this very important scene.

ACT 4, SCENE 4

Setting: Verona; a hall in Capulet's house.

In this **scene**, you will:

- Identify Capulet's **mood**.
- Learn about **juxtaposition**.

Action – What Happens?

This is a transition scene, in which we find the Capulet household busily preparing for the wedding feast. This provides the audience with a break between Juliet's taking of the potion and the discovery of her 'death'. It is a scene full of energy compared with the stillness of the previous scene.

Useful Words

pastry – the part of the kitchen where pastry was made

curfew bell – a bell rung to indicate that daylight had arrived

cot-quean – a slang term for a man who did 'women's work'

hood – a woman

Enter LADY CAPULET and NURSE.

LADY CAPULET

Hold, take these keys, and fetch more spices, Nurse.

NURSE

They call for dates and quinces in the pastry.[1]

1. pastry kitchen

Enter CAPULET.

CAPULET

Come, stir, stir, stir! The second cock hath crowed.

The curfew bell hath rung. 'Tis three o'clock.

Look to the baked meats, good Angelica.[2]   5

Spare not for cost.

2. (Angelica might be the name of the Nurse or Lady Capulet.)

NURSE

                 Go, go, you cot-quean,[3] go.

Get you to bed. Faith, you'll be sick to-morrow

For this night's watching.[4]

3. old housewife

4. From staying up all night

CAPULET

No, not a whit. What, I have watched ere now

All night for lesser cause, and ne'er been sick.   10

LADY CAPULET

Ay, you have been a mouse-hunt[5] in your time,

But I will watch[6] you from such watching now.

5. womaniser

6. guard

Exeunt LADY CAPULET and NURSE.

CAPULET

A jealous-hood,[7] a jealous-hood!

7. jealous woman

Enter three or four SERVINGMEN, with spits, logs and baskets.

Now, fellow, what is there?

FIRST SERVINGMAN

Things for the cook, sir, but I know not what.   15

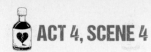

CAPULET

Make haste, make haste.

Exit FIRST SERVINGMAN.

Sirrah, fetch drier logs.
Call Peter. He will show thee where they are.

SECOND SERVINGMAN

I have a head, sir, that will find out logs,
And never trouble Peter for the matter.

CAPULET

20 Mass,[8] and well said! A merry whoreson,[9] ha!
Thou shalt be logger-head.[10]

Exit SECOND SERVINGMAN.

Good faith! 'Tis day.
The County will be here with music straight,
For so he said he would.

Music plays within.

I hear him near.
Nurse! Wife! What ho, what, Nurse, I say!

Enter NURSE.

25 Go waken Juliet. Go and trim her up.
I'll go and chat with Paris. Hie, make haste,[11]
Make haste! The bridegroom he is come already.
Make haste, I say.

Exeunt.

8. By the mass (an oath)
9. rascal
10. blockhead

11. hurry up

OVERVIEW OF ACT 4, SCENE 4

- This very short scene is a **transition scene**, in which we see the Capulet household busily preparing for the wedding feast. It provides the audience with a break between Juliet's taking of the potion and the discovery of her 'death'.

- Capulet has stayed up all night seeing to the wedding preparations. He tells the Nurse to wake Juliet and get her ready for her marriage to Paris. The scene ends with Capulet leaving to 'go and chat with Paris' (line 26).

Juxtaposition

This scene of activity, hustle and bustle forms a contrast with the sombre next scene. This device of placing contrasting scenes side by side is known as **juxtaposition**. Shakespeare does this to maximise the dramatic effect.

REVIEWING

1. What kind of preparations are being made for the wedding?
2. How would you describe Capulet's **mood** in this scene?

ACT 4, SCENE 5

Setting: Verona; Juliet's chamber.

In this **scene**, you will:

- Record the **characters' reactions** to the discovery of Juliet's 'death'.
- Identify language techniques such as **simile, personification and repetition**.
- Perform a **group reading** of parts of the scene.

Action – What Happens?

In this scene, Juliet's 'corpse' is discovered. Juliet's parents and the Nurse are completely distraught. Friar Laurence comes to find out what the delay is and offers words of comfort to the family. When Paris is informed of the tragic news, he feels cheated that his wife-to-be has been taken from him prematurely. The scene ends with the musicians, who were supposed to provide music for the wedding, deciding to stay to perform the funeral music.

Useful Words

lamentable – tragic/awful

aqua vitae – alcohol

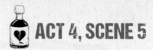

Enter NURSE.

NURSE

Mistress, what, mistress! Juliet! Fast,[1] I warrant[2] her, she.

Why, lamb! Why, lady! Fie, you slug-abed![3]

Why, love, I say! Madam! Sweetheart! Why, bride!

What, not a word? You take your pennyworths[4] now.

Sleep for a week, for the next night, I warrant,   5

The County Paris hath set up his rest

That you shall rest but little. God forgive me!

Marry, and amen. How sound is she asleep!

I needs must wake her. Madam, madam, madam!

Ay, let the County take[5] you in your bed.   10

He'll fright[6] you up, i' faith. Will it not be?

What, dressed and in your clothes, and down again?

I must needs wake you. Lady! Lady! Lady!

Alas, alas! Help, help! My lady's dead!

O weraday[7] that ever I was born!   15

Some aqua-vitae,[8] ho! My lord! My lady!

Enter LADY CAPULET.

LADY CAPULET

What noise is here?

NURSE

       O lamentable[9] day!

LADY CAPULET

What is the matter?

NURSE

       Look, look! O heavy[10] day!

LADY CAPULET

O me, O me, my child, my only life!

Revive, look up, or I will die with thee.   20

Help, help! Call help!

Enter CAPULET.

---

1. Asleep
2. guarantee
3. lazybones

4. naps

5. catch

6. startle

7. alas the day (unlucky day)

8. (an alcoholic drink)

9. tragic/dreadful

10. sorrowful

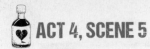
11. (an expression of regret)

12. still

13. unseasonable (unusual)

CAPULET

For shame, bring Juliet forth. Her lord is come.

NURSE

She's dead, deceased. She's dead, alack[11] the day!

LADY CAPULET

Alack the day! She's dead, she's dead, she's dead!

CAPULET

25 Ha, let me see her! Out, alas, she's cold.

Her blood is settled,[12] and her joints are stiff.

Life and these lips have long been separated.

Death lies on her like an untimely[13] frost

Upon the sweetest flower of all the field.

NURSE

O lamentable day!

LADY CAPULET

30   O woeful time!

CAPULET

Death, that hath ta'en her hence to make me wail,

Ties up my tongue, and will not let me speak.

Enter FRIAR LAURENCE and PARIS, with MUSICIANS.

FRIAR LAURENCE

Come, is the bride ready to go to church?

CAPULET

Ready to go, but never to return.

35 O son, the night before thy wedding day

Hath Death lain with thy wife. There she lies,

Flower as she was, deflowerèd[14] by him.

Death is my son-in-law, Death is my heir.

My daughter he hath wedded. I will die,

40 And leave him all. Life, living,[15] all is Death's!

14. seduced

15. property

PARIS

Have I thought long[16] to see this morning's face,

And doth it give me such a sight as this?

16. longed

LADY CAPULET

Accursed, unhappy, wretched, hateful day!

Most miserable hour, that e'er time saw

In lasting labour of his pilgrimage![17]

45

17. In all of time's journey (This is the worst hour of all time.)

But one, poor one, one poor and loving child,

But one thing to rejoice and solace[18] in,

18. take comfort

And cruel death hath catched[19] it from my sight!

19. snatched

NURSE

O woe! O woeful, woeful, woeful day!

Most lamentable day! Most woeful day

50

That ever, ever, I did yet behold!

O day, O day, O day, O hateful day!

Never was seen so black a day as this!

O woeful day, O woeful day!

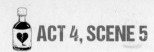
PARIS

55 Beguiled,[20] divorcèd, wrongèd, spited, slain![21]

Most detestable death, by thee beguiled,

By cruel, cruel thee quite overthrown![22]

O love! O life: not life, but love in death![23]

CAPULET

Despised, distressèd, hated, martyred, killed!

60 Uncomfortable time, why cam'st thou now

To murder, murder our solemnity?[24]

O child, O child, my soul, and not my child!

Dead art thou, alack, my child is dead,

And with my child my joys are burièd!

FRIAR LAURENCE

65 Peace, ho, for shame! Confusion's[25] cure lives not

In these confusions.[26] Heaven and yourself

Had part in this fair maid. Now heaven hath all,

And all the better is it for the maid.

Your part in her[27] you could not keep from death,

70 But heaven keeps his part[28] in eternal life.

The most you sought was her promotion,[29]

For 'twas your heaven[30] she should be advanced,[31]

And weep ye now, seeing she is advanced

Above the clouds, as high as heaven itself?

75 O, in this love you love your child so ill[32]

That you run mad, seeing that she is well.

She's not well married that lives married long,

But she's best married that dies married young.[33]

Dry up your tears, and stick your rosemary[34]

80 On this fair corpse, and, as the custom is,

In all her best array[35] bear[36] her to church;

For though fond[37] nature bids us all lament,

Yet nature's tears are reason's merriment.[38]

CAPULET

All things that we ordainèd festival,[39]

85 Turn from their office[40] to black funeral.

Our instruments[41] to melancholy bells,

Our wedding cheer[42] to a sad burial feast,

Our solemn[43] hymns to sullen dirges[44] change;

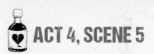

Our bridal flowers serve for a buried corpse,

And all things change them to the contrary. 90

FRIAR LAURENCE

Sir, go you in; and, madam, go with him.

And go, Sir Paris. Everyone prepare

To follow this fair corpse unto her grave.

The heavens do lour[45] upon you for some ill;[46]

Move[47] them no more by crossing their high will.[48] 95

Exeunt CAPULET, LADY CAPULET, PARIS and FRIAR LAURENCE.

Enter MUSICIANS.

FIRST MUSICIAN

Faith, we may put[49] up our pipes, and be gone.

NURSE

Honest good fellows, ah, put up, put up!

For, well you know, this is a pitiful case.

Exit NURSE.

FIRST MUSICIAN

Ay, by my troth,[50] the case[51] may be amended.[52]

Enter PETER.

PETER

Musicians, O, musicians! 'Heart's ease',[53] 'Heart's ease'; 100

O, an you will have me live, play 'Heart's ease.'

FIRST MUSICIAN

Why 'Heart's ease?'

PETER

O, musicians, because my heart itself plays 'My heart is full

of woe'. O, play me some merry dump,[54] to comfort me.

SECOND MUSICIAN

Not a dump we. 'Tis no time to play now. 105

45. frown/look dark and threatening
46. offense/sin
47. Anger
48. Command

49. pack

50. in truth
51. (This is a pun on the word 'case', meaning either a situation or a case for storing an instrument. The musician is trying to be funny and is deliberately misinterpreting what the Nurse said.)
52. mended/fixed

53. (the name of a popular song at that time)

54. sad tune (The phrase 'merry dump' is an oxymoron.)

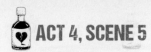
PETER

You will not then?

MUSICIANS

No.

PETER

I will then give it you soundly.[55]

FIRST MUSICIAN

What will you give us?

PETER

110 No money, on my faith, but the gleek![56] I will give you the minstrel.[57]

FIRST MUSICIAN

Then will I give you the serving-creature.[58]

PETER

Then will I lay the serving-creature's dagger on your pate.[59] I will carry no crotchets. I'll re you, I'll fa you. Do

115 you note[60] me?

FIRST MUSICIAN

An you re us, and fa us, you note us.

SECOND MUSICIAN

Pray you, put up your dagger and put out your wit.

PETER

Then have at you[61] with my wit. I will dry-beat[62] you with an iron wit, and put up my iron dagger. Answer me like men:

120 [sings] 'When griping grief the heart doth wound,
And doleful dumps[63] the mind oppress,
Then music with her silver sound' –
Why 'silver sound', why 'music with her silver
sound?' What say you, Simon Catling?[64]

FIRST MUSICIAN

125 Marry, sir, because silver hath a sweet sound.

---

55. in sounds/completely

56. but an insult

57. (lines 110–111) I will call you a 'minstrel' (which also meant a good-for-nothing).

58. I will call you what you are: a servant.

59. head

60. hear

61. I'll attack you
62. thrash

63. melancholy tunes

64. lute

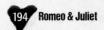

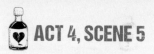

PETER

Prates![65] What say you, Hugh Rebeck?[66]

SECOND MUSICIAN

I say 'silver sound,' because musicians sound for silver.[67]

PETER

Prates too! What say you, James Soundpost?[68]

THIRD MUSICIAN

Faith, I know not what to say.

PETER

O, I cry you mercy,[69] you are the singer. I will say for you.   130

It is 'music with her silver sound' because musicians

have no gold for sounding:[70]

[*sings*] 'Then music with her silver sound

With speedy help doth lend redress'.[71]

Exit PETER.

FIRST MUSICIAN

What a pestilent knave[72] is this same!   135

SECOND MUSICIAN

Hang him, Jack! Come, we'll[73] in here, tarry[74] for the

mourners, and stay[75] dinner.

Exeunt.

---

65. Nonsense!
66. fiddle

67. play for money

68. (part of a violin/stringed instrument)

69. I beg your pardon

70. are given no gold for playing (i.e. Musicians are poor.)

71. gives comfort

72. an annoying fool

73. we'll go
74. wait
75. wait for

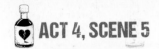

OVERVIEW OF ACT 4, SCENE 5 – JULIET'S 'DEATH' IS DISCOVERED

- At the beginning of this scene, the Nurse goes into Juliet's chamber to wake her. She is surprised to find Juliet dressed and lying on the bed. To her horror, she discovers that Juliet is dead:

  > *I must needs wake you. Lady! Lady! Lady!*
  >
  > *Alas, alas! Help, help! My lady's dead!* (lines 13–14)

- Lady Capulet is next to arrive in Juliet's chamber. She seems genuinely distraught at the news of her daughter's death. Despite her dismissive attitude to Juliet earlier in Act 4, we feel some sympathy for her as she mourns the loss of her only child:

  > *But one, poor one, one poor and loving child,*
  >
  > *But one thing to rejoice and solace in,*
  >
  > *And cruel death hath catched it from my sight!* (lines 46–48)

- Capulet is **incredulous** (in disbelief):

  > *O child, O child, my soul, and not my child!*
  >
  > *Dead art thou, alack, my child is dead,*
  >
  > *And with my child my joys are burièd!* (lines 62–64)

- Paris arrives to wed Juliet, only to find out that his bride is dead. He feels cheated by death:

  > *Beguiled, divorcèd, wrongèd, spited, slain!*
  >
  > *Most detestable death, by thee beguiled* (lines 55–56)

- Next, Friar Laurence enters on the scene and offers words of comfort to the mourners. He tries to make them see that Juliet is in a better place and tells them that they should be happy for her. He gently **rebukes** (scolds) the family for making such a commotion and advises them to bring her to church to be buried. He does his part in ensuring that the plan is successful. So far, all is going to plan, as Juliet is to be brought to the tomb for burial.

- The final part of this scene (lines 100–137) is often cut from productions of the play. The musicians lament the fact that there will be no need for them at the wedding ceremony. However, they stay to perform music at the funeral. The dramatic function of the musicians is perhaps to remind the audience that Juliet is not really dead, although the reactions and grief of the mourners are real.

A. EXPLORING

1. Reactions to the Discovery of Juliet's 'Death' |P|

Pair Activity

Turn to **page 68** of your portfolio and record each character's response to the discovery of Juliet's 'death'.

2. Language Devices |P|

Pair Activity

This scene features many language devices, such as simile, personification and repetition. Turn to **page 69** of your portfolio and complete the short activity on language devices.

B. ORAL LANGUAGE

Performing in Groups of Four

Group Activity

In groups of four, prepare a reading of the following lines, which capture each character's response to Juliet's death:

- **Lady Capulet** – lines 43–48
- **The Nurse** – lines 49–54
- **Paris** – lines 55–58
- **Capulet** – lines 59–64.

Decide as a group how you will perform them aloud. Consider the following:

- Will you read them all at the same time, or take turns?
- Will you interact with the other characters, or remain focused on yourself?

C. LOOKING BACK AT ACT 4

1. Overview |P|

Pair Activity

With your partner, turn back to **page 4** of your portfolio and write one sentence or phrase in the box for each scene in Act 4. This sentence or phrase should sum up the main action in that scene.

2. What If…?

Pair Activity

What if Juliet had been overcome by fear and she had called the Nurse back to inform her of Friar Laurence's plan? How would the Nurse have reacted? **Improvise** the scene (make it up as you go along) in pairs.

A map showing
the location of
Verona and Mantua

◎ The distance from Verona to Mantua is approx. 45km

Mantua

MANTVA.

Mantua, Lombardiæ Transpada:
næ vrbs clarißima et antiquißima,
venustißimum, in medio paludium,
situm obtinet Anno salutis ꝯꝯ
ꝯ.LXXV. ad viuum delineata.

ACT 5

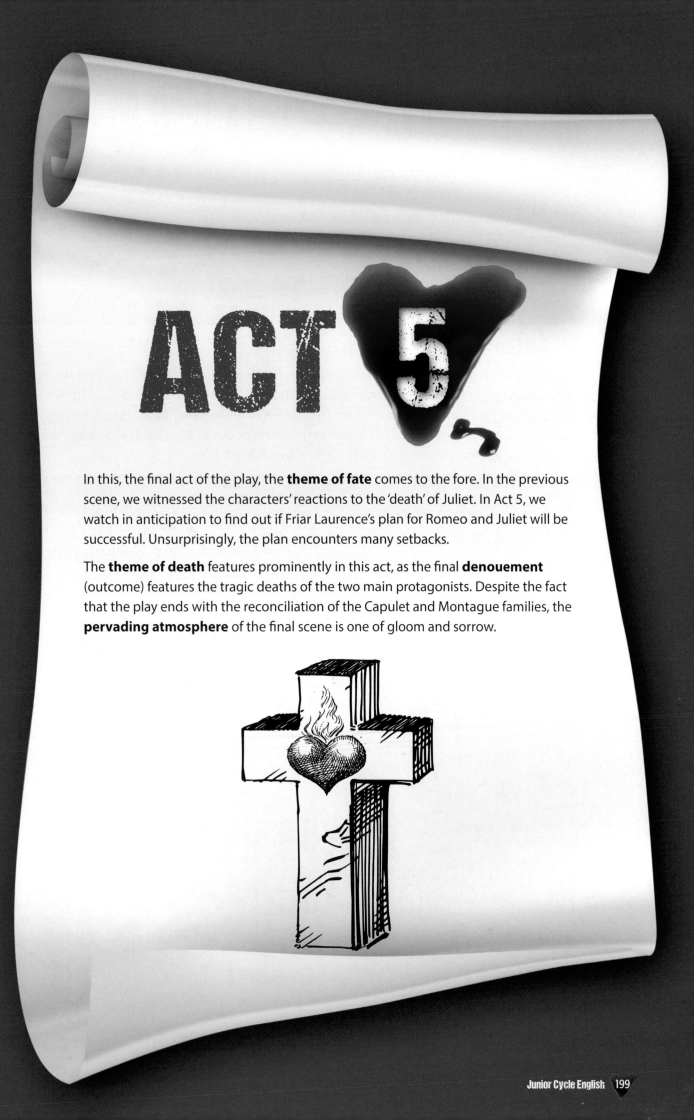

In this, the final act of the play, the **theme of fate** comes to the fore. In the previous scene, we witnessed the characters' reactions to the 'death' of Juliet. In Act 5, we watch in anticipation to find out if Friar Laurence's plan for Romeo and Juliet will be successful. Unsurprisingly, the plan encounters many setbacks.

The **theme of death** features prominently in this act, as the final **denouement** (outcome) features the tragic deaths of the two main protagonists. Despite the fact that the play ends with the reconciliation of the Capulet and Montague families, the **pervading atmosphere** of the final scene is one of gloom and sorrow.

ACT 5, SCENE 1

Setting: Mantua; a street.

In this **scene**, you will:

- Examine the **description** of the Apothecary's shop and illustrate it.

Action – What Happens?

This scene is set in Mantua, a city close to Verona, where Friar Laurence instructed Romeo to go following his banishment from Verona. Romeo is anxiously awaiting news from Friar Laurence when Balthasar, his servant, comes to tell him that Juliet is dead. Romeo immediately wishes to die with Juliet. He goes to seek out an **apothecary** to obtain the lethal drugs that he needs to fulfil his **macabre** (morbid) plan.

Useful Words

penury – poverty

apothecary – a person who prepared and sold medicines and drugs

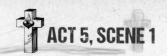

Enter ROMEO.

ROMEO

If I may trust the flattering truth of sleep,

My dreams presage[1] some joyful news at hand.

My bosom's lord[2] sits lightly in his throne.[3]

And all this day an unaccustomed spirit[4]

Lifts me above the ground with cheerful thoughts.   5

I dreamt my lady came and found me dead –

Strange dream, that gives a dead man leave[5] to think! –

And breathed such life with kisses in my lips

That I revived and was an emperor.

Ah me, how sweet is love itself possessed   10

When but love's shadows are so rich in joy![6]

Enter BALTHASAR, booted.

News from Verona! How now, Balthasar?

Dost thou not bring me letters from the friar?

How doth[7] my lady? Is my father well?

How fares my Juliet? That I ask again,   15

For nothing can be ill[8] if she be well.

BALTHASAR

Then she is well, and nothing can be ill.

Her body sleeps in Capel's monument,

And her immortal part[9] with angels lives.

I saw her laid low in her kindred's vault,   20

And presently took post to tell it you.[10]

O, pardon me for bringing these ill news,

Since you did leave it for my office,[11] sir.

ROMEO

Is it e'en so? Then I defy you, stars![12]

Thou knowest my lodging.[13] Get me ink and paper,   25

And hire posthorses. I will hence[14] tonight.

BALTHASAR

I do beseech[15] you, sir, have patience.

Your looks are pale and wild, and do import

Some misadventure.[16]

---

1. predict
2. heart
3. My heart is at ease in my chest.
4. an unusually good mood

5. the ability

6. (lines 10—11) Love is such a wonderful thing when even dreams about love give you so much joy!

7. How is

8. bad

9. soul

10. immediately set off to tell you

11. duty

12. Is it really true? Then damn my fate!

13. where I am staying

14. leave here

15. beg

16. suggest something bad

ROMEO

        Tush, thou art deceived.

30   Leave me, and do the thing I bid thee do.

Hast thou no letters to me from the friar?

BALTHASAR

No, my good lord.

ROMEO

        No matter. Get thee gone,

And hire those horses. I'll be with thee straight.[17]

Exit BALTHASAR.

Well, Juliet, I will lie with thee tonight.

35   Let's see for means.[18] O mischief, thou art swift

To enter in the thoughts of desperate men![19]

I do remember an apothecary,[20]

And hereabouts a dwells,[21] which late I noted

In tattered weeds,[22] with overwhelming brows,[23]

40   Culling of simples.[24] Meagre[25] were his looks.

Sharp misery had worn him to the bones,

And in his needy[26] shop a tortoise hung,

An alligator stuffed, and other skins

Of ill-shaped fishes; and about his shelves

45   A beggarly account[27] of empty boxes,

Green earthen pots, bladders,[28] and musty seeds,

Remnants of packthread,[29] and old cakes of roses,

Were thinly scattered to make up a show.

Noting this penury,[30] to myself I said

50   'An if a man did need a poison now,

Whose sale is present death[31] in Mantua,

Here lives a caitiff wretch[32] would sell it him.'

O, this same thought did but forerun[33] my need,

And this same needy man must sell it me.

55   As I remember, this should be the house.

Being holiday, the beggar's shop is shut.

What ho, apothecary!

Enter APOTHECARY.

---

17. straight away

18. Let me think how I will arrange it.

19. (lines 35–36) Oh mischief, you are quick to enter the minds of desperate men.
20. (someone who sold medicines and drugs)

21. he lives

22. clothes
23. bushy eyebrows
24. Gathering herbs
25. Thin/emaciated

26. poor

27. very small amount

28. containers

29. Bits of twine

30. poverty

31. The sale of which is punishable by immediate execution
32. a poor, miserable fellow

33. predict/anticipate

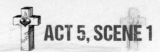

APOTHECARY

Who calls so loud?

ROMEO

Come hither, man. I see that thou art poor.

Hold, there is forty ducats.[34] Let me have

A dram[35] of poison – such soon-speeding[36] gear   60

As will disperse itself through all the veins,

That the life-weary taker may fall dead,

And that the trunk[37] may be discharged of breath

As violently as hasty powder fired

Doth hurry from the fatal cannon's womb.   65

APOTHECARY

Such mortal[38] drugs I have, but Mantua's law

Is death to any he[39] that utters[40] them.

ROMEO

Art thou so bare and full of wretchedness,[41]

And fear'st to die? Famine is in thy cheeks,

Need and oppression[42] starveth in thine eyes,   70

Contempt and beggary[43] hangs upon thy back.

The world is not thy friend, nor the world's law.

The world affords[44] no law to make thee rich.

Then be not poor, but break it, and take this.

APOTHECARY

My poverty but not my will consents.[45]   75

34. coins

35. dose
36. fast-acting

37. body

38. fatal

39. man
40. offers to sell

41. poverty

42. hardship/misery

43. poverty

44. provides

45. The fact that I am poor forces me to give it to you.

ROMEO

I pay thy poverty and not thy will.

APOTHECARY [*handing ROMEO poison*]

Put this in any liquid thing you will

And drink it off, and if you had the strength

Of twenty men, it would dispatch you straight.[46]

ROMEO

80   There is thy gold – worse poison to men's souls,

Doing more murder in this loathsome[47] world,

Than these poor compounds that thou mayst not sell.

I sell thee poison; thou hast sold me none.

Farewell, buy food, and get thyself in flesh.[48]

Exit APOTHECARY.

85   Come, cordial[49] and not poison, go with me

To Juliet's grave, for there I must use thee.

Exit.

46. it would kill you immediately

47. hateful

48. gain some weight

49. medicine

Romeo buys poison from the Apothecary

OVERVIEW OF ACT 5, SCENE 1

- In this scene, Balthasar wrongly informs Romeo that Juliet is dead. This news will have devastating consequences for all.

- On hearing that Juliet is dead, Romeo decides to take control of his own destiny:

  Is it e'en so? Then I defy you, stars! (line 24)

- His immediate wish is to join Juliet. He devises a plan to buy poison from an apothecary, which he intends to take at the Capulet tomb.

- When Romeo arrives at the Apothecary's shop, the Apothecary is wary of Romeo and is unwilling to part with the poison. He says that he would be put to death if he were discovered to have sold it. However, it does not take long for Romeo to convince him to sell it. The promise of forty **ducats** (gold coins) is too big a temptation for the poverty-stricken, **emaciated** (thin) Apothecary, so he agrees, saying:

  My poverty but not my will consents. (line 75)

A. REVIEWING

1. Briefly describe Romeo's dream, which he mentions at the beginning of this scene (lines 1–11).

2. What effect does this dream have on him?

3. How does Balthasar break the news to Romeo that Juliet is dead?

4. How does Romeo react to this news?

5. Why is the Apothecary reluctant to sell the poison to Romeo?

6. How does Romeo manage to convince him to give him the poison?

7. What effects will the poison have?

8. Where does Romeo want to go to take the poison?

B. EXPLORING

Imagery of the Apothecary's Shop |P|

Turn to **page 70** of your portfolio and draw a cartoon/picture of the **Apothecary** in his shop. (Look back over lines 37–56.) Label your cartoon/picture using quotes from the scene. Also, include a speech bubble for Romeo and another for the Apothecary, each containing an **important quote** from this character in the scene.

ACT 5, SCENE 2

Setting: Verona; Friar Laurence's cell.

In this **scene**, you will:

- **Write Friar Laurence's letter** to Romeo.

Action – What Happens?

In this brief scene, we learn that Friar Laurence's letter to Romeo has not been delivered. Friar John, who was supposed to deliver it, was delayed. Tragedy now seems unavoidable for Romeo and Juliet.

Useful Words

pestilence – disease/the plague

import – importance/significance

beshrew – curse

iron crow – crowbar

Enter FRIAR JOHN.

FRIAR JOHN

Holy Franciscan friar, brother, ho!

Enter FRIAR LAURENCE.

FRIAR LAURENCE

This same should be the voice of Friar John.

Welcome from Mantua! What says Romeo?

Or, if his mind be writ,[1] give me his letter.

1. if his thoughts are written down

FRIAR JOHN

Going to find a barefoot brother[2] out –   5

One of our order – to associate[3] me

Here in this city visiting the sick,

And finding him, the searchers[4] of the town,

Suspecting that we both were in a house

Where the infectious pestilence[5] did reign,[6]   10

Sealed up the doors, and would not let us forth,

So that my speed to Mantua there was stayed.[7]

2. (Franciscan friars travelled barefoot, because they swore a vow of poverty.)
3. accompany

4. (The searchers were health officers, who examined dead bodies and identified homes in which people were infected with the plague.)

5. the plague
6. was present

7. my journey to Mantua was delayed

FRIAR LAURENCE

Who bare[8] my letter then to Romeo?

8. delivered

FRIAR JOHN

I could not send it – here it is again –

Nor get a messenger to bring it thee,   15

So fearful were they of infection.

FRIAR LAURENCE

Unhappy fortune! By my brotherhood,

The letter was not nice,[9] but full of charge,

Of dear import,[10] and the neglecting it

May do much danger. Friar John, go hence.   20

Get me an iron crow,[11] and bring it straight

Unto my cell.

9. insignificant/unimportant

10. Of great importance

11. crowbar

FRIAR JOHN

        Brother, I'll go and bring it thee.

Exit FRIAR JOHN.

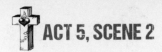

ACT 5, SCENE 2

12. I must go

13. curse/give out to

14. happenings

FRIAR LAURENCE

Now must I[12] to the monument alone.

Within this three hours will fair Juliet wake.

25 She will beshrew[13] me much that Romeo

Hath had no notice of these accidents.[14]

But I will write again to Mantua,

And keep her at my cell till Romeo come.

Poor living corpse, closed in a dead man's tomb!

Exit FRIAR LAURENCE.

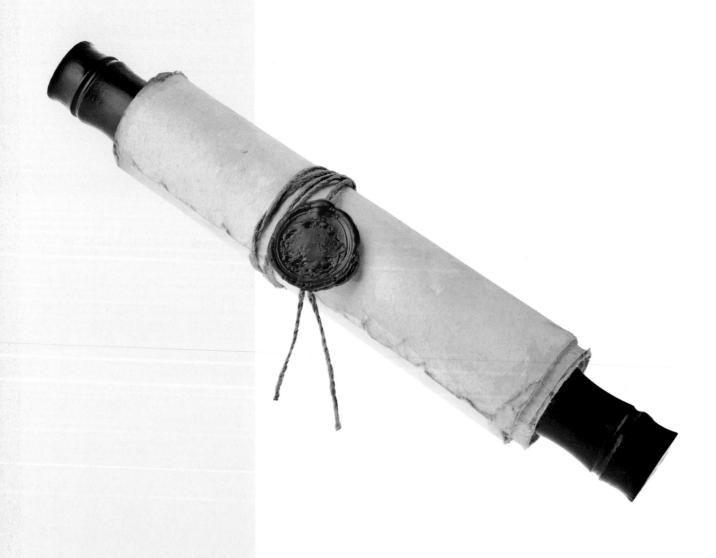

OVERVIEW OF ACT 5, SCENE 2

- Friar Laurence's plan is falling apart, due to Friar John's failure to deliver the letter to Romeo informing him that Juliet is not really dead. Friar Laurence warns:

  The letter was not nice, but full of charge,

  Of dear import, and the neglecting it

  May do much danger. (lines 18–20)

- Friar Laurence now realises that danger is fast approaching. Juliet is due to wake, but Romeo will not be there to rescue her. He fears that she will be a 'Poor living corpse, closed in a dead man's tomb!' (line 29).

- He decides to go the Capulet tomb to rescue Juliet and take her to his cell until Romeo comes for her. Although previously calm and philosophical, Friar Laurence is now genuinely worried and panic-stricken.

A. CREATING

Friar Laurence's Letter to Romeo 〡P〡

Friar Laurence says that he will 'write again to Mantua' (line 27). Turn to **page 71** of your portfolio and write his letter to Romeo in Mantua.

B. ORAL LANGUAGE

Discussing

Pair Activity

What would you advise Friar Laurence to do now? Do you think he is right to go straight to the Capulet tomb?

ACT 5, SCENE 3

Setting: Verona; a churchyard.

In this **scene**, you will:

- Compare the **characters** of Romeo and Paris.
- **Paraphrase** lines from Romeo's speech.
- Identify examples of **personification**.
- Find **images** of Romeo and Juliet's tomb.
- **Summarise** Friar Laurence's speech.
- **Write a letter** from Romeo to his father.
- Examine the **setting** and **design the stage set** for this, the final scene.

Action – What Happens?

This is the final scene of the play. The action takes place in the churchyard and in the Capulet tomb. A morbid, **macabre** atmosphere is created throughout as tragedy strikes the main characters. Paris has come to lay flowers on Juliet's grave and Romeo has come there to die. Paris mistakenly thinks that Romeo has come to **desecrate** (damage/disrespect) the Capulet tomb, so he challenges him. A fight **ensues** (follows) and Romeo kills Paris. Paris's page calls the Watch. Romeo enters the tomb, takes the poison and dies beside Juliet. Friar Laurence, meanwhile, is desperate to reach the tomb before Juliet wakes up, but is unable to stop her from taking her own life. At the end of the scene, the Prince arrives with the Capulet and Montague families, and the true extent of the tragedy is revealed. The play ends on a slightly hopeful note, as the families realise the error of their ways and reconcile their differences.

Useful Words

obsequies – funeral rites/religious practices

enmity – hatred/hostility

strew – scatter

apprehend – arrest

sepulchre – tomb

paramour – lover

conjuration – warning

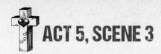

Enter PARIS, and his PAGE, bearing flowers and a torch.

PARIS

Give me thy torch, boy. Hence, and stand aloof.[1]

Yet put it out, for I would not be seen.

Under yond yew trees lay thee all along,[2]

Holding thy ear close to the hollow ground.

So shall no foot upon the churchyard tread,   5

Being loose, unfirm, with digging up of graves,

But thou shalt hear it. Whistle then to me,

As signal that thou hear'st something approach.

Give me those flowers. Do as I bid thee. Go.

PAGE

[*aside*] I am almost afraid to stand alone   10

Here in the churchyard, yet I will adventure.[3]

[*PAGE hides himself at a distance from PARIS.*]

PARIS

Sweet flower, with flowers thy bridal bed I strew,[4]

O woe! Thy canopy[5] is dust and stones,

Which with sweet water nightly I will dew,

Or, wanting[6] that, with tears distilled by[7] moans.   15

The obsequies[8] that I for thee will keep[9]

Nightly shall be to strew thy grave and weep.

PAGE whistles.

The boy gives warning. Something doth approach.

What cursèd foot wanders this way tonight

To cross[10] my obsequies and true love's rite?[11]   20

What, with a torch? – Muffle[12] me, night, a while.

[*He stands aside.*]

Enter ROMEO and BALTHASAR, with a torch, mattock, and a crow of iron.

ROMEO

Give me that mattock[13] and the wrenching iron.[14]

Hold, take this letter. Early in the morning

See thou deliver it to my lord and father.

1. stand back

2. lie flat on the ground

3. risk it

4. scatter

5. bed canopy

6. lacking
7. emanating from/produced by
8. mourning rites (the things/acts that Paris will do/ perform to express his sadness over Juliet's death)
9. perform

10. interrupt
11. mourning
12. Hide

13. pickaxe
14. crowbar

Junior Cycle English **211**

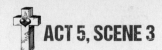
25 Give me the light. Upon thy life I charge[15] thee,

Whate'er thou hearest or seest, stand all aloof,[16]

And do not interrupt me in my course.[17]

Why I descend into this bed of death

Is partly to behold my lady's face,

30 But chiefly to take thence[18] from her dead finger

A precious ring, a ring that I must use

In dear employment.[19] Therefore hence, be gone.

But if thou, jealous,[20] dost return to pry

In what I further shall intend to do,

35 By heaven, I will tear thee joint by joint,[21]

And strew[22] this hungry churchyard with thy limbs.

The time[23] and my intents are savage-wild,

More fierce and more inexorable[24] far

Than empty[25] tigers or the roaring sea.

BALTHASAR

40 I will be gone, sir, and not trouble ye.

ROMEO

So shalt thou show me friendship. Take thou that.

[*He gives money.*]

Live and be prosperous, and farewell, good fellow.

BALTHASAR

[*aside*] For all this same, I'll hide me hereabout.

His looks I fear, and his intents I doubt.

[*He hides himself at a distance from ROMEO.*]

ROMEO begins to open the tomb.

ROMEO

45 Thou detestable maw,[26] thou womb of death,

Gorged[27] with the dearest morsel of the earth,

Thus I enforce thy rotten jaws to open,

And, in despite,[28] I'll cram thee with more food.

PARIS

[*aside*] This is that banished haughty Montague

50 That murdered my love's cousin, with which grief

It is supposèd the fair creature died;

And here is come to do some villainous shame[29]

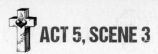

To the dead bodies. I will apprehend[30] him.

[*He comes forward.*]

Stop thy unhallowed toil,[31] vile Montague!

Can vengeance be pursued further than death?   55

Condemnèd villain, I do apprehend thee.

Obey, and go with me, for thou must die.

ROMEO

I must indeed, and therefore came I hither.[32]

Good gentle youth, tempt not[33] a desperate[34] man.

Fly hence, and leave me. Think upon these gone.[35]   60

Let them affright[36] thee. I beseech[37] thee, youth,

Put not another sin upon my head

By urging me to fury.[38] O, be gone.

By heaven, I love thee better than myself,

For I come hither armed against myself.   65

Stay not, be gone. Live, and hereafter[39] say

A madman's mercy bid thee run away.

PARIS

I do defy thy conjuration,[40]

And apprehend thee for a felon[41] here.

ROMEO

[*drawing*] Wilt thou provoke me? Then have at thee, boy!   70

They fight.

PAGE

O Lord, they fight! I will go call the Watch.[42]

Exit PAGE.

PARIS

[*falls*] O, I am slain! – If thou be merciful,

Open the tomb, lay me with Juliet.

ROMEO

In faith, I will.

PARIS dies.

30. arrest/capture

31. unholy work

32. here

33. do not provoke
34. violent/despairing
35. Think about these dead bodies.

36. scare
37. beg

38. (lines 62–63) Do not make me kill you, by angering me.

39. afterwards

40. plea/request

41. criminal

42. (citizens who patrolled/guarded the streets – the police)

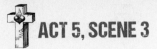

43. look at

44. troubled

45. listen to

46. One whose name is written along with mine in the book of misfortune/bad luck
47. magnificent

48. lighthouse

49. a royal chamber suitable for a feast

50. (Romeo is referring to himself.)
51. buried

52. jailers

53. Elation/euphoria

Let me peruse[43] this face.

75   Mercutio's kinsman, noble County Paris!

What said my man when my betossèd[44] soul

Did not attend[45] him as we rode? I think

He told me Paris should have married Juliet.

Said he not so? Or did I dream it so?

80   Or am I mad, hearing him talk of Juliet,

To think it was so? O, give me thy hand,

One writ with me in sour misfortune's book.[46]

I'll bury thee in a triumphant[47] grave.

[*He opens the tomb.*]

A grave? O no, a lantern,[48] slaughtered youth,

85   For here lies Juliet, and her beauty makes

This vault a feasting presence[49] full of light.

[*He lays PARIS in the tomb.*]

Death, lie thou there, by a dead man[50] interred.[51]

How oft, when men are at the point of death,

Have they been merry, which their keepers[52] call

90   A lightning[53] before death! O, how may I

Call this a lightning? O my love, my wife!

Death, that hath sucked the honey of thy breath,

Hath had no power yet upon thy beauty.

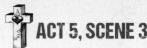

Thou art not conquered. Beauty's ensign[54] yet

Is crimson in thy lips and in thy cheeks,   95

And death's pale flag is not advancèd[55] there.

Tybalt, liest thou there in thy bloody sheet?

O, what more favour can I do thee

Than with that hand that cut thy youth in twain[56]

To sunder his that was thine enemy?[57]   100

Forgive me, cousin! Ah, dear Juliet,

Why art thou yet[58] so fair? Shall I believe

That unsubstantial[59] Death is amorous,[60]

And that the lean abhorrèd[61] monster keeps

Thee here in dark to be his paramour?[62]   105

For fear of that I still will stay with thee,[63]

And never from this palace of dim night

Depart again. Here, here will I remain

With worms that are thy chambermaids.[64] O, here

Will I set up my everlasting rest,   110

And shake the yoke of inauspicious stars[65]

From this world-wearied flesh.[66] Eyes, look your last.[67]

Arms, take your last embrace, and lips, O you

The doors of breath, seal with a righteous[68] kiss

A dateless bargain[69] to engrossing[70] death!   115

Come, bitter conduct,[71] come, unsavoury[72] guide!

Thou desperate pilot,[73] now at once run on

The dashing rocks thy seasick weary bark![74]

Here's to my love! [*drinks*] O true[75] apothecary,

Thy drugs are quick![76] Thus with a kiss I die.   120

54. flag

55. raised

56. in two

57. To destroy the life of he who was your enemy (i.e. to kill himself)

58. still

59. invisible
60. loving/romantic
61. hateful

62. lover

63. I will stay with you forever

64. servants

65. shake off the burden of bad luck/reject my cruel fate (The word 'inauspicious' means 'unlucky'.)
66. body
67. for the last time

68. an honourable

69. An eternal contract
70. all-consuming
71. poison
72. unpleasant/revolting
73. sailor

74. ship

75. truthful

76. fast-acting

Romeo dies.

Enter FRIAR LAURENCE, with a lantern, crow, and spade.

FRIAR LAURENCE

Saint Francis be my speed![77] How oft[78] tonight

Have my old feet stumbled at graves! Who's there?

77. help me
78. often

BALTHASAR

Here's one, a friend, and one that knows you well.

FRIAR LAURENCE

Bliss be upon you! Tell me, good my friend,

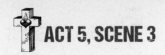
79. maggots
80. make out

125 What torch is yond, that vainly lends his light
To grubs[79] and eyeless skulls? As I discern,[80]
It burneth in the Capels' monument.

BALTHASAR

It doth so, holy sir, and there's my master,
One that you love.

FRIAR LAURENCE

      Who is it?

BALTHASAR

                Romeo.

FRIAR LAURENCE

How long hath he been there?

BALTHASAR

130   Full half an hour.

FRIAR LAURENCE

Go with me to the vault.

BALTHASAR

         I dare not, sir.

81. My master thinks that I have left

82. threatened

83. to watch what he was doing

My master knows not but I am gone hence,[81]
And fearfully did menace[82] me with death
If I did stay to look on his intents.[83]

FRIAR LAURENCE

135 Stay then, I'll go alone. Fear comes upon me.
O, much I fear some ill unthrifty[84] thing.

84. unfortunate

BALTHASAR

As I did sleep under this yew tree here,
I dreamt my master and another fought,
And that my master slew[85] him.

85. killed

FRIAR LAURENCE

         Romeo!
[*He stoops and looks on the blood and weapons.*]

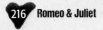

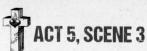

Alack, alack, what blood is this which stains   140

The stony entrance of this sepulchre?[86]

What mean these masterless[87] and gory[88] swords

To lie discoloured by this place of peace?

[*He enters the tomb.*]

Romeo! O, pale! Who else? What, Paris, too,

And steeped in blood? Ah, what an unkind hour   145

Is guilty of this lamentable chance![89]

The lady stirs.

JULIET wakes.

JULIET

O comfortable[90] friar, where is my lord?

I do remember well where I should be,

And there I am. Where is my Romeo?   150

FRIAR LAURENCE

I hear some noise. Lady, come from that nest

Of death, contagion, and unnatural sleep.

A greater power than we can contradict

Hath thwarted our intents.[91] Come, come away.

Thy husband in thy bosom there lies dead,   155

And Paris, too. Come, I'll dispose of thee[92]

Among a sisterhood of holy nuns.

Stay not to question, for the Watch is coming.

Come, go, good Juliet. I dare no longer stay.

JULIET

Go, get thee hence, for I will not away.[93]   160

Exit FRIAR LAURENCE.

What's here? A cup, closed in my true love's hand?

Poison, I see, hath been his timeless[94] end.

O churl![95] – drunk all, and left no friendly drop

To help me after? I will kiss thy lips.

Haply[96] some poison yet doth hang on them,   165

To make me die with a restorative.[97]

[*She kisses him.*] Thy lips are warm!

---

86. tomb

87. abandoned
88. bloody

89. unfortunate coincidence

90. comforting/reassuring

91. Has ruined our plans

92. hide you

93. I will not leave

94. premature

95. brute (a term of mild abuse)

96. Perhaps

97. medicine/kiss (lines 165–166: Juliet is saying that if there is a trace of poison on Romeo's lips, it may cure her by helping her to be reunited with him.)

FIRST WATCHMAN

[*within*] Lead, boy. Which way?

JULIET

Yea, noise? Then I'll be brief.

[*She takes ROMEO's dagger.*]

O happy[98] dagger!

170 This is thy sheath! There rust, and let me die.

[*She stabs herself, falls and dies.*]

Enter WATCH, with the PAGE of PARIS.

PAGE

This is the place, there where the torch doth burn.

FIRST WATCHMAN

The ground is bloody. Search about the churchyard.

Go, some of you. Whoe'er you find, attach.[99]

Exeunt some WATCHMEN.

Pitiful sight! Here lies the County slain,

175 And Juliet bleeding, warm, and newly dead,

Who here hath lain this two days burièd.

Go, tell the Prince. Run to the Capulets,

Raise up the Montagues. Some others search.

98. lucky

99. arrest

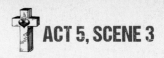

Exeunt other WATCHMEN.

We see the ground[100] whereon these woes do lie,

But the true ground[101] of all these piteous woes   180

We cannot without circumstance descry.[102]

Enter WATCHMEN, with BALTHASAR.

SECOND WATCHMAN

Here's Romeo's man. We found him in the churchyard.

FIRST WATCHMAN

Hold him in safety, till the Prince come hither.

Enter another WATCHMAN, with FRIAR LAURENCE.

THIRD WATCHMAN

Here is a friar, that trembles, sighs, and weeps.

We took this mattock and this spade from him   185

As he was coming from this churchyard's side.

FIRST WATCHMAN

A great suspicion. Stay[103] the friar, too.

Enter the PRINCE and ATTENDANTS.

PRINCE

What misadventure[104] is so early up,

That calls our person[105] from our morning rest?

Enter CAPULET, LADY CAPULET and OTHERS.

CAPULET

What should it be that is so shrieked abroad?[106]   190

LADY CAPULET

O, the people in the street cry 'Romeo',

Some 'Juliet', and some 'Paris', and all run

With open[107] outcry toward our monument.

PRINCE

What fear is this which startles in our ears?

---

100. soil

101. cause

102. understand (lines 180–181: We won't understand the cause of these deaths until we investigate the circumstances surrounding them.)

103. Hold

104. accident

105. me

106. What is everybody shouting about?

107. public

Juliet's Tomb, Verona

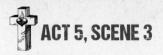
FIRST WATCHMAN

Sovereign, here lies the County Paris slain, 195

And Romeo dead, and Juliet, dead before,

Warm, and new killed.

PRINCE

Search, seek, and know how this foul murder comes.

FIRST WATCHMAN

Here is a friar, and slaughtered Romeo's man,

With instruments upon them, fit to open 200

These dead men's tombs.

CAPULET

O, heavens! O wife, look how our daughter bleeds!

This dagger hath mista'en,[108] for lo, his house[109]   108. has been misdirected
                                                                    109. its sheath (cover)

Is empty on the back of Montague,

And it mis-sheathèd in my daughter's bosom. 205

LADY CAPULET

O me, this sight of death is as a bell,

That warns[110] my old age to a sepulchre.[111]   110. calls
                                                                            111. tomb

Enter MONTAGUE and OTHERS.

PRINCE

Come, Montague, for thou art early up

To see thy son and heir more early down.

MONTAGUE

Alas, my liege,[112] my wife is dead tonight. 210   112. lord

Grief of my son's exile hath stopped her breath.

What further woe conspires against mine age?

PRINCE

Look, and thou shalt see.

MONTAGUE

[*seeing ROMEO's body*] O thou untaught![113] What manners is in this,   113. rude boy

To press before thy father to a grave?[114] 215   114. die before your father

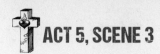
115. confusing matters
116. And find out how these events began and how they unfolded

117. be patient
118. bad luck
119. (lines 220–221) Let us remain calm in the face of sorrow.
120. the suspects

121. accuse
122. excuse

123. (lines 229–230) I will be brief because I won't live long enough to tell a long-winded story.

124. secret

125. day of death

126. Promised her
127. against her will

128. guided by my skills (with plants and herbs)

129. gave her

130. appearance

131. should come here
132. (as this = this)
133. temporary

PRINCE

Seal up the mouth of outrage for a while,

Till we can clear these ambiguities[115]

And know their spring, their head, their true descent;[116]

And then will I be general of your woes,

220 And lead you even to death. Meantime forbear,[117]

And let mischance[118] be slave to patience.[119]

Bring forth the parties of suspicion.[120]

FRIAR LAURENCE

I am the greatest, able to do least,

Yet most suspected, as the time and place

225 Doth make against me, of this direful murder;

And here I stand, both to impeach[121] and purge[122]

Myself condemnèd and myself excused.

PRINCE

Then say at once what thou dost know in this.

FRIAR LAURENCE

I will be brief, for my short date of breath

230 Is not so long as is a tedious tale.[123]

Romeo, there dead, was husband to that Juliet,

And she, there dead, that Romeo's faithful wife.

I married them, and their stolen[124] marriage day

Was Tybalt's doomsday,[125] whose untimely death

235 Banished the new-made bridegroom from this city;

For whom, and not for Tybalt, Juliet pined.

You, to remove that siege of grief from her,

Betrothed[126] and would have married her perforce,[127]

To County Paris. Then comes she to me,

240 And with wild looks bid me devise some mean

To rid her from this second marriage,

Or in my cell there would she kill herself.

Then gave I her – so tutored by my art,[128] –

A sleeping potion, which so took effect

245 As I intended, for it wrought on her[129]

The form[130] of death. Meantime I writ to Romeo

That he should hither come[131] as this[132] dire night

To help to take her from her borrowed[133] grave,

Being the time the potion's force should cease.

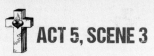

But he which bore my letter, Friar John,   250

Was stayed[134] by accident, and yesternight

Returned my letter back. Then all alone

At the prefixèd[135] hour of her waking,

Came I to take her from her kindred's vault,[136]

Meaning to keep her closely[137] at my cell   255

Till I conveniently could send to Romeo.

But when I came, some minute ere the time

Of her awakening, here untimely lay

The noble Paris and true Romeo dead.

She wakes, and I entreated[138] her come forth,   260

And bear this work of heaven with patience.

But then a noise did scare me from the tomb,

And she, too desperate, would not go with me,

But, as it seems, did violence on herself.[139]

All this I know, and to the marriage   265

Her nurse is privy;[140] and if aught in this

Miscarried by my fault,[141] let my old life

Be sacrificed, some hour before his[142] time,

Unto the rigour[143] of severest law.

PRINCE

We still[144] have known thee for a holy man.   270

Where's Romeo's man? What can he say to this?

BALTHASAR

I brought my master news of Juliet's death,

And then in post[145] he came from Mantua

To this same place, to this same monument.

This letter he early bid me give his father,   275

And threatened me with death, going in the vault,

If I departed not and left him there.

PRINCE

Give me the letter. I will look on it.

Where is the County's page that raised the Watch?

Sirrah, what made your master in this place?[146]   280

PAGE

He came with flowers to strew[147] his lady's grave,

And bid me stand aloof,[148] and so I did.

---

134. delayed

135. pre-arranged

136. family's tomb

137. secretly

138. begged

139. stabbed herself

140. witness to

141. Went wrong because of me

142. its

143. harshness

144. always

145. quickly

146. Why was your master here?

147. scatter over

148. back

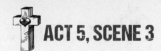
149. Soon
150. open
151. And soon

152. proves

153. news

154. with it

155. curse/punishment

156. happiness/children

157. for ignoring your fighting

158. two of my relatives (He is referring to Mercutio and Paris.)

159. wedding gift (i.e. 'This handshake is my daughter's wedding gift.')

160. hostility/hatred

161. Leave here

Anon,[149] comes one with light to ope[150] the tomb,

And by and by[151] my master drew on him,

285 And then I ran away to call the Watch.

PRINCE

This letter doth make good[152] the Friar's words,

Their course of love, the tidings[153] of her death;

And here he writes that he did buy a poison

Of a poor 'pothecary, and therewithal[154]

290 Came to this vault to die, and lie with Juliet.

Where be these enemies? – Capulet, Montague,

See what a scourge[155] is laid upon your hate,

That heaven finds means to kill your joys[156] with love.

And I, for winking at your discords[157] too,

295 Have lost a brace of kinsmen.[158] All are punished.

CAPULET

O brother Montague, give me thy hand.

This is my daughter's jointure,[159] for no more

Can I demand.

MONTAGUE

        But I can give thee more,

For I will raise her statue in pure gold,

300 That whiles Verona by that name is known

There shall no figure at such rate be set

As that of true and faithful Juliet.

CAPULET

As rich shall Romeo's by his lady's lie,

Poor sacrifices of our enmity.[160]

PRINCE

305 A glooming peace this morning with it brings.

The sun for sorrow will not show his head.

Go hence,[161] to have more talk of these sad things.

Some shall be pardoned, and some punishèd;

For never was a story of more woe

310 Than this of Juliet and her Romeo.

Exeunt.

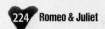

OVERVIEW OF ACT 5, SCENE 3
KEY SCENE OF TRAGEDY

Part 1 – Paris arrives in the churchyard with his page (servant).

- Paris has come to the graveyard to place flowers at Juliet's tomb. He claims that he will come every night and mourn for her:

  The obsequies that I for thee will keep

  Nightly shall be to strew thy grave and weep. (lines 16–17)

- Paris's page warns Paris that someone is coming, and so Paris hides.

Part 2 – Romeo arrives with Balthasar.

- Romeo arrives at the graveyard with a **mattock** (pick-axe) and a crowbar. He instructs Balthasar to deliver a letter to his father and asks him to leave. He warns him that he will 'tear [him] joint by joint' (line 35) if he does not obey his orders. There is a sense of wildness in Romeo's behaviour.

- Balthasar says that he will leave, but decides to stay, because he is concerned about Romeo's rash behaviour. Aside, Balthasar says:

  For all this same, I'll hide me hereabout.

  His look I fear, and his intents I doubt. (lines 43–44)

Part 3 – Paris and Romeo fight; Romeo kills Paris.

- As Romeo is beginning to open the tomb, Paris emerges from his hiding place and confronts him. Paris is convinced that Romeo has come to 'do some villainous shame to the dead bodies' (lines 52–53) and challenges Romeo to a fight. Romeo, who is determined to die with Juliet, pleads with Paris to leave him be:

  I beseech thee, youth,

  Put not another sin upon my head

  By urging me to fury. (lines 61–63)

- Paris, however, disregards Romeo's words and they fight. At the sight of his master and Romeo fighting, Paris's page goes to call the Watch. Before he dies from his wounds, Paris asks Romeo to place him inside the tomb with Juliet:

  If thou be merciful,

  Open the tomb, lay me with Juliet. (lines 72–73)

- Romeo agrees to grant Paris's dying request. He identifies with Paris, who, like him, was in love with Juliet. To Paris's corpse, Romeo says:

  O, give me thy hand,

  One writ with me in sour misfortune's book. (lines 81–82)

Part 4 – Romeo enters the tomb and dies.

- Romeo enters the tomb and reflects on how Juliet looks beautiful even in death:

  Death, that hath sucked the honey of thy breath,

  Hath had no power yet upon thy beauty.

  Thou art not conquered. (lines 92–94)

- He describes death as an 'abhorrèd monster', who has taken Juliet to be his 'paramour' (lover) (lines 104–105). In order to protect Juliet, he will stay with her forever. This is a very **poignant** (moving) moment. Romeo, about to take his own life, is unaware that Juliet is not really dead. He drinks the poison and dies:

> *O true apothecary,*
>
> *Thy drugs are quick! Thus with a kiss I die.* (lines 119–120)

Part 5 – Friar Laurence arrives and tries to rescue Juliet; Juliet dies.

- Friar Laurence arrives too late to avert disaster. In the graveyard, he meets Balthasar, who tells him he had a dream that his master, Romeo, fought and killed someone. Friar Laurence sees the 'masterless and gory swords' (line 142) lying on the ground and realises that he has come too late to save Romeo.

- Juliet awakes and asks for Romeo. Friar Laurence pleads with her to leave the tomb, which he describes as a 'nest of death, contagion, and unnatural sleep' (lines 151–152).

- He informs Juliet that the plan has failed:

> *A greater power than we can contradict*
>
> *Hath thwarted our intents.* (lines 153–154)

- Friar Laurence tells Juliet that Romeo is dead and begs her to leave the tomb. Worried that the Watch is coming, he hurries out of the tomb and leaves her behind, saying:

> *Stay not to question, for the Watch is coming.* (line 158)

- Juliet sees the cup of poison that Romeo drank. She kisses Romeo's lips, and then, hearing a noise, takes his dagger and stabs herself:

> *O happy dagger!*
>
> *This is thy sheath! There rust, and let me die.* (lines 169–170)

Part 6 – The Watch arrives, followed by Montague, the Prince and the Capulets.

- The Watch (guards) arrive with Paris's page and survey the scene of tragedy. They find Balthasar and Friar Laurence in the churchyard and **apprehend** (arrest) them. Prince Escalus arrives next, followed by Juliet's parents and Montague. We find out that Romeo's mother has died of grief over Romeo's banishment.

- The Prince asks for the suspects to be brought forward. First, Friar Laurence speaks:

> *And here I stand, both to impeach and purge*
>
> *Myself condemnèd and myself excused.* (lines 226–227)

- Friar Laurence's **ensuing** speech acts as a summary of the main events in the play. He is willing to face the consequences of his actions if the Prince believes that he acted inappropriately:

> *… if aught in this*
>
> *Miscarried by my fault, let my old life*
>
> *Be sacrificed, some hour before his time,*
>
> *Unto the rigour of severest law.* (lines 266–269)

- The Prince reassures Friar Laurence that he knows he has always been a holy man.

- Balthasar **corroborates** (backs up) Friar Laurence's story and gives Romeo's letter – which was supposed to be delivered to his father – to the Prince to **peruse** (look at).

- Next, Paris's page explains what took place between his master and Romeo.

- The Prince reveals that the contents of Romeo's letter confirm what the Friar has told them, and asks the families to reflect on their roles in the tragedy:

Capulet, Montague,

See what a scourge is laid upon your hate,

That heaven finds means to kill your joys with love. (lines 291–293)

… All are punishèd. (line 295)

- The Montague and Capulet families reconcile. Capulet shakes Montague's hand, and Montague says that he will erect a gold statue of Juliet. Similarly, Capulet says that he will erect a statue of Romeo to be placed by Juliet's side, describing the lovers as 'Poor sacrifices of our enmity' (line 304).

- The final words of the play, uttered by the Prince, provide a fitting conclusion and sum up the tragedy:

    For never was a story of more woe

    Than this of Juliet and her Romeo. (lines 309–310)

- However, despite this glimmer of optimism, the ending is overwhelmingly bleak and sorrowful, and the audience is left contemplating the extent of the **tragedy**.

A. REVIEWING

1. What does Romeo ask Balthasar to do at the beginning of the scene?

2. Why has Paris come to the churchyard?

3. How does Paris react when he sees Romeo?

4. What does Romeo do with Paris's corpse?

5. What happens when Romeo enters the tomb and sees Juliet?

6. Why do you think Juliet refuses to leave the tomb?

7. What happened to Lady Montague, according to Montague?

8. How do the families react when the full extent of the tragedy is revealed to them?

9. Do you think that Prince Escalus is sympathetic to the families? Explain your answer.

10. Is there anything positive about the ending, in your opinion?

B. EXPLORING

1. Comparing Romeo and Paris as Love Rivals │P│

In what ways are Romeo and Paris similar in this scene? Compare their **actions** and their **words**. Turn to **page 72** of your portfolio to help you with this task.

2. Language and Imagery │P│

Turn to **page 73** of your portfolio and complete the following activities:

(a) Romeo's Soliloquy

Read back over Romeo's **soliloquy** (lines 87–120) and **paraphrase** two of the questions that he asks in this speech.

(b) Personification

There are many examples of **personification** throughout this scene, which help to create vivid images and contribute to the atmosphere of the scene. For example, Death is seen as a creature that is keeping Juliet to be his 'paramour' (Romeo, line 105). Find **two** examples of personification in this scene and comment on the **effect** of each one.

(c) Imagery of the Tomb

This scene contains many interesting **descriptions of the tomb**, such as a 'maw' that has swallowed up Juliet, 'the dearest morsel of the earth' (Romeo, lines 45–46), and a 'palace of dim night' (Romeo, line 107). Find two descriptions of the tomb and discuss the image that is created by each one in your mind.

3. The Dramatic Scene of Tragedy

Write about the aspects of this scene that make it so dramatic. You might consider some of the following:

- The **setting** – the churchyard at night
- The **sounds**
- The **imagery** of death and blood
- The **tragic deaths** that occur
- The **role of fate/timing** in the tragedy.

C. CREATING

1. Romeo's Letter to his Father |P|

Turn to **page 74** of your portfolio and write Romeo's letter to his father.

2. Sketching |P| the Scene

(a) **Design a stage set** suitable for the final scene of *Romeo and Juliet*. Look at the images on the right to help you. Bear in mind that your design will have to incorporate ideas to show the audience the exterior of the graveyard as well as the interior of the tomb. Sketch your design on **page 75** of your portfolio.

(b) Turn to **page 76** of your portfolio and write a **short piece** to accompany your design, indicating how the distinct parts of the scene could be played.

(c) Pick out a few **important lines** from Paris, Romeo, Juliet, Friar Laurence and Prince Escalus, and say how you would expect the actors to deliver these lines.

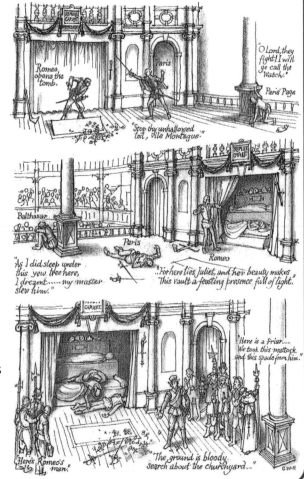

D. REFLECTING

Character File

Turn to the Character File section of your portfolio and continue recording your impressions of **(a) Romeo (page 88)** and **(b) Friar Laurence (page 101)** based on this scene.

E. ORAL LANGUAGE

1. Friar Laurence's Speech |P|

Pair Activity

Turn to **page 77** of your portfolio and summarise each section of Friar Laurence's speech (lines 229–269).

2. Performing the Trial of Friar Laurence |P|

Group Activity

Charge: The murders of Romeo and Juliet

Bring forth the parties of suspicion. (Prince Escalus, line 222)

Participants in the Trial		
Judge: Prince Escalus	**Accused:** Friar Laurence	**Accusers:** Capulet and Montague families
Lawyers: Lawyers for Capulet and Montague families Lawyers for Friar Laurence	**Witness 1:** the Nurse **Witness 2:** Benvolio **Witness 3:** Balthasar **Witness 4:** Paris's page	**Jury:** The rest of the class

(a) Lawyers for both sides prepare **two questions** for each witness.

(b) Each team takes it in turn to **cross-examine** (question) each witness.

(c) Each witness improvises answers, based on his/her knowledge of events in the play. The answers that each witness gives will provide the evidence.

(d) When all witnesses have given evidence, each side will examine their evidence and formulate a closing speech/statement to try to convince the jury of their viewpoint.

(e) Turn to **page 78** of your portfolio to help with this task.

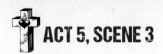

F. LOOKING BACK AT ACT 5

1. Overview P

Pair Activity

With your partner, turn back to **page 4** of your portfolio and write one sentence or phrase in the box for each scene in Act 5. This sentence or phrase should sum up the main action in that scene.

2. What If…?

Group Activity

In groups, re-write Act 5, Scene 3, so that it does not end in tragedy for the lovers. Perform/read your revised script aloud.

DELVING DEEPER

1. Comparing Film Versions

(a) Write a **review** of one film version of *Romeo and Juliet*. Compare it to the play.

OR

(b) Compare the **final scene of tragedy** in two film versions of *Romeo and Juliet*. For example, you may wish to choose the 1996 film directed by Baz Luhrmann and one other film.

2. Designing a Soundtrack

Group Activity

In groups, choose **five** songs that you think would be suitable to depict the key stages of Romeo and Juliet's relationship. The key stages might include when Romeo and Juliet first meet, the Balcony Scene, when Romeo leaves for Mantua, etc. Explain each song choice, referring to the play where possible. You could present this as a slideshow.

Examining the Play

· Plot Structure · Characters · Themes ·
· Approaching Exam Questions ·

Important Vocabulary

Plot: The sequence of events in a story.

Protagonist: The main character or one of the main characters in a literary work.

Theme: A recurring topic, message or idea in a literary work. Examples from *Romeo and Juliet* are love, conflict and fate.

Looking at the Plot Structure

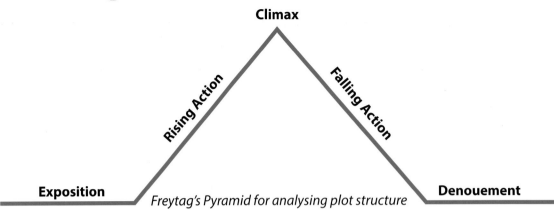

Freytag's Pyramid for analysing plot structure

The plot is the sequence of events in a story. The German writer **Gustav Freytag** (1816–1895) devised the diagram above to examine the plot structure in Shakespearean plays. He identified the following five elements:

1. **Exposition** refers to the audience's introduction to the characters, main setting and events. The main themes may also be introduced.

2. **Rising action** refers to important events (or inciting actions) that cause the story to develop. Rising action leads to the play's climax.

3. The **climax** is the high point of the play. It is also known as the crisis. It may include a dramatic turning point. The climax scene often occurs in the third act of a play.

4. **Falling action** includes the events that occur after the climax. These lead to the play's ending. In scenes of falling action, the main protagonist (character) suffers a period of bad luck or misfortune.

5. **Resolution** (or **denouement**) is the ending of the story, during which the plot details are tied up. Themes and conflicts are resolved and explained.

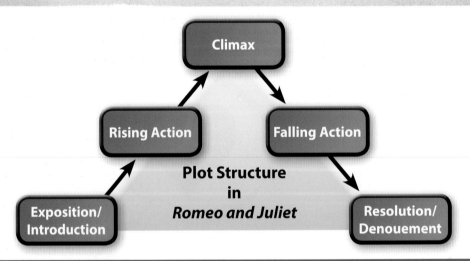

 # EXPLORING

Plot Structure /P\

Pair Activity

Turn to **page 104** of your portfolio and complete the activity on plot structure.

Looking at Character Development

Think about **how and why the characters develop** as they do in the play. Use the Character File in your portfolio to reflect on the characters and to form a response to them.

Character Checklist

Think about:

- What the **character does** or how he/she **behaves** in each key scene.
- The **adjectives** that you would use to describe the character.
- Something that **stands out** to you in a key scene.
- How the character **reacts to situations**.
- A significant **change** in the character.
- Your personal response to the character – reflecting on something that **confuses or surprises you** about the character.
- How the character interacts with other characters – his/her **relationships, both positive and negative**.

CHARACTER TRACKER |P|

Turn to **pages 105–107** of your portfolio and fill in the diagram based on your **favourite character** from the play. (Use the grids showing characters and their scenes on **page 111** of your portfolio as well as the Character File section to help you.)

Juliet

'Give me, give me! O, tell me not of fear!'
(Juliet, Act 4, Scene 1, line 121)

devoted

genuine

realistic

loving

caring

dutiful

impulsive

rational

clear-thinking

Juliet is a character who **changes dramatically** from the start to the end of the play. At the start of the play, she is an **obedient, dutiful** daughter, but by the end of the play, she has transformed into an **independent, courageous tragic heroine**.

When we first meet Juliet, she appears to be an **obedient** daughter who has given no thought to marriage, which is not surprising as she is only 13 years old. When her mother **broaches** (brings up) the subject of marriage, Juliet informs her that: 'It is an honour that I dream not of' (Act 1, Scene 3, line 67).

However, Juliet's attitude to love and marriage changes when she meets Romeo Montague in Act 1, Scene 5. By the end of this scene, she makes it clear that she has fallen deeply in love with him:

> *My only love sprung from my only hate!*
> *Too early seen unknown, and known too late!*
> *Prodigious birth of love it is to me*
> *That I must love a loathèd enemy.* (Act 1, Scene 5, lines 138–141)

At the start of the Balcony Scene, Juliet muses about giving up her family name for Romeo:

> *O Romeo, Romeo, wherefore art thou Romeo?*
> *Deny thy father and refuse thy name,*
> *Or, if thou wilt not, be but sworn my love,*
> *And I'll no longer be a Capulet.* (Act 2, Scene 2, lines 33–36)

This declaration can be interpreted in two ways: either as deep devotion or intense foolishness. Either way, Juliet has become more **independent** and **decisive** as a character at this point. She also appears grounded and down-to-earth in this scene, cautioning Romeo about being too impulsive. She thinks that their vows of love are 'too rash, too unadvised, too sudden' (Act 2, Scene 2, line 118), but reassures Romeo that she loves him deeply.

While her **devotion** to Romeo is **admirable**, we must also remember that Juliet is quite **secretive** and **rebellious** in hiding her marriage from her family.

Juliet is presented as a **realistic, three-dimensional character** in **Act 3, Scene 2,** as she responds to the news that Romeo has killed her cousin, Tybalt. Despite her initial anger, she realises that she has a lot to be grateful for, because Romeo could have been killed.

Arguably, the most challenging scene for Juliet comes in **Act 3, Scene 5,** when she is informed of her arranged marriage to Paris. She is very emotional at this point in the play, as she has just said farewell to Romeo. She is then subjected to a torrent of verbal abuse from her father, who is outraged at her refusal to marry Paris:

> *Hang thee, young baggage, disobedient wretch!*
> *I tell thee what: get thee to church a' Thursday,*
> *Or never after look me in the face.*
> *Speak not, reply not, do not answer me!* (Act 3, Scene 5, lines 160–163)

Her mother, too, dismisses her coldly, taking her husband's side, and even her trusted Nurse abandons her in her time of need. At the end of this scene, Juliet is **isolated** and alone, but still finds the courage to seek help from Friar Laurence. This shows her **maturity** and **independence**.

Juliet's **fearlessness** and **courage** are most evident in the Potion Scene (Act 4, Scene 3) and in the final scene (Act 5, Scene 3), when she decides to stay with Romeo and join him in death. She achieves the status of **tragic heroine**, as she sacrifices herself for love.

Romeo

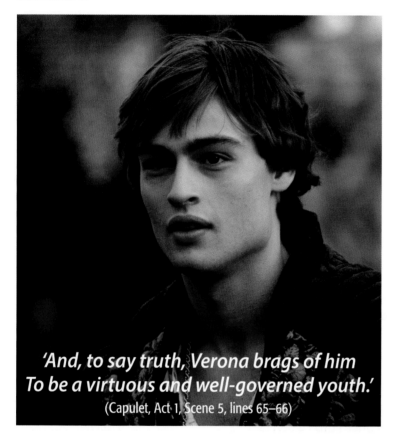

'And, to say truth, Verona brags of him
To be a virtuous and well-governed youth.'
(Capulet, Act 1, Scene 5, lines 65–66)

melancholy
impulsive
spontaneous
devoted
loving
passionate
reckless
impetuous

When we first meet Romeo, he is **lovelorn** and **melancholy** because of his unrequited love for a girl, whom we later find out, is named Rosaline. However, Romeo's character changes for the better when he meets Juliet Capulet at the Capulet feast. He is immediately captivated by her beauty and dismisses all other loves as false:

> *Did my heart love till now? Forswear it, sight,*
> *For I ne'er saw true beauty till this night.* (Act 1, Scene 5, lines 50–51)

This may suggest that Romeo is **fickle**, or that he genuinely feels that he has fallen in love for the first time and that his love for Rosaline was mere infatuation.

When he finds out that Juliet is a Capulet, he realises that his life is in the hands of his enemy:

> *Is she a Capulet?*
> *O dear account! My life is my foe's debt.* (Act 1, Scene 5, lines 117–118)

Romeo reveals himself to be an **impulsive, spontaneous** youth when he and Juliet exchange vows of love in the Balcony Scene. Whereas Juliet comes across as grounded and down-to-earth, Romeo uses **hyperbolic** (exaggerated), over-the-top language:

> *I am no pilot [sailor], yet wert thou as far*
> *As that vast shore washed with the farthest sea,*
> *I should adventure for such merchandise.* (Act 2, Scene 2, lines 82–84)

He becomes more mature as a result of his relationship with Juliet. Mercutio comments on Romeo's **transformation** in Act 2, Scene 4:

> *Why, is not this better now than groaning for love?*
> *Now art thou sociable, now art thou Romeo.* (Act 2, Scene 4, lines 78–79)

Another positive effect of Romeo's relationship with Juliet is his reluctance to fight with the Capulets. Unfortunately, his position has negative repercussions. In the Fight Scene, Mercutio is so outraged by what he perceives as Romeo's 'vile submission' (Act 3, Scene 1, line 69) that he fights on Romeo's behalf and gets killed by Tybalt. At this point, Romeo blames his relationship with Juliet for making him cowardly:

> *O sweet Juliet,*
> *Thy beauty hath made me effeminate*
> *And in my temper softened valour's steel!* (Act 3, Scene 1, lines 111–113)

Later, in Friar Laurence's cell (Act 3, Scene 3), Romeo becomes **hysterical** and loses all self-control. He seems to have **regressed** as a character, as he appears **immature** and helpless. His **impulsiveness** is seen once again when he threatens to take his own life:

> *O tell me, Friar, tell me,*
> *In what vile part of this anatomy*
> *Doth my name lodge? Tell me, that I may sack*
> *The hateful mansion.* (Act 3, Scene 3, lines 105–108)

However, when he is forced to consider his good fortune by Friar Laurence, and when the Nurse gives him the ring from Juliet, he regains his **composure** (calmness) and becomes more **optimistic**.

Romeo is absent for the entire fourth act of the play. When we meet him again in Act 5, Scene 1, he is distraught at the news of Juliet's supposed death. He curses fate and decides to take control of his own destiny:

> *Is it e'en so? Then I defy you, stars!* (Act 5, Scene 1, line 24)

Here, we see his **impulsive** nature once again, as he seeks out the Apothecary in order to get a poison to take at Juliet's tomb. However, we could also interpret this as an act of **true love** and **devotion**, because he would rather die than live without Juliet.

Mercutio

witty
defensive
loyal
argumentative
violent
rash
impulsive
threatening
provocative

Mercutio, Romeo's close friend, is related to Prince Escalus. He is a witty, imaginative character, and is prone to quarrelsome and impulsive behaviour. He tries to cheer Romeo up when he is feeling down about his unrequited love for Rosaline, saying, 'If love be rough with you, be rough with love' (Act 1, Scene 4, line 27). He shows a **whimsical, imaginative** side in his Queen Mab speech (Act 1, Scene 4, lines 55–96).

Mercutio's language is also **bawdy** (rude) and filled with sexual **innuendo** (double meaning) as he focuses on the physical side of love. However, he proves himself a **brave** and **honourable** character when he stands up for Romeo in Act 3, Scene 1:

> *O calm, dishonourable, vile submission!* (Act 3, Scene 1, line 69)

Mercutio fights Tybalt and gets killed. As he is dying, he curses the Capulets and the Montagues, saying, 'A plague o' both your houses!' (Act 3, Scene 1, line 88), but he retains his good humour to the very end:

> *Ask for me tomorrow, and*
> *you shall find me a grave man.* (Act 3, Scene 1, lines 95–96)

It has been suggested that Shakespeare 'kills off' Mercutio at this point in the play because he is such an interesting character that he could overshadow other more important characters. His death prompts Romeo to kill Tybalt in revenge, thus **precipitating** (causing) the tragedy.

The Nurse

The Nurse is one of Shakespeare's finest comic characters. She is a **maternal** figure for Juliet who acts as her confidante and loves her deeply. She seems much closer to Juliet than Lady Capulet, who is more formal and distant in her dealings with her daughter. The Nurse's amusing account of Juliet's childhood reveals her intimate knowledge of the girl's life. It is clear that the Nurse wants Juliet to be happily married:

> *Thou wast the prettiest babe that e'er I nursed.*
> *An I might live to see thee married once,*
> *I have my wish.* (Act 1, Scene 3, lines 61–63)

The Nurse acts as a **go-between** in the relationship between Romeo and Juliet. When she seeks Romeo out in Act 2, Scene 4, she is quite protective of Juliet and warns him to be true to her.

Despite her good points, the Nurse proves herself to be **fickle (changeable)** when she turns against Romeo and advises Juliet to marry Paris. She says that Juliet would be 'happy in this second match' for it 'excels' her first match (Act 3, Scene 5, lines 223–224). The Nurse is simply being practical, but Juliet feels suddenly **estranged** from her, and so seeks out the help of Friar Laurence.

However, the Nurse's devotion to Juliet is again evident in **Act 4, Scene 5**, when she discovers Juliet's 'dead' body. She is inconsolable in her loss:

> *Alas, alas! Help, help! My lady's dead!*
> *O weraday that ever I was born!* (Act 4, Scene 5, lines 14–15)

Despite her contradictions, the Nurse is a well-meaning character who displays genuine love and affection for her 'lamb' and 'ladybird', Juliet Capulet.

Friar Laurence

Friar Laurence is Romeo's **confidant** and spiritual advisor. He is also a kind of **surrogate father** to Romeo. When we first meet Friar Laurence, he is gathering herbs and plants while meditating on the existence of good and evil. He appears to be a **wise and philosophical** character. When Romeo tells him of his secret relationship with Juliet and his desire to marry her, Friar Laurence is at first surprised and hesitant. However, it is not long before he agrees to marry Romeo and Juliet, believing that the marriage may bring an end to the long-held feud between their families:

> *For this alliance may so happy prove,*
> *To turn your households' rancour to pure love.*
> (Act 2, Scene 3, lines 91–92)

humorous
maternal
loving
talkative
sensitive/insensitiv
critical
fickle
changeable

paternal
philosophical
deep
wise
quick-thinking
reckless
optimistic
trustworthy
dependable
deceitful

In **Act 2, Scene 6,** as Friar Laurence prepares to marry Romeo and Juliet, he seems to have a sense of **foreboding** (worry), as he says:

> *So smile the heavens upon this holy act,*
> *That after-hours with sorrow chide us not!* (Act 2, Scene 6, lines 1–2)

It is almost as if he realises that no good can come of this secret marriage. He commits **deception** by performing this marriage ceremony for Romeo and Juliet without their parents' knowledge.

Friar Laurence proves an **invaluable support** to Romeo, who, distraught at the news of his banishment, threatens to end his life. He uses all of his skills of persuasion to appeal to Romeo and help him to see the positive side of the situation. He gives Romeo **spiritual comfort** and **practical help** by formulating a plan for Romeo to go to Mantua.

Juliet, too, receives help and comfort from Friar Laurence. Feeling abandoned by those around her, she looks to him for advice on how to avoid marrying Paris. Seeing that Juliet is desperate, he devises a hasty plan to help her escape the marriage. While one may criticise his plan, it is possible that Juliet would have taken her own life if she were not given some kind of practical solution. However, we must remember that Friar Laurence commits **deception** yet again by offering the Capulets spiritual comfort even though he knows that Juliet is not really dead.

When it is revealed towards the end of the play that Romeo did not receive his letter, Friar Laurence acts quickly to **avert** (prevent) danger. He arrives at the Capulet tomb just as Juliet is waking, informs her of the unlucky turn of events and asks her to leave. Here, it may be argued that Friar Laurence displays a degree of **cowardice**, with devastating consequences. On hearing a noise, he is concerned about his own safety and rushes out of the tomb, leaving a **vulnerable** Juliet to deal with the reality of Romeo's death alone.

He is **repentant**, however, and willing to take responsibility for his actions when he confesses to his part in the tragedy:

> *And here I stand, both to impeach and purge*
> *Myself condemnèd and myself excused.* (Act 5, Scene 3, lines 226–227)

The Prince responds, 'We still have known thee for a holy man' (Act 5, Scene 3, line 270), suggesting that he does not blame Friar Laurence for the tragedy.

Like the Nurse, Friar Laurence displays many contradictory characteristics, being both wise and foolish, and deceitful yet honest. He appears to be an **inherently** (essentially) good character.

Benvolio

truthful
honest
loyal
trustworthy
diplomatic
encouraging
selfless
sensitive
supportive
peacemaker

Benvolio is Romeo's cousin and acts as his **confidant** (advisor) in the play. At the start of the play, when Romeo's parents are worried about their sad, withdrawn son, Benvolio offers to find out what is wrong with him.

Benvolio is a **peacemaker** and always tries to avoid conflict. In **Act 1, Scene 1**, when Tybalt arrives at the scene of the street brawl, Benvolio tells him:

> *I do but keep the peace. Put up thy sword,*
> *Or manage it to part these men with me.*
> (Act 1, Scene 1, lines 61–62)

Again, in Act 3, Scene 1, he is anxious to leave, as he is worried that a fight might break out. He tries to reason with Tybalt and Mercutio, urging them to discuss their differences away from the public gaze:

> *We talk here in the public haunt of men.*
> *Either withdraw unto some private place,*
> *Or reason coldly of your grievances,*
> *Or else depart. Here all eyes gaze on us.* (Act 3, Scene 1, lines 46–49)

Benvolio's **truthful, honest** nature is evident when he faithfully recounts, to the Prince and others, the events that transpired in Act 1, Scene 1 and Act 3, Scene 1. He does not feature again in the play after Act 3, Scene 1.

Tybalt

fiery
quarrelsome
argumentative
defiant
hot-tempered
vengeful

Tybalt is Juliet's cousin. His **fiery** nature makes him the **embodiment** (symbol/personification) of conflict in the play. His influence in the play is far-reaching, even though he has only 36 lines of dialogue. From the first time we meet him, we are aware that he is **hot-tempered** and **quarrelsome**. In Act 1, Scene 1, he forms a contrast with Benvolio, the peacemaker, when he says:

> *What, drawn and talk of peace? I hate the word*
> *As I hate hell, all Montagues, and thee.* (Act 1, Scene 1, lines 63-64)

Tybalt is **incensed** at Romeo's appearance at the Capulet feast. His rage **manifests** (shows) itself again in **Act 3, Scene 1** and has devastating consequences for Romeo and Juliet. Romeo's reluctance to fight Tybalt causes Mercutio to step in for him, which results in Mercutio's death. Romeo then fights Tybalt and kills him. Benvolio's account of the incident provides a good insight into Tybalt's character:

> *... the unruly spleen*
> *Of Tybalt, deaf to peace* (Act 3, Scene 1, lines 155–156)

Romeo's killing of Tybalt sets off a chain of events that **culminates** (ends) with his own death and the death of his beloved Juliet.

Prince Escalus

Prince Escalus is in charge of law and order in Verona. He appears in the play at its three **moments of crisis**: after the street brawl in Act 1, Scene 1, after the Fight Scene in Act 3, Scene 1, and at the end in Act 5, Scene 3. He is related to both Mercutio and Paris, so he is personally affected by the deaths in the play. However, this does not stop him from being honest and fair in his dealings.

merciful
fair
just
firm
honest
impartial
dignified
self-possessed

In Act 1, Scene 1, Prince Escalus speaks **ominous** words of warning:

> *If ever you disturb our streets again*
> *Your lives shall pay the forfeit of the peace.*
> (Act 1, Scene 1, lines 89–90)

He proves himself a **merciful** and **fair** ruler when it emerges that Romeo has killed Tybalt. Rather than sentencing Romeo to death, he banishes him from Verona.

He also warns the Montagues and the Capulets that he will be 'deaf to pleading and excuses' (Act 3, Scene 1, line 190), showing that he is **impartial** and **firm**.

At the end of the play, he sums up the entire tragedy with two **poignant** (moving) lines:

> *For never was a story of more woe*
> *Than this of Juliet and her Romeo.* (Act 5, Scene 3, lines 309–310)

Paris

Paris's role in the play is to act as a **love rival** to Romeo. Paris is quite a **two-dimensional** (flat and not fully developed) character, whose main goal is to marry Juliet. When we first meet Paris, he is asking Capulet for Juliet's hand in marriage. Capulet says that Juliet is still very young, but he advises Paris to woo her. Capulet tells him that he thinks it will be two more years before Juliet is 'ripe to be a bride' (Act 1, Scene 2, lines 10–11).

Paris is considered to be a **handsome, eligible** bachelor. In Act 1, Scene 3, Lady Capulet informs Juliet that 'the valiant Paris' seeks her to be 'his love' (line 75). The Nurse describes him as a 'man of wax' (line 77), suggesting that he is perfect!

In Act 3, Scene 4, shortly after Tybalt's death, Paris is still pursuing his suit for Juliet's hand in marriage. However, he does so with great consideration, acknowledging that 'These times of woe afford no time to woo' (line 8).

In Act 4, Scene 1, Paris is delighted at his chance meeting with Juliet at Friar Laurence's cell. However, the tension in this scene is obvious to the audience. Paris displays compassion for Juliet, whom he believes has been weeping over Tybalt's death. However, when he leaves, Juliet reveals just how hateful the prospect of marrying him is to her:

> *O, bid me leap, rather than marry Paris,*
> *From off the battlements of any tower* (Act 4, Scene 1, lines 77–78)

We must bear in mind that Juliet does not know Paris well, is already married to Romeo, and is in a very vulnerable mental state.

Paris's reaction to Juliet's death also reveals his love for her. He feels cheated by death, which he personifies as a love rival:

> *Beguiled, divorcèd, wrongèd, spited, slain!*
> *Most detestable death, by thee beguiled,*
> *By cruel, cruel thee quite overthrown!*
> *O love! O life: not life, but love in death!* (Act 4, Scene 5, lines 55–58)

In the final scene of the play, we learn that he intends to visit her tomb each night to mourn for her. He proves himself to be **valiant** by standing up to Romeo, whom he thinks plans to desecrate the Capulet tomb. When Romeo tells Paris to leave him alone and warns him to 'tempt not a desperate man' (Act 5, Scene 3, line 59), Paris flatly refuses. A fight ensues and Romeo kills Paris. His final thoughts are of Juliet:

> *O, I am slain! – If thou be merciful,*
> *Open the tomb, and lay me with Juliet.* (Act 5, Scene 3, lines 72–73)

Romeo finally recognises Paris and identifies with his suffering. He agrees to place him in the tomb with Juliet, realising that both of them are victims of fate. He aptly describes Paris as 'One writ with [him] in sour misfortune's book' (Act 5, Scene 3, line 82).

sensitive

compassionate

loving

devoted

noble

virtuous

honourable

valiant

tactful

Capulet

In the play, we witness two sides to Capulet: the good-humoured, loving side, and the tyrannical, authoritarian side.

As a father, it is Capulet's duty to choose the right husband for his daughter. We learn early on that Juliet is an only child. Capulet informs us that the 'Earth hath swallowed all my hopes but she' (Act 1, Scene 2, line 14). This might explain his determination to ensure that she has the best possible future. When she refuses to marry Paris, Capulet flies into a rage. He believes that she is ungrateful in disregarding his efforts to find her a suitable match. He shows himself to be a tyrannical bully and uses language towards Juliet that is shockingly abusive. He gives her an ultimatum: either marry Paris – his choice of husband for her – or be disowned:

authoritarian
abusive
caring
devoted
practical
impulsive
inconsistent
cruel

> *An you be mine, I'll give you to my friend.*
> *An you be not, hang, beg, starve, die in the streets,*
> *For, by my soul, I'll ne'er acknowledge thee* (Act 3, Scene 5, lines 192–194)

Later, Capulet is overjoyed when Juliet returns from seeing Friar Laurence and reconciles with her parents. Unfortunately, his joy is short-lived, as he learns of his daughter's 'death' the following morning:

> *… alack, my child is dead,*
> *And with my child my joys are burièd!* (Act 4, Scene 5, lines 63–64)

Capulet, realising the futility of his feud with Montague and the true cost of their conflict, reconciles with his old enemy in the final scene. He has come to the heartbreaking realisation that Romeo and Juliet were 'Poor sacrifices of [their] enmity' (Act 5, Scene 3, line 304).

Lady Capulet

Lady Capulet and Juliet do not appear to have a close bond. When we first meet Lady Capulet, she asks the Nurse to leave while she has an intimate discussion with her daughter about marriage. However, she soon calls the Nurse back again, suggesting that such a conversation would be awkward without the Nurse being present. Her language when speaking to her daughter is quite formal:

dismissive
superficial
pragmatic
practical
formal

> *Tell me, daughter Juliet,*
> *How stands your disposition to be married?*
> (Act 1, Scene 3, lines 65–66)

Lady Capulet takes a very **practical approach** to marriage, seeing it as an economic arrangement. She is hopeful that her daughter will consider a match with Paris.

Lady Capulet is dismissive and lacks sensitivity in Act 3, Scene 5. When she thinks Juliet is grieving excessively over the death of Tybalt, she tells her to 'have done' and says that 'much of grief shows still some want of wit' (Act 3, Scene 5, lines 72–73).

Juliet turns to her mother for help after her father insults her and threatens to disown her, but Lady Capulet is unsympathetic and dismissive:

> *Talk not to me, for I'll not speak a word.*
>
> *Do as thou wilt, for I have done with thee.* (Act 3, Scene 5, lines 203–204)

However, Lady Capulet is genuinely upset to hear that her only child has 'died':

> *But one, poor one, one poor and loving child,*
>
> *But one thing to rejoice and solace in,*
>
> *And cruel death hath catched it from my sight!* (Act 4, Scene 5, lines 46–48)

We get the impression that Juliet meant the world to Lady Capulet and that she 'rejoiced' in having her. Like Capulet, Juliet's mother wanted what was best for Juliet. We must also remember that Juliet deceived her parents by faking her death, causing them extreme grief and anguish.

Looking at Themes

Love

Romeo and Juliet's True Love

Love is a **central theme** in *Romeo and Juliet*. The story charts the relationship between Romeo and Juliet, the 'star-cross'd lovers' (Act 1, Prologue, line 6). Their love is described as 'death-mark'd' (Act 1, Prologue, line 9), suggesting that it is doomed from the start. However, because they 'Doth with their deaths bury their parents' strife' (Act 1, Prologue, line 8), their love eventually brings peace and harmony to Verona.

When Romeo and Juliet meet for the first time in **Act 1, Scene 5,** their identities are unknown to one another. Romeo is mesmerised by Juliet's beauty and quickly forgets about Rosaline:

> *Did my heart love till now? Forswear it, sight,*
>
> *For I ne'er saw true beauty till this night.* (Act 1, Scene 5, lines 50–51)

An important point to remember about Romeo and Juliet's love is that it is mutual, whereas Romeo's love – or infatuation – for Rosaline was **unrequited**.

In the Feast Scene, Juliet accepts Romeo's advances, saying, 'You kiss by th' book' (Act 1, Scene 5, line 110). Romeo uses **religious imagery** in this scene, suggesting that their love is **sacred** and special.

The **Balcony Scene** (Act 2, Scene 2) is a key scene of love in the play. Romeo, unable to bring himself to leave the Capulet grounds since meeting Juliet at the feast, spies her standing on her balcony. His language is full of religious imagery:

> *O, speak again, bright angel* (Act 2, Scene 2, line 26)

Juliet realises that she is willing to renounce her family name, if that is what it will take to be with Romeo:

> *O Romeo, Romeo, wherefore art thou Romeo?*
>
> *Deny thy father and refuse thy name,*
>
> *Or, if thou wilt not, be but sworn my love,*
>
> *And I'll no longer be a Capulet.* (Act 2, Scene 2, lines 33–36)

Although Juliet is worried that they are moving too quickly and their love 'is too rash, too unadvised, too sudden' (Act 2, Scene 2, line 118), she also realises that she loves Romeo deeply, and it is she who proposes marriage.

Sensual Love

The Nurse and Mercutio take delight in the sensual side of love and enjoy making sexual innuendos and using bawdy language.

The Nurse refers to the physical side of love when she says that 'Women grow by men' (Act 1, Scene 3, line 96), meaning that women become pregnant by men. Her comment to Juliet, 'Go, girl, seek happy nights to happy days' (Act 1, Scene 3, line 106), also has sexual undertones.

In Act 2, Scene 1, when Mercutio is trying to make Romeo appear, his language also focuses on the physical side of love:

> *I conjure thee by Rosaline's bright eyes,*
>
> *By her high forehead, and her scarlet lip,*
>
> *By her fine foot, straight leg, and quivering thigh,*
>
> *And the demesnes that there adjacent lie* (Act 2, Scene 1, lines 17–20)

Parental Love

At the start of the play, Romeo's parents are extremely worried about their son's behaviour. They express their concern to Benvolio in the hope that he might find out what is bothering their son.

> *And private in his chamber pens himself,*
>
> *Shuts up his windows, locks far daylight out* (Montague, Act 1, Scene 1, lines 131–132)

Romeo shows consideration and respect for his parents when he gives Balthasar a letter to give to his father, outlining his relationship with Juliet and the events that have led to his impending death. We learn that Lady Montague, upset at the news of Romeo's exile, has died.

Likewise, Juliet's parents' chief concern is for their daughter's happiness. Their wish is to secure her future by finding her the best match possible. Initially, Capulet tells Paris that Juliet is too young to marry, but that he would like him to 'woo her' and 'get her heart' (Act 1, Scene 2, line 16). This suggests that Capulet wants Juliet to love her future husband.

Despite Capulet's angry outburst at Juliet, we know that he loves his daughter dearly. The depth of both her parents' love is made clear when they discover her 'death':

> *… alack, my child is dead,*
>
> *And with my child my joys are burièd!* (Capulet, Act 4, Scene 5, lines 63–64)

Conventional Love

Paris epitomises conventional love in the play. He is mainly concerned with arranging an advantageous match with the daughter of the rich Capulets. His conventional love contrasts greatly with Romeo's spontaneous, passionate love. Romeo risks danger in climbing the walls of his enemy's orchard just to catch a glimpse of the girl he loves, whereas Paris applies formally to Juliet's father for Juliet's hand in marriage, as was the convention of the time.

Throughout the play, Shakespeare **juxtaposes** (contrasts) different types of love to highlight the superiority and depth of Romeo and Juliet's true love.

Conflict

The theme of conflict pervades the play. The play opens with a dramatic, violent street brawl. This reminds us that violence affects everyone, from master to servant. Prince Escalus comes to **quell** (calm) the violence, informing us that 'three civil brawls' have 'thrice disturbed the quiet of our streets' and warning that if there is further violence, then citizens' 'lives shall pay the forfeit of the peace' (Act 1, Scene 1, lines 82–90).

In **Act 1, Scene 5**, tension is brewing as Tybalt **recognises** Romeo's voice at the Capulet feast. He is so **incensed** (angry) at this intrusion that he wants to fight him then and there. However, Capulet forces him to contain his temper. Tybalt warns:

> *I will withdraw, but this intrusion shall*
>
> *Now seeming sweet convert to bitterest gall.* (Act 1, Scene 5, lines 91–92)

We learn in Act 2, Scene 4 that Tybalt has issued a challenge to Romeo, which creates tension and an ominous sense of foreboding. The tension between Tybalt and Romeo will ultimately prove a major obstacle to the lovers' happiness.

Act 3, Scene 1 is the climax of the play and is a **key scene of conflict**. Mercutio, who is outraged at Romeo's apparent cowardice, challenges Tybalt to fight and is killed. Romeo, seeking revenge, goes after Tybalt and kills him. This event has **devastating consequences** for Romeo and Juliet, as Romeo gets banished from Verona.

The **final scene of tragedy** (Act 5, Scene 3) underlines the **consequences of violence.** At the beginning, we witness a **fight** between Paris and Romeo, which results in Paris's death. When Friar Laurence arrives, he comments on the bloody scene before him:

> *What mean these masterless and gory swords*
>
> *To lie discoloured by this place of peace?* (Act 5, Scene 3, lines 142–143)

Prince Escalus later calls on the Montague and Capulet families to reflect on the consequences of their feud:

> *Where be these enemies? – Capulet, Montague,*
>
> *See what a scourge is laid upon your hate,*
>
> *That heaven finds means to kill your joys with love.* (Act 5, Scene 3, lines 291–293)

The two families finally understand the futility of their conflict now that 'All are punishèd' (Prince Escalus, Act 5, Scene 3, line 295), and agree to put aside their differences.

Fate

What do we mean by 'fate'?

The word 'fate' is often linked to events in an individual's life that may be seen as being beyond his/her control. Words related to fate include: destiny, luck, fortune, providence and future.

Fate is an important theme in *Romeo and Juliet*. In Shakespeare's time, people were often very **superstitious**. Many believed that one's fate or future was mapped out in the stars or that some higher being or **supernatural** force controlled one's destiny.

In the very first lines of the play, we learn that fate will play an important role in the story. In Act 1, Prologue, Romeo and Juliet are described as 'a pair of star-cross'd lovers' (line 6), which means that they are ill-fated. The term 'star-cross'd' comes from the belief that the position of the stars could influence one's life. In this way, Romeo and Juliet could be considered to be **victims of fate**.

Romeo is **apprehensive** about the prospect of attending the Capulet feast. He feels that his fate has been mapped out in the stars and that going to the feast is destined to bring him bad luck and result in his 'untimely death':

> *I fear too early, for my mind misgives*
> *Some consequence yet hanging in the stars*
> *Shall bitterly begin his fearful date*
> *With this night's revels, and expire the term*
> *Of a despisèd life, closed in my breast,*
> *By some vile forfeit of untimely death.* (Act 1, Scene 4, lines 107–112)

Romeo is proved correct. By attending the feast he meets Juliet. This eventually leads to his death.

In **Act 3, Scene 1**, we see another example of ill fate. Romeo is reluctant to fight Tybalt, because he is Juliet's cousin. When Mercutio gets killed fighting on his behalf, Romeo kills Tybalt and is subsequently banished from Verona. Soon after, he calls himself 'fortune's fool' (Act 3, Scene 1, line 134).

In **Act 3, Scene 5**, Juliet has a strange premonition of Romeo's death as he is leaving to travel to Mantua:

> *O God, I have an ill-divining soul!*
>
> *Methinks I see thee, now thou art so low,*
>
> *As one dead in the bottom of a tomb.* (Act 3, Scene 5, lines 54–56)

Immediately after he leaves, she calls on **fortune** (fate) to be 'fickle', hoping that her luck will change and that Romeo will soon return.

Bad luck strikes yet again when Romeo fails to receive Friar Laurence's letter telling him of Juliet's plan to fake her own death. Friar John has been unable to deliver the letter because of fears that he might spread the plague. When Romeo hears from Balthasar in **Act 5, Scene 1** that Juliet is dead, he decides to take control of his own fate by ending his life. He buys a lethal potion from the Apothecary to take to Juliet's tomb.

In **Act 5, Scene 3**, Romeo says that he will lie with Juliet:

> *And shake the yoke of inauspicious stars*
>
> *From this world-weared flesh.* (Act 5, Scene 3, lines 111–112)

When Friar Laurence later goes to the tomb to rescue Juliet, he informs her that:

> *A greater power than we can contradict*
>
> *Hath thwarted our intents.* (Act 5, Scene 3, lines 153–154)

This seems to capture the idea that **misfortune** or bad luck has gained the upper hand.

Language and Imagery in Romeo and Juliet

The play *Romeo and Juliet* abounds with imagery and figurative language. Imagery can tell us about a character, help to establish a particular mood or atmosphere, or add drama or tension to a scene.

Imagery in the play comes from **language devices** such as:

- **Simile**
- **Metaphor**
- **Personification**
- **Antithesis**
- **Oxymoron**
- **Hyperbole**

Can you remember what they mean? (Turn to **page viii** of this book if you need reminding.)

EXPLORING

Language Devices

Pair Activity

Choose three language devices from the list on the previous page. Identify **two** examples of each and write about how each device contributes to the play overall. For example, if you choose **personification**, you could discuss the effect of death being personified, or if you choose **oxymoron** you could talk about how it is used to capture the characters' conflicting emotions at various points in the play.

Approaching Examination Questions

KEY AREAS FOR STUDY

- **Characters**
- **Key scenes**
- **Themes**
- **Relationships – positive or negative**
- **Your evaluation of the play**

The TED Approach to Answering Examination Questions

For each main point:

include a	**Topic sentence**
give	**Examples/evidence**
and then	**Discuss**

A **topic sentence** expresses the main **idea/point** of the paragraph in which it occurs. It usually comes at the **start** of the paragraph, but can also be found at the end of the paragraph. For example, if I wish to write about the **challenges** that Juliet faces as a character, I might write a topic sentence such as: **'Juliet's relationship with Romeo causes her many problems in the play.'**

Next, try to include **examples** to support your point. These could be quotes or references to the play.

Finally, discuss how your examples help to expand on your topic sentence.

Approaching a Romeo and Juliet *Character Question*

EXPLORING AN IMPORTANT CHARACTER

(a) Identify an important character from a play that you have studied and outline some of the **obstacles or challenges** faced by him/her in the course of the play.

(b) What do we **learn about this character** from the way in which he/she deals with one or more of these **obstacles** or **challenges**?

Before you begin, read the information that follows. We will explore Juliet's character.

1. Planning Your Answer

Brainstorm your points. Make brief notes for yourself about Juliet's challenges, such as:

- Her relationship with Romeo – forbidden love.
- Tybalt's death and Romeo's banishment.
- Her arranged marriage to Paris – feeling isolated, betrayed and abandoned.
- Friar Laurence's plan – the Potion Scene.
- Ending – the plan has failed.

2. Writing Your Answer

Now that you have brainstormed your points, decide which ones you will discuss in detail. Your answer needs:

- An **introduction**.
- Three or four developed **points** (one per paragraph).
- A brief **conclusion**.

3. Getting Started ⏏P

Turn to **page 108–110** of your portfolio to complete **part (a)** of the question. Read the **introduction** and then **elaborate on three of the topic sentences provided**. Include plenty of **quotes or references** and expand on each point, **discussing** the problems that Juliet faces.

Next, complete **part (b)** of the question in your **copy**. Stay focused on what you have found out about Juliet's personality. Mention the many obstacles that she has to overcome. (Each paragraph should link to the points that you have made in your portfolio.) The following are tips to help you to complete this task:

- Discuss how we see Juliet's love/devotion to Romeo. She is willing to risk everything for him.
- Describe how Juliet reacts to the news of Tybalt's death. What does this tell us about her? (Hint: That she is a realistic character. She is logical but, like real people, she experiences conflicting emotions.)
- What does the Potion Scene reveal about Juliet? (Hint: She faces her greatest fears. She is brave and courageous.)
- Think of adjectives to describe Juliet towards the end of the play. (Hint: Loyal and devoted to Romeo; courageous.)

Writing about an Important Scene in the Play

When writing about an important scene, consider the following:

Characters

Who are the main characters in this scene? What do they say and do? How do the characters interact with each other in this scene? For example, a scene might show how a character has changed or developed. Where do we see this in the scene?

Action

What happens in this scene to further the plot? Is this a climax scene? Is this a key scene for a major theme in the play such as love or conflict?

Does anything **surprising/shocking/memorable/unexpected** take place in this scene?

Atmosphere

How is the atmosphere created? Is the mood tense or calm, romantic or sorrowful? How is this mood established? What images contribute to this mood?

Audience's Response

How did you respond to this scene? How do you feel about the events that take place in the scene and the characters?

Staging the Scene

Imagine that you will be staging/directing this scene. How would you stage it to maximise its impact? Consider the type of stage, advice to characters, visual and sound effects, the positioning of the characters on the stage, etc.

ROMEO AND JULIET TIMELINE

	SUNDAY	MONDAY	TUESDAY	WEDNESDAY	THURSDAY
MORNING		Romeo visits Friar Laurence to arrange marriage.	Romeo must leave for Mantua. Juliet is informed that she is to wed Paris. Juliet argues with her parents.	Juliet's 'dead' body is discovered. Friar Laurence comforts the family.	Early hours: Prince Escalus, the Capulets and Montague arrive and the full extent of the tragedy is revealed.
AFTERNOON	Benvolio and Romeo decide to go to the Capulet feast.	Romeo jokes with friends. The Nurse comes looking for Romeo. Romeo and Juliet meet to get married.	Juliet goes to Friar Laurence's cell and formulates a plan. Friar Laurence sends Friar John with a letter to Romeo in Mantua.	Juliet is brought to the Capulet tomb. Balthasar informs Romeo about Juliet's death. Romeo visits the Apothecary and heads for the Capulet tomb in Verona.	
EVENING	The **Feast Scene**.	The **Fight Scene.** Juliet wishes for night to come. The Nurse informs Juliet about the fight. Romeo is distraught at Friar Laurence's cell.	Juliet reconciles with her father.	Friar Laurence hears that his letter was not sent to Romeo. Friar Laurence rushes to the Capulet tomb.	
NIGHT	The **Balcony Scene**.	Romeo and Juliet spend the night together.	Juliet arranges to be alone in her room and **takes the potion.** Capulet stays up to oversee preparations for the wedding.	Romeo arrives at the Capulet tomb. He fights Paris and kills him. Romeo dies. Juliet wakes. Friar Laurence arrives. Tragedy in the churchyard.	

The first cell in the MORNING row reads: "Brawl on the streets of Verona." under SUNDAY.